HOUSING FIRST

Housing First

ENDING HOMELESSNESS, TRANSFORMING SYSTEMS, AND CHANGING LIVES

Deborah K. Padgett, Benjamin F. Henwood,
and Sam J. Tsemberis

OXFORD
UNIVERSITY PRESS

OXFORD
UNIVERSITY PRESS

Oxford University Press is a department of the University of
Oxford. It furthers the University's objective of excellence in research,
scholarship, and education by publishing worldwide.

Oxford   New York
Auckland   Cape Town   Dar es Salaam   Hong Kong   Karachi
Kuala Lumpur   Madrid   Melbourne   Mexico City   Nairobi
New Delhi   Shanghai   Taipei   Toronto

With offices in
Argentina   Austria   Brazil   Chile   Czech Republic   France   Greece
Guatemala   Hungary   Italy   Japan   Poland   Portugal   Singapore
South Korea   Switzerland   Thailand   Turkey   Ukraine   Vietnam

Oxford is a registered trademark of Oxford University Press
in the UK and certain other countries.

Published in the United States of America by
Oxford University Press
198 Madison Avenue, New York, NY 10016

Library of Congress Cataloging-in-Publication Data
Padgett, Deborah.
Housing first : ending homelessness, transforming systems, and changing lives / Deborah K. Padgett,
Benjamin F. Henwood, and Sam J. Tsemberis.
    pages cm
Includes bibliographical references and index.
ISBN 978-0-19-998980-5 (alk. paper)
1. Homeless persons—Housing—United States.   2. Homeless persons—Services for—United
States.   3. Homeless persons—Housing.   I. Henwood, Benjamin F.   II. Tsemberis, Sam J.
III. Title.
HV4505.P23 2016
363.50973—dc23
2015014797

9 8 7 6 5 4 3 2
Printed in the United States of America
on acid-free paper

Contents

Preface

Pathways to Housing and the Rise of Housing First

Consider the following questions:

- How often in the vast landscape of health and human services does a small programmatic innovation become the leading approach in less than 20 years, making waves in a multibillion-dollar service sector?
- How often is a fundamental change in social policy attributed to research findings?
- How often does a successful evidence-based practice address human rights and consumer choice as central to its philosophy?
- How often does an innovative social program obtain endorsements from conservative *and* left-leaning political leaders?
- How often in recent history has an innovative social program originated in the United States and become widely adopted in Canada, Australia, and Europe?

The answers to these questions range from "not often" to "almost never." Yet they all apply to the subject of this book: an approach to ending homelessness known as "Housing First." Many ambitious social programs have started small, taken root and flourished, but few have shown positive and robust results from empirical research and subsequent dissemination. As we approach the fourth decade of what was supposed to be a troubling but transitory epidemic, homelessness in America has not gone away. But there are promising signs that it can be ended for many.

In 1992, Housing First was developed as a new program by psychologist Dr. Sam Tsemberis, who founded Pathways to Housing, Inc. Hundreds of nonprofit social services agencies existed in New York and around the United States, offering a range of programs from emergency shelters to transitional housing and permanent housing. Support services ranged from minimal-to-absent (usually in shelters) to comprehensive, for example, help in accessing housing, case management support when housed, as well as job training, mental health treatment, and more. Single adults, mostly men, were the most visible segment of the homeless population and a significant minority had serious mental illnesses such as schizophrenia. It was these men and women whom Tsemberis had tried with middling success to persuade to go to a shelter or a psychiatric hospital. After years of directing New York City's emergency outreach team for the homeless, Tsemberis was converted to a consumer-driven approach known as psychiatric rehabilitation, and he started taking homeless persons at their word. When they insisted that what they really needed was a place to live, not a shelter or a hospital ward, he searched for a way to make that a reality.

Now jump ahead some 20-odd years. Pathways to Housing is still a small player on the multimillion-dollar homeless services scene in New York City, but the "housing first" model it spawned has begun to transform homeless services nationally and internationally. What set Pathways on this transformative course was its philosophical premise and programmatic approach: to provide *immediate access to housing*—most often an independent apartment—*and support services* to individuals with mental illness living on the streets. This "housing first" model was in direct opposition to the mainstream approach to homeless services in the United States and most other nations. The mainstream approach, variously known as the "continuum of care" or "staircase model" mandated treatment and behavior change as prerequisites to moving toward the longed-for top step—independent permanent housing.

The problem with the mainstream model was that for many people the climb was too steep, the journey too long, or the difficulty level too high. Repeatedly trying and failing discouraged many, and they eventually stopped trying, remained homeless, and withdrew into hopelessness. The net result: The mainstream model had a steadily growing number of dropouts, and the people it failed were becoming more visible on the streets (Johnsen & Teixeira, 2010; Sahlin, 1998).

Pathways to Housing honored the desire for choice by moving homeless men and women directly into their own furnished apartment and enveloping them in support services. The consumer choice ethos was further employed by not requiring medication adherence or abstaining from drugs or alcohol to keep one's apartment. This was not an incremental change, a softening of demands. It was a reversal of fortune, something completely different.

Pathways was also groundbreaking in its embrace of rigorous self-evaluation early on. In 1997, the young program became the experimental "arm" of a four-year randomized trial funded by the Federal government's Substance Abuse and Mental Health Services Administration (SAMHSA).[1] Half-way through, the New York Housing Study was already yielding striking results of 80% housing stability for "housing first" clients (Tsemberis, Gulcur, & Nakae, 2004). This and subsequent findings propelled Pathways onto the center stage of homeless services, a novel approach in what had been a long, expensive, and often futile effort to end homelessness. In an era of evidence-based practice, "housing first" (HF) earned the credential, endorsed by the U.S. Federal Government as the "clear solution" to chronic homelessness.[2]

This complicated and ongoing story of systems change is the subject of this book. To this end, we scoured the literature on HF to ensure full coverage of the topic. We also interviewed a few key implementers of the approach to tap into various perspectives and experiences. Regrettably, we could not interview everyone—the number of people who have made significant contributions in homelessness research, practices, and policies in the past two decades would require a book in and of itself. And another volume would be needed just to interview and credit the many hundreds of people who work quietly under the radar introducing HF programs to their communities.

The three coauthors are uniquely qualified to tell the story of HF through our extensive research on Pathways and the model it spawned. One of us (Tsemberis) is the founder of Pathways to Housing. Another of us (Henwood) has extensive practice and administrative experience in the agency in its New York City and Philadelphia programs and has gone on to become a researcher on HF. Finally, the lead author (Padgett) was initially involved as a Pathways board member, departing the board in 2005 to engage in qualitative research on HF for the next 10 years and counting. For these reasons, we reasonably could be considered biased in favor of "housing first." Cognizant of this, we have sought to present opposing viewpoints, to explore criticism of the HF model, and to acknowledge its limitations when and where they exist. We hope the reader agrees that this story is one worth telling and reading about. It is not often that such a story arises.

Notes

1. http://usich.gov/usich_resources/fact_sheets/opening_doors_chronic_homelessness/

2. This acronym provides us with the opportunity to warn the reader than an alphabet soup of acronyms will appear in the chapters to come. To ease this unfortunate but necessary abbreviating, we have put a List of Abbreviations in the front of the book for reference.

List of Abbreviations

ACA	Affordable Care Act
ACO	Accountable Care Organization
ACT	Assertive Community Treatment
ADA	Americans with Disabilities Act
AEIPS	Associação para o Estudo e Integração Psicossocial
AH/CS	At Home/Chez Soi
CASES	Center for Alternative Sentencing and Employment
CCH	Colorado Coalition for the Homeless
CCNV	Center for Creative Non-Violence
CG	Common Ground
CM	case manager
CSH	Corporation for Supportive Housing
CTI	Critical Time Intervention
CUCS	Center for Urban Community Services
DES	Vancouver's Downtown East Side
DESC	Seattle Downtown Emergency Service Center
DHCR	Division of Housing and Community Renewal
DHFC	Denver Housing First Collaborative
DMH	New York City Department of Mental Health
EBP	evidence-based practice
EC	European Commission
ETHOS	European Typology of Homelessness and Housing Exclusion
EU	European Union
FEANTSA	European Federation of National Organizations Working with the Homeless
HCH	Health Care for the Homeless

HEARTH	Homeless Emergency and Rapid Transition to Housing Program
HF	Housing First
HFE	Housing First Europe
HFPC	Housing First Partners Conference
HPD	New York City Department of Housing and Preservation Development
HPRP	Homelessness Prevention and Rapid Re-Housing Program
HPS	Canada's Homeless Partnering Strategy
HRA	Human Resources Administration
HSIC	Homeless Services Institutional Complex
HTH	Howie the Harp training program
HUD	U.S. Department of Housing and Urban Development
HUD-VASH	HUD-Veterans Administration Supportive Housing Program
ICM	intensive case management
IE	institutional entrepreneur
IPS	independent placement and support
LAC	Los Angeles County
MHCC	Mental Health Commission of Canada
NAEH	National Alliance to End Homelessness
NAMI	National Alliance for the Mentally Ill
NREBPP	National Registry of Evidence-based Programs and Practices
NCH	National Coalition for the Homeless
NGO	nongovernmental organization
NIH	National Institutes of Health
NIMBY	not in my back yard
NIMH	National Institute of Mental Health
NUH	National Union of the Homeless
NWRO	National Welfare Rights Organization
NYHS	New York Housing Study
NY/NY	New York–New York Agreement
NYHS	New York Housing Study
NYRS	New York Recovery Study
NYSS	New York Services Study
OMH	Office of Mental Health
PHF	Pathways Housing First
PIT	point-in-time
RCT	randomized controlled trial
RHF	Robin Hood Foundation
RSI	Rough Sleepers Initiative

RWJ	Robert Wood Johnson Foundation
S2H	Street to Home–New York City or Streets to Homes–Toronto
SAMHSA	U.S. Substance Abuse and Mental Health Services Administration
SE	supported employment
SMI	serious mental illness
SP	study participant
SRO	single-room occupancy
SSA	Social Security Administration
SSI/SSDI	Supplemental Security Income/Social Security Disability Insurance
SSVF	Supportive Services for Veteran Families
TAU	treatment as usual
TF	treatment first
USICH	U.S. Interagency Council on Homelessness
VA	U.S. Veterans Administration
VAMC	Veterans Administration Medical Centers

HOUSING FIRST

1 Paradigm Shifts and Systems Change
UNDERSTANDING HOUSING FIRST AND ITS IMPACT

WHAT DO THESE cities have in common: Casper (Wyoming), Charlotte (North Carolina) Burlington (Vermont), Salt Lake City (Utah), Lexington (Kentucky), Honolulu (Hawaii), and Medicine Hat (Alberta, Canada)? All have endorsed Housing First as their approach to ending rather than managing homelessness. Little more than two decades ago, the "housing first" (HF) approach to homeless services was deemed irresponsible and doomed to failure. Today, some may still believe the first part about irresponsibility but no one can say HF has been a failure. The sea change in policy and practice wrought by this approach brought much-needed optimism to many homeless service providers for too long accustomed to revolving doors and patchwork solutions. Especially in its early years, HF unleashed reactions ranging from lingering doubts to outright hostility. From its humble beginnings in New York City in 1992, HF has become a catchword internationally; its promise fulfilled in some places and untested (or considered unnecessary) in others.

In this book we propose that the systems change wrought by HF is tantamount to a paradigm shift. The term, made popular through Thomas Kuhn's (1962) *Structure of Scientific Revolutions*, has become a modern-day trope, shorthand for massive change that occurs relatively rapidly rather than gradually and incrementally. Kuhn challenged long-held perceptions that change in scientific knowledge was gradual, linear, cumulative, and orderly. Instead, he argued, major changes in science happen as sudden and profound turning points or "paradigm shifts" needed to overcome natural conservatism.

Services for the homeless encompass not only shelter but assistance in meeting other basic needs such as food, clothing, and health care. Few social problems draw in as many stakeholders and service systems as homelessness; ameliorating the problem requires action at multiple levels involving multiple agencies. And few social problems and their solutions are as beset by definitional disagreement, starting with the term "homeless" itself.

The Contested World of Defining and Counting
Who is Homeless (and Who is Not)

The subject of innumerable essays, policy initiatives, and researchers' headaches, estimates depend upon consensus in defining who is (and is not) homeless (Hopper, 2003). Consensus is hard to come by, resulting in an uneasy compromise between governments (with lower estimates) and advocates (with higher estimates) (Hopper, Shinn, Laska, Meisner, & Wanderling, 2008). Even agreement on the definition does not mean that the counting is done well or accurately. The point-in-time (PIT) count method favored by federal, state, and municipal governments in the United States involves a dead-of-winter, late-night outreach in which trained volunteers canvass likely locations, adding these numbers to the census of shelter users. During the count, the balance of the ideal (effective outreach) with the real (holding back due to fears of intrusion or safety) often tilts toward the latter. Because funding allocations depend on the results, PIT counts are highly politicized as are the data.

Not surprisingly, definitions have been codified by government entities to reduce ambiguity about who might be eligible for services. Government definitions are also influenced, however, by the willingness to acknowledge the magnitude of the problem and to provide services. This propensity narrows or increases estimates as a function of cultural norms, attitudes concerning the deserving and undeserving poor, and availability of safety net services. According to the U.S. Federal government 1994 definition (Stewart B. McKinney Act, 42 U.S.C. § 11301, et seq.), a person is considered homeless if he or she "lacks a fixed, regular, and adequate nighttime residence and ... has a primary nighttime residency that is: (a) a supervised publicly or privately operated shelter designed to provide temporary living accommodations ... (b) an institution that provides a temporary residence for individuals intended to be institutionalized, or (c) a public or private place not designed for, or ordinarily used as, a regular sleeping accommodation for human beings."

The vast majority of homeless adults and families exit homelessness in a few days or weeks and find a way to get re-housed through the help of informal or formal support (Culhane, 2014). As a result, the contours of homeless services are shaped by the needs of those who are left behind, a group more likely to include persons with serious mental illness, substance abuse, health problems, or some combination of these. Most "single" homeless adults have families and children but when they enter the system solo, they are served in that way, not in the way that homeless families are treated. The latter group tends to be younger, female-headed, and relatively healthy by comparison. Their needs are by no means simple, but they are different from the needs of adults who are chronically homeless and high-service users. These individuals are the focus of this book.

Defining Housing First (HF) and Pathways Housing First (PHF)

Beginning with Pathways to Housing ("Pathways"), the HF approach has since come to be defined in differing ways such that we reserve "PHF" for the original model or direct and faithful replications. Not all HF programs follow PHF (hence the need for the distinction). As we will see in subsequent chapters, HF has recently been invoked by programs seeking to align themselves with the zeitgeist. As the term has come into vogue, so has its usage become stretched, at times beyond recognition, testifying to snowballing HF endorsements from high government entities. So where—and how—do we draw the definitional line(s)?

As noted by its founder, PHF is a complex clinical and housing intervention that comprises three major components: (1) program philosophy and practice values emphasizing *consumer choice*; (2) *community based, mobile support services*; and (3) *permanent scatter-site*[1] *housing* (Tsemberis, 2010). Permanent housing is necessary but not sufficient to fulfill what PHF means in practice—housing must be paired with adequate support services. Because PHF does not require psychiatric treatment or sobriety as preconditions for attaining housing, the model includes a fourth component, *harm reduction,* so that support services can help reduce risks associated with psychiatric or addiction-related behavior.

Although merged into a novel approach, each of these four components has its own history predating and transcending its use by PHF, and several were innovations supported by research evidence in their own right. Consumer choice, for example, stems from a wider movement for patient and human rights dating to the 1970s and is a core principle in psychiatric rehabilitation (Anthony et al., 1982; Anthony, Cohen, & Farkas, 2002). Community-based mobile services originated with Assertive Community Treatment (ACT) as developed in the 1970s (Stein & Test, 1980) to support persons with serious mental illness living in the community, thereby reducing the need for hospitalization. The idea of scatter-site apartments as permanent housing came from consumer advocates who argued that persons with psychiatric disabilities should have the same "normalized" housing choices as those with other disabilities (Carling, 1993; Howie the Harp, 1993; Ridgway & Zipple, 1990). Thus, a version of permanent and independent supportive housing (PSH)—community-based living with flexible support services—was promoted as an ideal before PHF made it a reality. The alternative—congregate living and on-site services—risks recreating the institutionalization that undermines social integration and independent living.

Harm reduction achieved greater acceptance in the United States during the HIV/AIDS epidemic through clean-needle sharing and safe sex practices (Inciardi & Harrison, 1999; Marlatt, 1996). Still considered controversial in some circles, the principle of working with clients to minimize harm rather than forbid or extinguish the targeted behavior was extended to substance abuse and influenced by the "Dutch model" from the Netherlands (Marlatt, Larimer, & Witkiewitz, 2011). Harm reduction has aroused suspicion within the abstinence-based addiction treatment community, where it is viewed as condoning or enabling use. Although tolerant programs (and case workers) no doubt existed before PHF, the incorporation of harm reduction as programmatic policy was new.

The synergy of these four essential but disparate components endowed PHF with a unique purpose and approach to housing and services, one that required a sea change in the organizational culture of existing programs serving homeless adults. The environment from which PHF emerged operated under very different assumptions, including the role of consumers.

Consumer Input in the Development of Pathways Housing First: The Earliest Days

The Pathways Housing First model emerged from an ongoing dialogue among consumers, staff, and researchers (Barrow, McMullin, Tripp, & Tsemberis, 2007; Lovell & Cohen, 1998; Tsemberis et al., 2003) who initially developed an outreach and drop-in center program (known as "Choices") as a research demonstration project (Shern et al., 2000). An ethos of respect for consumers and their ideas was fostered by training staff in consumer-centric clinical approaches such as psychiatric rehabilitation (Anthony et al., 2002), trauma-informed care, and harm reduction as well as including consumer advocates like "Howie the Harp" (Howard Geld) as members of the project's advisory board.

Hiring people with lived experience to provide case management services further contributed to the inclusion and incorporation of consumer input in the Choices program. Moreover, the governance and day-to-day operation of the program included regularly scheduled community meetings that served a quality improvement function. At these meetings, when issues were raised that required a vote, consumers were included as voting members. Staff, administrators, and program participants acted as decision makers and thus shared responsibility for policy and program decisions. In addition to advocacy, Howie the Harp and others brought to the program a commitment to social justice and a revolutionary fervor to change the mental health system (Tsemberis & Asmussen, 1999).

In the Choices drop-in center where the Pathways HF program was originally conceived, neither status nor salary distinguished peer specialist staff from non-peer staff. Every effort was made to reduce power differentials and operate as collaboratively as possible. This approach blurred boundaries between staff and program participants and fostered a program culture where proposals and ideas were evaluated on the merit of their content rather than by the social or professional status of the source.

Lengthy conversations and debates ensued over how best to secure access to the existing supportive housing programs. The harm reduction practice at Choices was very effective for engagement but conflicted with the sobriety or abstinence requirements of housing providers. Program participants and staff were aware of and deeply unhappy that existing housing providers used the need for housing as leverage to ensure consumer acquiescence to treatment and abstinence requirements (Allen, 2003). After repeated failures to secure housing either by persuading programs to change their admission requirements or by convincing consumers that they had to comply with the rules, the group began a trial and error discussion centered around designing a housing program that would be both desirable and acceptable to consumers and manageable by staff.

In the course of these conversations about the stigma associated with single-site housing set aside for the "mentally ill," the decision was made to seek out a supported housing contract that provided rent stipends and the possibility of renting an apartment of one's own with case management support. The scatter-site supported housing model met consumers' requirements for normal housing ("We just want a simple ordinary apartment."), tenancy rights ("a place that is mine"), privacy ("I can wake up when I want."), freedom separate from program demands ("I don't want to have to hide my beer under the couch when you come to visit."), off-site rather than on-site services ("I may want to go to treatment but I don't want to be living in treatment."), and affordable rent contributions (30% of income).

Consumers and staff worked collaboratively on the operational details including occupancy policies and program and consumer fiscal responsibilities. This included setting up a bank account to pay the consumer's portion of the rent and required both staff and consumer signatures for checks to be cashed.

Once Housing First was launched by creating Pathways to Housing, Inc., steps had to be taken to ensure and sustain the continued input of consumer voices within the program. The program was designed collaboratively and steps were taken to ensure that this ethos would be carried forward to all levels of the operation and management of the nascent Pathways. This was considered central to sustaining the consumer-centered origins of the program.

Several administrative practices were used to promote consumer voices more broadly within the agency: (1) as tenants, consumers participated on an advisory committee that met regularly with agency heads to express tenant concerns and provide programmatic input; (2) every executive officer of the organization had an open door policy for consumers; (3) people with lived experience (peers) were hired as service providers and managers and were elected to the Pathways board of directors.

In everyday group or program meetings accommodations were made to ensure full participation by appointing a moderator, taking turns speaking, and having an active, moderated, question-and-answer period. In addition, social and recreational events provided opportunities for staff and consumers to meet informally and expand the repertoire of their dialogue. Both the service approach and the organizational environment were designed to foster empowerment for greater community, civic, and political participation.

The Linear Approach to Homeless Services

PHF came to life at a time when services for the homeless operated according to the principle of a "linear continuum of care" predicated on consumers' behavior change as the key to progress made—step-by-step—to the idealized endpoint of independent living in one's own dwelling. This arrangement has been characterized as a staircase[2] (Sahlin, 1998), starting with low demand and low service provision (such as in an emergency shelter, safe haven, or drop-in center) and ascending through increasing demands and more services associated with transitional housing programs (Atherton & MacNaughton

Nicholls, 2008). The staircase's top step is the attainment of one's own housing and a minimum of services required to maintain independent living (see Figure 1.1). Most of the services along the continuum are delivered in supervised settings where residents are required to follow the rules of congregate living and show progress toward "housing readiness" or "housing worthiness" (Dordick, 2002).

The intuitive draw of the continuum approach was and remains powerful. It also aligns closely with the step-by-step ethos of personal responsibility and behavioral change deeply rooted in American values. Thus, homeless men and women with serious mental illness and co-occurring substance abuse are the authors of their destinies, arriving at such a debased state of existence through bad luck, poor decisions, and avoidable circumstances. Only with the expert assistance of psychiatrists, social workers, case managers, and addiction counselors can their lives be turned around. Complying with treatment and program requirements serves as a demonstration of the willingness to work harder and this effort leads to a reward (i.e., moving a step up the staircase). Refusal to comply is seen as further evidence of poor decision-making and a lack of "housing readiness," typically resulting in discharge and cautions that a return signals that the consumer is ready and willing to change his or her behavior.

The reality on the ground in cities across America was a hodgepodge of services heavily weighted toward the bottom of the continuum with varying access to anything beyond an emergency shelter (e.g., transitional housing such as a single-room occupancy building or a halfway house). Thus, the principle of a

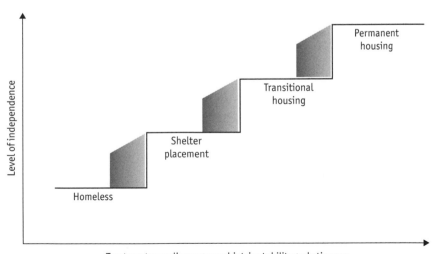

FIGURE 1.1 The Continuum or Staircase Approach to Homeless Services.

linear continuum or staircase existed even if individuals did not always proceed through it in an orderly fashion or encounter anything beyond the lowest step. Some never got beyond that first step, some skipped steps, and far too many fell off the "staircase." For these individuals, life is lived on the "institutional circuit" (Hopper, Jost, Hay, Welber, & Haugland, 1997), travelling from shelter to hospital to jail and back to the streets. The linear continuum was (and continues to be) a cruel and costly circle of futility.

The rise of the continuum service philosophy was probably inevitable given deeply rooted Anglo-Saxon values requiring a demonstration of worthiness by the poor and destitute. Yet, even as the limitations of this approach became evident, it not only continued but also became entrenched as the normative mainstream in homeless services. From a supply and demand perspective, the number of homeless people who needed services far exceeded the slots available so that programs having even the strictest rules were able to enroll clients and operate at full capacity. In turn, operating at full capacity was accepted as the definition of a successful program. But this "success" was predicated on a form of creaming (i.e., selecting applicants who were willing and able to comply with treatment and sobriety demands). This left the more troubled, and those less able or willing, on the streets to fend for themselves.

Whether for reasons of economy or efficiency, transitional housing programs toward the bottom end of the staircase typically placed consumers in tight living quarters within a single building, an arrangement well-suited to the careful supervision deemed necessary to help consumers adjust to their posthomeless living situation. Congregate living also required rules—curfews, meal times, bed checks, treatment attendance, sobriety, limited or no guests—in order to ensure the safety and comfort of all residents. Relapse into substance abuse or a psychiatric crisis meant discharge (to hospitalization, street, or rehabilitation facility). Once discharged from the program, the consumer returned to the bottom of the staircase and started all over again. Despite or because of these demands, dropout rates were high (Hopper et al., 1997).

That the continuum service model was predisposed to excluding (or ejecting) those with the most problems resulted in a greater concentration of severely disabled people living on the streets. Advocates for the homeless were quick to point this out, but governments appeared stymied and unable or unwilling to move toward more permanent solutions. Instead, they did more of the same, giving rise to more and more homeless service programs and to thousands of jobs in a homeless "industry" (e.g., outreach workers, caseworkers, van drivers, security guards, maintenance staff, cooks, building managers, and other supervisory positions). In the next section, we expand our framework to understand how an innovation such as HF can set in motion fundamental changes in policies and practices.

Institutional and Organizational Change

Thomas Kuhn's (1962) *Structure of Scientific Revolutions* offers an oft-cited thesis on change that has proven to be influential far beyond his original intent. Similar to Kuhn's cycle of long stretches of stability marked by disruptive paradigm shifts, institutional change does not come easily or inevitably. Max Weber (1952) referred to the "iron cage" that bureaucratization brings to institutions, an image that DiMaggio and Powell (1983) invoked to explain the increasing homogeneity of institutions acting within a common sphere. Large institutions may have bricks-and-mortar visibility for example, the Roman Catholic Church, but they can also be defined through social meanings and connections, such as the institutions of marriage or the nuclear family. The challenge in institutional theory is less one of explaining endurance—inertia alone can be powerful—than in understanding how institutions change at all. The most expedient explanations are external events—wars, natural disasters, epidemics, and economic depressions. There are also internally disruptive forces such as social movements that can overthrow institutions if powerful enough.

DiMaggio and Powell's (1983) neo-institutional theory refers to three pillars or structures that maintain institutions: (a) *regulative*—laws and contractual obligations; (b) *normative*—assumption or ideals governing behavior; and (c) *cultural–cognitive*—schemas or taken-for-granted scripts underlying behavior. Accordingly, institutional change can be *coercive* (top-down enforcement), *normative* (altering perceptions of what is expected and desirable), or *mimetic* (copying best-practice models). Whatever the pathway to institutional change, its success is heralded by the appearance of a new *institutional logic* and set of norms. Together, these confer legitimacy to the new institutional form. Without such legitimacy, institutional change will founder.

So how and why did the regulative, normative, and cultural–cognitive pillars that supported the staircase approach shift such that HF became a legitimate (and legitimizing) force with its own distinctive institutional logic? In order to understand this shift—where obtaining federal dollars became contingent upon adopting a HF approach, where there was an expectation that HF would be implemented, and where immediate access to housing became ingrained as the go-to response of homeless service providers—one must understand not just the larger institutional forces that were at play, but also those individuals who served as catalysts for change. See Box 1.1 for a discussion of organizations and the nonprofit distinction.

BOX 1.1

ORGANIZATIONS: FOR-PROFIT AND NON-PROFIT

According to Scott (2001), scholarly interest in organizations is relatively recent (dating to the 1940s) compared with a longstanding sociological preoccupation with institutions and their stabilizing role in society (Spencer, Durkheim, Weber, and Marx come to mind). *Organizations* are defined as having a shared purpose or goal, their size dependent upon their scope of activity. Organizational theorists concern themselves with the structure, function, internal culture, and broader social context of organizations (Scott, 2001). The staying power of organizations depends upon their cohesiveness and ability to operate within the larger social environment.

In the late 20th century, a veritable industry of inquiry arose focused on studies of organizations, including the fields of business, economics, public administration, and political science. Not surprisingly, the volatility and variety of organizational types provided fertile ground for theorists of change. Organizations driven by the pursuit of profit are of interest (especially to the fields of business and economics) because of the ways in which decisions are made and their consequences made known, the latter ranging from robust growth to decline, bankruptcy, and organizational death.

Organizations in the nonprofit realm may be governmental or private, the latter receiving tax exemptions in recognition of their nonprofit status. Harking back to Max Weber, government organizations are known for bureaucratic entrenchment. To the extent that private nonprofits rely on a steady and reliable stream of public funds, they may come to resemble government entities in their staying power.

Just as the public versus private distinction gets blurry in defining organizations, so can the meaning of profit versus nonprofit. The privatization of prisons and schools illustrates how public services get contracted or outsourced to profit-driven companies. Similarly, nonprofit hospitals are bought by and absorbed into large healthcare corporations. Closer to the topic of this book, many organizations that offer public services—such as adult homes, halfway houses, general hospitals, and residential treatment centers—enjoy the tax-free benefits of a nonprofit status even though they can be highly profitable for their executives and vendors. When organizations enrich some and employ many others, change brings threats that are personal as well as organizational.

Institutional Logics, Actors, and Entrepreneurs

Neo-institutional theory encompasses various levels of activity: macro (institutions), meso (organizations), and micro (individuals or small groups). It is considerably harder to apply empirical research methods to the study of large-scale systems and institutions compared with the meso-level of organizations or the micro-level of individual actions (Macfarlane, Barton-Sweeney, Woodard, & Greenhalgh, 2013). At any level, it is not uncommon for multiple, even conflicting institutional logics to develop—all fertile ground for researchers seeking to understand change. Institutions, organizations, and practices often endure, but the rise of multiple logics can introduce volatility and seed change (Binder, 2007; Greenwood, Díaz, Li, & Lorente, 2010).

Too much focus on logics and norms, however, can overlook the role of individual actors and personal agency (Suddaby, 2010). Although institutional actors are presumed to reinforce dominant logics, *institutional entrepreneurs* (IEs) are change agents (Rao & Giorgi, 2006). Working from the outside or from within, IEs take advantage of weaknesses or contradictions within the dominant cultural logic of an institution. The stability of taken-for-granted behaviors that form the glue of institutional stability thereby becomes disrupted (Battilana, Leca, & Boxenbaum, 2009; Clemens & Cook, 1999).

Successful entrepreneurs frame the issues convincingly and mobilize support, drawing on new or revised cultural logics to advance their cause (Lockett, Currie, Waring, Finn, & Martin, 2012). Unlike economic entrepreneurs who take risks to reap profits, IEs are more often driven by ideology. Suddaby and Greenwood (2005) refer to issue-framing by IEs as using rhetoric to achieve legitimacy—rhetoric that may draw on values or ideological arguments.

By definition, IEs seek to reframe a problem and stimulate fresh thinking about new and different solutions to the problem. Their message may be reformist or subversive. Of course, success depends not solely upon rhetorical skills so much as upon timing and the context or receptivity to the message. The message's capacity to stimulate change and attain legitimacy may come from broad grassroots agreement, from powerful elites, or from both. Its impact may be immediate or need time to take hold. One thing is certain: There is almost always resistance from individuals and organizations seeking to defend the status quo. Failure for an IE implies that the message was not welcome, was inadequately framed, was resisted successfully, or all of the above. Kuhn and Weber pertain here, given that the inherent conservatism of bureaucratic institutions serves as a bulwark against change.

IEs may be insiders familiar with the inner workings of the institution or they may be less knowledgeable outsiders seeking change (Rao & Giorgi, 2006). Following Maguire, Hardy, and Lawrence (2004), outsider IEs have less to lose and greater exposure to innovative ideas, but insider IEs have greater knowledge of how the system works and its flaws. Optimal impact is likely to come from insider IEs at the top of the hierarchy (using knowledge plus coercive authority) but they also have the most to lose in power and resources.

All of this emphasis on individual agency is at risk of being oversold. Its centrality to traditional American values renders it an often-invoked yet facile explanation, obscuring the role of social and structural factors. This tension between micro- and macro-level explanations, with their contrasting values of individualism and collectivism, animates public policy debates. The challenge is to contextualize individual actions, to understand what came before and what comes after and what larger forces enable and impinge on these actions.

A Framework for Understanding Housing First and its Impact

Two decades and counting after the founding of Pathways, HF has spread so quickly that one has to ask the question: What exactly is HF? Is it a program model? An approach? A paradigm shift? All of the above? HF had its beginnings in a specific program at a specific time and place and its model of practice (including an overarching philosophy) is one that can now be replicated (Tsemberis, 2010). Over time, however, HF has acquired a much broader and deeper meaning, perhaps inevitable given its marked departure from business as usual and its widespread adoption.

The growing momentum supporting HF has spawned a propensity for homeless service providers to: (a) invoke HF in a vague way to indicate they are "on board" with what funders expect regardless of how much HF is actually in place at their particular program; and (b) view HF as having an unfair competitive advantage in funding decisions. With respect to the former, the staff of a rescue mission could insist that they "do HF" because they provide immediate access to a bed and hot meals. Or consider the proprietor of a board and care home saying they "do HF" because residents have minimal rules to follow and are rarely evicted. Such invocations of HF are understandably made but incorrect. Yet they are likely to increase in number as HF expands nationally and internationally.

As this book will demonstrate, HF has acquired the gravitas of a paradigm shift. Its widespread adoption has inspired systems change well beyond what a model could accomplish. That said, HF started out as a program model—that was the only way it could become embodied or realized in the first place. This book is about that journey from a small but determined opponent of the status quo to the challenges that come with success as well as critical scrutiny. Figure 1.2 depicts how HF skipped over the steps and placed consumers directly into their own independent housing. Going directly from "streets to homes" (Tsemberis, 1999) was, for its time, virtually unheard of.

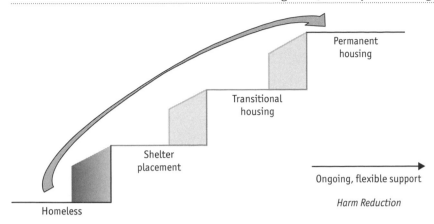

FIGURE 1.2 The Housing First Approach.

Conclusion: Opening the Door to Broader Considerations

A coauthor of this book, Sam Tsemberis, was an institutional entrepreneur who worked on the margins of an expansive service system in New York City to establish Pathways to Housing. Pathways was based on an institutional logic that stood in opposition to the mainstream or staircase continuum then dominant in homeless services. The HF program, however, was not developed solely to enact a new theoretical perspective.

As described earlier in this chapter, many of Pathways' original staff members had been working in crowded drop-in centers where they kept trying and failing to refer their clients to existing continuum programs. It was this experience of repeated failure that moved Pathways staff and consumers to work together to bring about change. Although some of the central components of this alternative logic were not new, their combination and actualization into a real-world service organization, one that considered housing as a basic human right, was unprecedented. In keeping with the power of the status quo ante, the rise of HF was not without resistance, its institutional logic contested.

As we will see in Chapter Two, the homelessness epidemic (as it was called) had diverse and poorly understood causes but its impact was undeniable. Not surprisingly, the policies and practices designed to end or at least manage the epidemic were rooted in a sense of urgency and finitude. In Chapter Three, we describe the institutional actors and entrepreneurs who charted the mainstream or dominant course in homeless services, starting from various lineages or premises but ultimately converging into an unwieldy but massive bureaucracy. Chapter Four is devoted to HF and its evidence base, a body of research that helped shape the new paradigm and set in motion wide dissemination and occasional contestation.

Chapter Five summarizes the qualitative research on HF and non-HF programs, providing themes derived from research that gives a voice to consumers as study participants. In Chapter Six, we feature consumer experiences in their own words through vignettes of life experiences before and after enrolling in a HF or non-HF program. Chapter Seven employs implementation and diffusion theories to describe HF as it spread to other cities in the United States and underwent the inevitable alterations and divergent opinions regarding the core ingredients of the model. Chapter Eight covers the adoptions of HF internationally, introducing new complications in culture and social norms surrounding definitions of homelessness and the services deemed appropriate to help those most in need. Chapter Nine takes a longer view of HF and the problem of homelessness in a world characterized by increasing disparities and inequality.

This broader context is critical to understanding the success as well as the limitations of HF. It is also necessary to avoid decontextualizing, that is, implying that individual actions are all that matter. Changes in the modalities of behavioral and social services usually happen at the micro-level, for example, family preservation programs to prevent foster care placement or cognitive-behavioral treatment for depression. This is a logical consequence of a fundamental premise of these services: The beliefs and behaviors of individuals and families need altering, not the environmental conditions that surround them. If the locus of change is the patient or client, its instigator is the provider—the social worker, psychiatrist, shelter director, or rehabilitation counselor whose authority is socially sanctioned.

HF changed these terms of engagement at the micro-level, but it also opened the door to broader considerations of power in determining access to a scarce and precious resource (housing). It spotlighted the individual client as agent of change as it rewrote the rules regarding access to what endowed that person with client-hood in the first place (homelessness). Shifting to a HF approach demanded major changes in funding priorities and policies. It also depended upon transforming organizational and practice culture, reaching down into the everyday interactions between a psychiatrist (or social worker or case manager) and a client (or tenant).

Beyond the individual and organizational levels are larger structural factors that shape the course of change. These factors often get lost in discourses on the causes of and solutions to homelessness. Structural barriers do not negate individual acts—whether committed by institutional entrepreneurs or homeless persons—but they do place profound constraints on how well or poorly such actions fare. Shortages of affordable housing and living wage jobs, when combined with negative attitudes and stigma, are hardly inconsequential. In the following chapter, we examine the historical antecedents of the homelessness "epidemic" of the 1980s in the United States, setting the stage for the beginning of Housing First.

Notes

1. PHF began as a scatter-site model, that is, clients were placed in apartments in diverse neighborhoods and no more than 20% of the apartments in any building could be PHF clients. As we will see, this aspect of the model underwent modification in later iterations of HF.

2. The term "staircase" is a metaphoric description of homeless services. In large cities like New York, the existence of the staircase is apparent because there is a full array of shelters and transitional housing programs offering step-wise increases in independence (immediate access to the topmost step—permanent independent housing—was rarely available before Housing First). In smaller cities and towns, the bottom steps, such as shelters and temporary apartments or rooms, are the most common form of homeless service.

2 Homelessness in America
TRUTHS AND CONSEQUENCES

Growing Inequality in America: Race, Poverty and Polarization

The story of Housing First (HF) must be set within the larger historical context of homelessness, and homelessness exists within a larger context of growing inequality and housing insecurity. The two major eras of homelessness—during the Great Depression and the 1980s and continuing today—represent key milestones along an historic upward trajectory in income inequality in the United States (Quigley & Raphael, 2004). The usual suspects—outsourcing of jobs overseas, economic recessions, low service-economy wages—intensified after the 1970s. The post-World War II middle-class flight to the suburbs began to reverse itself with the return of young professionals to colonize and gentrify neighborhoods once a haven for singles and working class families. Unable to pay rising taxes and rents, the latter were funneled toward low-income neighborhoods and the inner city (Wilson, 2012). Thus, "concentrated disadvantage" intensified in American cities (Sampson, Raudenbush, & Earls, 1997, p. 918).

For down-on-their-luck residents facing eviction and homelessness, old stand-bys were getting harder to find. Public housing units had years-long waiting lists. In New York City, single-room occupancies (SROs) declined by 60% between 1975 and 1981 (Wright, 1989), a turning point in the availability of affordable housing repeated in cities around the country. The usual restoration of jobs at the tail end of the 1970s recession did little to benefit those most in need (Burt & Aron, 2000).

16

It would be an understatement to say that African Americans fared less well amidst shrinking economic opportunities. The undertow of racism is evident in segregation and discrimination at each juncture, from the initial requirement that public housing developments be segregated to the fierceness of white resistance to integration (Wilkerson, 2011). Related events contributed to racial polarization. For example, draconian drug laws led to widespread incarcerations for low-level offenses and harsher penalties for crack (as opposed to powder) cocaine. A prime example of the effects of intersectionality, race and gender converged to produce a "feminization of poverty" in which women, especially single mothers, bore a disproportionate burden of income deprivation (Brenner, 1987).

Rarely benign in its effects, race consciousness was a not-so-subtle subtext to how the homelessness problem was framed in the 1980s and beyond (Hopper, 2003). The downward and blocked mobility adversely affecting people of color was reproduced and intensified among the homeless. Members of racial and ethnic minorities constitute about one third of the U.S. population, one half of the poor, and almost two thirds of the homeless. African Americans constitute 12% of the U.S. population, about one half of the homeless, and up to 85% of the long-term or chronically homeless (U.S. Department of Housing and Urban Development, 2010). African American women are underrepresented in the homeless adult shelter system but overrepresented in shelters for families.

Sociologists William J. Wilson, Robert Sampson, and their colleagues described inner city neighborhoods of the 1990s as beset by a shrinking job market, high crime, rising rents, and a growing availability of drugs (Sampson et al., 1997; Wilson, 1997). Childhood was lacking in security and stability—with one or both parents unable to support their families. Turbulent family life meant being on the move, living with relatives, foster parents, or friends. There have always been hardworking, law-abiding citizens living this way. But it was undeniable that more of these citizens were losing their grip on financial stability after the economic recessions of the 1970s.

What happened to make homelessness such a problem in the late 1980s? People have been evicted, succumbed to addiction, and run out of money for a long time without becoming homeless. Demographic changes in the U.S. population after World War II may have amplified the effects of increasing economic disparity (Culhane, Metraux, Byrne, Stino, & Bainbridge, 2013). The adult homeless of the 1980s were born at the tail end of the Baby Boom—one of the largest increases in birth rates in U.S. history. As economic opportunities shrank along with the usual safety net protections, the number of adults vulnerable to homelessness expanded.

Affordable Housing as Federal Government Responsibility

Federal government involvement in building and providing affordable housing began with the New Deal Public Works Administration and the Wagner-Stegall Housing Act of 1937. Cities took over vacant lands and built low-rise apartment complexes for poor and working class families—50,000 new units were built in 1939 alone. In New York City, the first public housing units—known as First Houses—opened in December 1935 in a ceremony presided over by Mayor Fiorello LaGuardia and First Lady Eleanor Roosevelt. Towering housing projects opened in large cities around the United States beginning in the 1940s, their height made possible by the invention of the elevator and architectural designs featuring steel frames and reinforced concrete rather than masonry and stone.

Although the New Deal was steeped in idealism about public works, the post-World War II era ushered in a contraction in government spending on housing. The return of military veterans and the Baby Boom gave rise to unprecedented demand for single-family homes and private developers obliged in meeting this demand as the suburbs spread farther from the city center. Meanwhile, the rising value of urban real estate ran up against growing concentrations of poor and near-poor in inner city areas, especially in the North where thousands of African Americans migrated to escape the Jim Crow South (Wilkerson, 2011).

By the 1950s, cities like Chicago, Milwaukee, Detroit, and Philadelphia were transformed, their European immigrant neighborhoods in demographic transition prompted by Southern migration and race-baited "white flight" to the suburbs. Earlier civic reforms bent on slum removal gave way to urban renewal as these same neighborhoods were targeted for demolition and population displacement. However, a civic duty to replace blight with livable neighborhoods was rarely in evidence; only a fraction of razed homes were replaced by new ones. Public housing developments were built on some of the cleared lands but the open space was more often used for new office buildings and highways linking suburbs and cities (Kusmer, 2003).

President Johnson's War on Poverty breathed new life into the Federal government's role in housing and community development—starting the cabinet-level Department of Housing and Urban Development (HUD) in 1965 was a key part of Johnson's Great Society initiatives. Meanwhile, the endurance of Section 8 of the Housing Act of 1937, a Federal rental assistance program, kept untold millions from becoming homeless.[1] This voucher program allowed tenants who qualified (had low income) to pay no more than 30% of their income toward rent assessed at fair market value. For some landlords, a Federal guarantee that rent would be paid was attractive but for others, visits from HUD housing inspectors, a cap on fair market rents, and resistance to poor families living in their properties were sufficient grounds for rejection.

Nixon's retrenchment policies and the economic recession of the 1970s put an effective halt to new public housing developments, and the Reagan years added an ideological hardening to this economic rationale. As neo-liberal policies[2] of the late 1970s and early 1980s gained traction, local and federal governments backed away from financing for public welfare—from income supports to affordable housing to health care. This ushered in an era of private market-driven federal housing and tax policies that contributed to homelessness then and up to the present day. Essentially, there was a sharp turn away from supporting public housing to supporting home ownership. Homeowners got deductions for mortgage interest, property taxes, exempted or deferred tax on capital gains from the sale of a home and other perquisites. In addition, real estate investors received deductions for tax-exempt housing bonds, depreciation, and other expenses. Simultaneously, there was a significant reduction in federal housing assistance expenditures such as development of low-income housing or rental assistance.

From 1976 to 2002, housing outlays rose from $7.2 billion to $32.1 billion and the housing assistance budget dropped from $55.6 billion to $27.6 billion (Dolbeare & Crowley, 2007). One of the few exceptions in the general decline of federal benefits has been the availability of disability income such as SSI (Supplemental Security Income) where growth in the number of recipients has been steady over the past four decades.

Disillusionment with urban renewal and high-rise public housing also hastened the decline in Federal investment. The infamous Pruitt-Igoe housing project in St. Louis, Missouri epitomized this. A 33-building complex built in 1954, Pruitt-Igoe became marred by crime, violence, and extreme segregation, its grand demolition televised in 1972 to international audiences. The equation of high-rise living with vandalism and crime was viewed as rendering public housing unsafe for children and families. The solution—to abandon public housing rather than invest to improve it—reaped profits for private developers. The net result was that working class families, the working poor, and individuals on fixed incomes were steadily displaced by upwardly mobile urbanites.

Notwithstanding long waiting lists, deteriorating conditions, and general neglect, public housing keeps many families from the streets and shelters where they might otherwise find themselves. Currently, there are about 1.2 million households in public housing overseen by 3,300 housing authorities (www.hud.gov). There has been no significant increase in public housing units in decades.

Homelessness as a Federal Government Responsibility

The reductions in affordable housing and rising rents permanently "priced out" of the rental market those living on fixed incomes such as disability payments, given that they would need almost 150% of their total income to simply afford a month's rent (O'Hara, 2007). Individuals working at full-time minimum wage jobs would have to hold 3.1 full-time jobs in order for the rent to comprise 30% of their income (Frazier, 2013). One need not be a mathematician to know that eviction is a real possibility for those living on fixed and low incomes—even homeowners without a mortgage must pay taxes, utilities, and insurance.

A pivotal event in Federal Government actions to address homelessness occurred in 1987 with the passage of the Stewart B. McKinney Homeless Assistance Act (renamed the McKinney–Vento Act by President Clinton in 2000 to honor Minnesota Senator Bruce Vento's work on behalf of the poor). The McKinney Act offered 350 million dollars in funds in its first year to enable states, along with public and private organizations, to open and operate emergency food and shelter programs for homeless persons.

Provisions of the Act included support for education of homeless adults and children, job training, demonstration projects in mental health and substance abuse for homeless persons, and sustainable funding for the pilot Health Care for the Homeless (HCH) program. This represented a fraction of what was needed to address the problem—and the bulk of funding was targeted to the needs of homeless families rather than single adults—but it was a start.

Last but not least, the Act included the creation of the United States Interagency Council on Homelessness (USICH), a consortium of 20 Federal agencies including HUD. The USICH was left unfunded and remained without staff under President Clinton and then HUD Secretary Andrew Cuomo; it was essentially dormant from 1988 until 2002. Then, in 2002, President G. W. Bush appointed Philip Mangano to head USICH. Mangano, a Massachusetts Republican and former director of the Massachusetts Housing and Shelter Alliance, had long advocated for the abolition of homelessness.

There were plenty of other distractions for the Bush administration, including the aftermath of the September 11 attacks and the war in Iraq, but this appointment reverberated widely among homeless advocates as an unusual sign of attention from the President. The *Wall Street Journal* referred to it as a "Nixon-goes-to-China" reversal of policy in which $4 billion annually was pledged to HUD and the effort to address homelessness (Vitullo–Martin, 2007). Ever the entrepreneur, Mangano used his bully pulpit for homeless advocacy and gave it a Federal imprimatur.

From Single-Room Occupancy to Emergency Shelters to Transitional Housing

In larger American cities, single-room occupancy buildings (SROs) were one of the few viable options for those living on the margins. An SRO is typically a large building consisting of dozens of small rooms containing a bed, a dresser, and a hot plate; the shared bathroom is down the hall. SROs afforded a place to keep one's possessions, stay warm in the winter, and have a bit of security and privacy at a low cost. The deterioration of SROs may have seemed inevitable given rising real estate prices and urban renewal, but their tarnished reputations and inadequate upkeep by their owners did little to endear them to city authorities. Moreover, as elderly SRO residents died off and some SROs became vacant, the buildings decayed further.

Without the SRO safety net (however tattered and shrunk in size by the 1980s), cities and communities grew desperate to address a problem that was no longer hidden from sight. Most cities set up temporary shelters and specialty programs such as outreach teams, drop-in centers, and safe havens to engage those among the homeless with psychiatric disabilities. In New York City, massive fortresses like the Fort Washington Armory—with a peak count of 1,000 men each night—were repurposed with cots lined up 18 inches apart on the vast open drill room floor. Such crowded conditions violated United Nations standards for refugee camps. Box 2.1 describes the early days of the homelessness crisis in New York City.

Complementing public shelter provision was a network of churches and synagogues that organized volunteers to serve an evening meal and accommodate about a dozen homeless guests on any given night. The guests would sleep on cots in the vestibule or basement of the building and as in city shelters they were required to leave the premises by dawn. This private voluntary network offered smaller, less dangerous venues for women and the elderly, but these were few and far between and "guests" were carefully screened.

Visitors to the public shelters were also immediately struck by the clearly intended message of enforced transience. Cots were lined up in rows, there was no storage space for personal belongings, meals consisted of little more than hot coffee and a cold sandwich, and clean bathrooms were in short supply. Possessions had to be closely guarded under the cot or pillow and residents had to leave the shelter early each morning and were permitted to return only at night. Shelter staff and security guards had little training; reports of theft, sale of contraband, or violence were common.

With crowded, unsanitary, and dangerous conditions, frustrations rose and fights often broke out. Weaker residents were preyed upon. AIDS, hepatitis, and

BOX 2.1
THE NEW YORK CITY EXPERIENCE IN THE 1980S

Land-scarce and surrounded by rivers and oceanfront, New York City has long endured shortages of housing and near-record occupancy rates. But the city in the 1970s suffered an acute case of urban decay, increasing crime and middle-class abandonment. Movies like *Midnight Cowboy, Needle Park, Fort Apache,* the *Bronx,* and *The French Connection* captured this gritty reality Hollywood-style. Graffiti-covered subways rumbled over- and underground, drug markets thrived on street corners, and the South Bronx looked like a postapocalyptic movie set. Along with San Francisco, New York was the epicenter of the AIDS epidemic of the 1980s, a plague that spread through the gay community and on to poor neighborhoods.

When drug dealers, faced with a glut of cocaine, developed a solid smokable form in the early 1980s, crack cocaine became one of the greatest successes in the history of drug marketing. Delivering an intense high at a low price (as little as $5 for a small "rock") meant that cocaine now ceased being a drug solely for the affluent, who continued to buy it in powder form. Starting in Los Angeles and Miami, crack spread quickly to the populous cities of the North. Crack addiction was devastating to poor minority communities, contributing to a rise in violent crimes, thefts, and burglaries. Although oversold as a cause of urban problems of the 1980s, there is little doubt that crack addiction sent many poor Latinos and African Americans over the edge into homelessness (Bourjois, 1996).

tuberculosis (TB) were common along with the usual respiratory problems, injuries, and skin infections. This was the environment where a strain of treatment-resistant TB first appeared, alarming residents, staff, and the general public. These conditions led to a seemingly irrational but entirely reasonable choice to stay away from the city shelters except under dire circumstances, like a freezing-cold winter night.

However unpleasant they might have been, the shelters were filled to over-flowing in the 1990s, a reflection of the numbers of new homeless, given that the majority of shelter residents stayed only a few days then found some place else to go. Those unable or unwilling to enter shelters sought help in other ways, visiting soup kitchens and crowded drop-in centers where they might take a shower, store some of their belongings, and nap on a chair.

Stability in funding for the shelter system was made possible by McKinney funds and dollars from state and local governments. A profound shift took place, however, in homeless services that allowed providers to go beyond emergency accommodations—not abandoning these altogether but supplementing them with longer-term housing combined with services. A stay in such a shelter was expected to last 30 days, more or less. Transitional housing could be offered for one or two years, sometimes longer (Ellen & O'Flaherty, 2010).

New York City and New York State led the way in making available new sources of funding for nonemergency supportive housing, but this came with a price. The historic 1990 New York–New York (NY/NY) Agreement called for 3,615 units of permanent and transitional housing for homeless mentally ill people in New York City. After delays prompted by disagreements over jurisdiction and funding, Mayor David Dinkins and Governor Mario Cuomo signed the agreement, an unprecedented collaboration between city and state. The price of such an agreement lay in its narrowing of eligibility to persons who are mentally ill among the homeless.

This was a politically strategic decision for a couple of reasons. First, the visibility of psychotic individuals on city streets, though hardly representative of all homeless persons, fueled public demands for more concerted action. Second, New York State's Office of Mental Health had a multibillion-dollar budget that was being reconfigured as state psychiatric hospitals were closed or being closed by the late 1980s. Although community mental health centers remained underfunded (and a few expensive upstate hospitals stayed open due to political pressure), there were state and city mental health dollars available when the political will was forthcoming.

The NY/NY agreement channeled state and city mental health funds to nonprofit organizations that won successful bids to build or renovate congregate residences with some additional scatter-site independent apartment units covered by rental subsidies. Prior to NY/NY, the State had mostly funded group homes, adult homes, and in some instances nursing homes for residents discharged from state psychiatric hospitals. Providing permanent housing with supports represented a new philosophical and practice approach for the state's outdated mental health services. The use of these state funds for capital improvement and the city's issuance of municipal bonds to build or renovate housing also marked a new era in government resourcefulness and cooperation in providing for the homeless.

Steeped in New York's traditional liberalism in public assistance, the NY/NY agreement met with little overt opposition. But public generosity did not always extend to the neighborhoods where these projects were slated to be developed, as local groups protested "not in my back yard" (NIMBY) and expressed concerns about safety and lower property values. The politically influential, wealthier neighborhoods were able to resist these programs; new projects were typically placed in mixed-use areas or low-income neighborhoods.

It is worth noting that the construction and occupancy of the NY/ NY-funded units did not reduce the number of people who were homeless according to annual street counts. As soon as some left homelessness, there were new entrants to take their places—and more. Less obvious was the fact that these new supportive housing programs used admissions criteria that were very demanding. Initially, applicants were required only to have a history of homelessness and a serious mental illness. Because these criteria applied to a very large pool of applicants, however, providers saw a need to narrow the admissions criteria. Most were new operators of supportive housing but they fully understood that their program's survival depended on maintaining a full census.

Ensuring that applicants would be reliable tenants meant screening for those who would not create a nuisance, need to be evicted, or disturb others in the building. Thus the successful applicant was one who was in treatment, medication compliant, did not use substances, and was willing to abide by the program rules. This screening for well-behaved tenants increased the proportion of more troubled and addicted men and women remaining on the street. Housing providers had plenty of terms for these people: "not-housing-ready," "hard-to-house," "housing resistant," and "treatment resistant" among others. Eventually, such persons also came to be known as the "chronically homeless."

Criminalizing the Homeless

New York City Mayor Guiliani's law and order rhetoric and "broken windows" policing became popular in many cities in the United States in the 1990s (see Box 2.2 for more on this subject). Yet most of the crimes committed by the homeless were minor offenses necessitated by their condition: theft of service (e.g., jumping the turnstile to ride the subway); theft of goods (e.g., stealing groceries); indecent exposure (e.g., urinating in public); or trespassing (e.g., sleeping in a public space). Once homeless men or women are charged with one of these offenses, the criminal justice system sets up a cascade of events that do not bode well for them (O'Sullivan, 2012). First, the fine goes unpaid. With no fixed address, the defendant never receives the notice to appear in court and misses the hearing date. Next, a bench warrant is issued and on the next encounter with the police the person is arrested and jailed. Without the cash for bail (sometimes as little as $10) homeless persons spend weeks and months in jail (at a cost to taxpayers of several hundred dollars a day).

The criminalization of homelessness in combination with woefully inadequate mental health care transformed many city jails into de facto mental institutions for the homeless. Seeing erratic behavior on the street and having little to do

BOX 2.2

NEW YORK CITY IN THE 1990S: CRIME, SQUEEGEE MEN AND GIULIANI

By the mid-1990s, rising crime rates were equated with homelessness (despite the absence of data to support this notion) and patience in some quarters was wearing thin. New York City's Rudolf Giuliani staked his successful 1994 mayoral campaign on law and order, in particular promising to rid the city of "squeegee men," the mostly African American men who frequented the city's busy traffic intersections, performing unsolicited windshield washings and expecting cash in return. Newspapers inflamed public hostility with stories of aggressive panhandling and public attitudes toward the homeless were souring.

Guiliani's police crackdown focused on lifestyle offenses—fare beating, public intoxication and trespassing—based upon the famous "broken windows" theory of criminology (Kelling & Wilson, 1982). Research has since called this into question (Harcourt & Ludwig, 2006) but the perception that police crackdowns for small offenses also tamped down serious crimes has stuck around. For the homeless, this was less about crime-fighting than criminalization.

besides make an arrest, police officers treat a jail stay as the least problematic response to local complaints. In contrast, the crimes to which the homeless were subjected—physical and sexual assault, theft, confiscation and destruction of their belongings—were of less public concern.

Cities found creatively punitive ways to discourage people from sleeping rough and an urban phenomenon of "hostile architecture" flourished in the United States and abroad (Quinn, 2014). Benches were redesigned with armrests or uneven surfaces to prevent reclining; low border walls had fencing or planters along their surfaces to prevent sitting. Use of security fencing, razor wire, and "no trespassing" signs went up as did security cameras and guard services. A social media storm erupted in June 2014 when a luxury apartment building and nearby grocery chain in London installed metal spikes on the surfaces of doorways and entrances to discourage "anti-social behavior." After petitions and online protests, the spikes were removed.

Under stricter antivagrancy laws, libraries and other public buildings forbade lingering too long or sleeping on the premises (although more tolerant communities resisted this). Public-access toilets became harder to find as shops and restaurants restricted use to paying customers. Abandoned buildings, attractive to squatters and the homeless, were sometimes violently vacated by fire departments or city officials.

Los Angeles's policy of segregating and corralling the homeless in Skid Row (see Box 2.3) represents a scaled-up version of 19th-century practices—tolerating a Bowery or run-down district where vagrancy and sleeping rough were allowed

BOX 2.3
THE LOS ANGELES EXPERIENCE: SKID ROW

Los Angeles's Skid Row, for over 100 years a destination for the poor, homeless, and addicted, was home to faith-based missions that provided charity as well as personal redemption. Located not far from the downtown business district, the area was largely left alone until the 1980s when the growing numbers of homeless led city officials to order police crackdowns and destruction of the camps. The rights-based litigation and advocacy that ensued kept Skid Row intact and the missions empowered as advocates and service providers.

This policy of containment and segregation continued as downtown LA began to gentrify and attract businesses and affluent residents in the 1990s. A few blocks from the vast canyons of sleek office buildings and luxury condominiums, Skid Row is unique. There is no greater concentration of homeless adults in America, about 5,000 give or take. Visitors—mostly social service workers and a few curious tourists—enter 50 square blocks of shopping carts and tents filled with personal belongings and hoardings, of people sitting or sleeping, intoxicated or sober, waiting in lines at the missions for food or services. Skid Row is predominantly African American even though African Americans comprise only 9.8% of the city's population.

as long as these practices did not spread to other parts of the city. The more common response by cities was to disperse their homeless shelters and use assertive outreach teams to convince or cajole street homeless to go to these shelters. Of course, "dispersing" was not random—zoning ordinances and NIMBY-ism ensured that shelters were located in lower-income (or more tolerant) neighborhoods. Some communities complained of becoming service ghettos, hosting a disproportionate number of half-way houses, congregate residences, or mental health and methadone clinics.

A Homeless Services Institutional Complex (or a Homeless Service "Industry") is Born

The homelessness crisis of the 1980s and subsequent governmental response set the stage for explosive growth in outreach, shelters, transitional housing, and support services in American cities. Such largesse did not extend to the general population of the poor—Reagan-era cuts in entitlements were followed by Clinton-era welfare reform (known as "workfare") in the mid-1990s. In this context, it is remarkable that the homeless received a measure of public sympathy

BOX 2.4

AN AMERICAN WAY OF CHANGING POLICY: LITIGATION AS ADVOCACY

A lesser-known benefit of the litigious bent in American society is the rapidity with which social change can be mandated by a court order. The U.S. Supreme Court's 1972 *Roe v. Wade* decision swept away most restrictions on abortion in the United States and its *Brown v. Board of Education* in 1954 mandated school desegregation. The 1979 *Callahan v. Carey* court decision was a defining moment for New York City's homeless, binding the city to a legal right to shelter that continues at this writing. This legacy of bringing about change via litigation has been a prime tactic of legal advocates such as the American Civil Liberties Union (ACLU).

A recent case in point is Miami, Florida and its strategy of using arrests as a means of evicting homeless men and women from its revitalizing downtown business district. Beginning in mid-2013, attorneys for the local ACLU challenged the city, citing a previous court decision designed to protect the rights of the homeless. This 1998 settlement (*Pottinger et al. v. City of Miami*) was the culmination of a class action lawsuit and a decade of litigation involving two trials, two appeals, and almost two years of mediation in which a federal court found intentional and systematic violations of the constitutional rights of homeless persons in Miami. The agreement afforded protection in carrying out "life-sustaining misdemeanors" such as sleeping, erecting a tent in a park, and urinating in public if a toilet was not available.

By 2013, the city's downtown business leaders were urging a clampdown on the hundreds of homeless men and women living in parks and on sidewalks. Miami police stepped up arrests for minor infractions—all violations of the *Pottinger* agreement—and seized and demolished campsites and belongings.[3] Negotiations between the ACLU and the city bogged down as the city proposed to bus homeless persons to a shelter miles away. Measuring the distance to a public toilet, a trash receptacle, or a shelter was the metric for determining whether an arrest could be made.

Ascertaining what constituted "available shelter" was a major sticking point. The city sought to expand the definition to include shelters that imposed mandatory mental health and drug addiction treatment (prohibited under the *Pottinger* agreement). Helping to support the city's case, a local religious shelter offered open-air mats for sleeping as appropriate for shelter referrals (along with treatment mandates).

The ACLU attorneys countered with "Housing First" as the evidence-based standard against which the city was falling short. The case drew to a close when a judge-mediated agreement was reached in November 2013. With some minor concessions, the *Pottinger* protections remain in place until 2016. For the longer-term, the Miami-Dade County Homeless Trust embarked on a major shift in strategy focusing on Housing First with the goal of ending chronic homelessness by the end of 2015.

and financial support, though conditionally given and temporary in nature. As described in Box 2.4, policy changes were not always prompted by legislative mandates. Indeed, the successful use of litigation on behalf of homeless persons could produce sweeping mandates.

The era of local responses to homelessness gave way to large-scale efforts and a vast industry of homeless services came into being. This was not a matter of planning or coordination; it was willy-nilly in its evolution but coalescent nonetheless. Closely resembling Willse's (2010) "non-profit industrial complex" and Stid's (2012) "social services industrial complex," this "homeless services institutional complex" comprised a self-perpetuating system (the term "institutional" used to indicate that levels of government and governmental organizations worked together with nonprofits in cross-institutional collaboration). Providing services to and for the homeless becomes an end in itself, sustaining thousands of jobs for those working in the "industry."

What began as service silos for various needs (e.g., mental illness, substance abuse, the lack of food and shelter) were joined together by a common thread of first temporary then stable streams of funding. State mental hospitals, public hospitals, community mental health clinics, and rehabilitation centers were joined by a burgeoning number of shelters, drop-in centers, soup kitchens, and food pantries. Along with jails and hospital emergency rooms, these became stopovers on an "institutional circuit" (Hopper, Jost, Hay, Welber, & Haugland, 1997) traversed by homeless men and women.

As the number of homeless adults increased, government agencies responded by aggregating temporary housing with services and supervision under (often literally) the same roof. New programs sprang up and existing ones grew to meet demand by building and renovating properties, while hiring more staff to secure grants and service contracts. This growth—in needs, in services, in jobs—was especially evident in large cities (U.S. Department of Housing and Urban Development, 2010). In the smaller cities and towns of America affected by homelessness, the "industry" emerged in the form of shelters, rescue missions, and soup kitchens.

Conclusion

The homeless services institutional complex had a cultural logic as well as norms and taken-for-granted behaviors. Owing much to institutional entrepreneurs with divergent motivations and constituencies, the complex evolved into an unwieldy yet curiously unified service system. The complex was fragmented enough to allow an innovative upstart such as Pathways to emerge but cohered sufficiently to present resistance to the changes wrought by the HF approach. Neo-institutional theory renders both action and reaction understandable but offers little in the way of predicting the course of change once the process is underway.

The next chapter traces the philosophical premises of the social response to homelessness in the United States. These overlapping yet contrasting visions had institutional logics that melded advocacy, altruism, and down-to-earth pragmatism.

Notes

1. The Section 8 program (now called Housing Choice) was a rare instance of government involvement in rental assistance for use in the private housing market. Though funded at levels far below need, such vouchers help millions of Americans to stay housed. For proponents of Housing First, the Section 8 program is a natural fit as it fosters scatter-site living in the private rental market.

2. The word "neoliberal" is a term of reference for conservative governments of the Reagan–Thatcher era and their policies of market-driven capitalist expansion, deregulation, reduced social programs, and privatization. As non-Western governments adopt such policies, the impact of globalization and rising poverty is attributed to neoliberalism.

3. Information on the ACLU-Miami legal standoff—all public documents—was available through the first author's preparation as an expert witness.

3 Three Lineages of Homeless Services

ENDING HOMELESSNESS IN the 1990s did not happen, but not for lack of trying. The civic response to the crisis was an unprecedented outpouring of public and private funds. The strictures attached to these funds steered efforts in certain directions (and away from others), but they also allowed institutional entrepreneurs and organizations sufficient latitude to address homelessness in differing ways.

In this chapter, we describe three broad forms this service response took, which we call: *extending the mission, advocacy with action,* and *business model* approaches. Each of these approaches is rooted in different but overlapping philosophies of service and each has its own institutional logic. The first is rooted in traditional faith-based charity and philanthropic giving, the second in a manifestation of human rights activism, and the third in representing public–private partnerships infused with business practices. The examples described in this chapter are archetypal, and there are many organizations that draw on elements of more than one approach. Not surprisingly, the presence of multiple logics can introduce volatility and seed change, especially if they are competing or contradictory.

Lineage 1: Extending the Mission

Charitable giving has taken many forms in the United States; religious doctrine has always been a powerful motivator, seeking to reform the destitute and shape their destinies toward becoming productive God-fearing citizens. Among the more visible and impenitent were the men who drank in excess, stumbling on the streets or passed out in doorways. The rescue missions run by religious charities were places to dry out, get a meal, and hear a sermon.

Long-term presence in the skid rows of American cities meant faith-based organizations were among the first to step up in the 1980s, already equipped to operate soup kitchens, food pantries, and small shelters. Many Christian missions and their volunteers were driven by compassion as well as an evangelical impulse. Well-meaning but morality-driven, these religious missions have been small-scale but determined stakeholders in the "homeless industry."

Included in this lineage are the much larger but still charity-driven philanthropic organizations. Generally secular and more broadly defined in purpose, wealthy foundations extend assistance through program development and evaluation, spending private endowments for public welfare. Some examples of charitable organizations are described below.

BOSTON'S PINE STREET INN. The Pine Street Inn in Boston's Chinatown neighborhood was founded in 1969 to help homeless men with alcohol problems but was later transformed by the influx of "new homeless"—younger men and women, mentally ill persons, and members of ethnic minorities. Expanding to include an emergency shelter for women in a repurposed fire department building, Pine Street Inn became a leading shelter and housing provider for Boston's homeless population. As in other U.S. cities, Boston's poor experienced the same life predicament—being priced out of the rental market and having reduced access to rental subsidies and low-cost housing. An estimated 20,000 single-room occupancy (SRO)-type rooms disappeared over a 10-year period in Boston alone. The new urbanites, mostly young professionals, paid well for apartments and condos in rehabilitated downtown buildings.

Pine Street Inn joined the supportive housing movement in 1984, setting up a residence in the nearby city of Brookline where 26 men and women had private rooms and shared kitchens, bathrooms, and commons areas with on-site staff support. Over time, the full continuum of services was offered, ranging from street outreach to emergency shelter to transitional and permanent housing.

LOS ANGELES: SKID ROW MISSIONS. Los Angeles offers a rare example of a big city that embraced faith-based missions as key partners in homeless services, not only in the past (as many cities had done) but continuing into the present (as few cities have done). This version of "extending the mission" was enacted on Los Angeles's Skid Row, where various ministries and churches operated. As described in Chapter 2, Skid Row in LA was and is a place of segregation and containment—50 square blocks where approximately 5,000 homeless men and women are allowed to camp out without being arrested for trespassing or vagrancy.

In recent years, the balance has tipped toward forming coalitions to provide housing, including the use of Housing First (HF),[1] but Skid Row missions continue to operate and advocate, including the Midnight Mission, Open Door Skid Row Ministry, Los Angeles Mission, and Union Rescue Mission to name a few. Recent moves to promote permanent housing and HF have met with resistance from these organizations, whose allegiance is with "treatment first" (or "spiritual redemption first"). A mission administrator expressed concern over the harm-reduction aspects of HF, saying that substance abuse and mental health treatment need to come first. "Our point is that if you can do that before they are housed, there will be a higher success rate." (Parvini, 2014).

THE ROBERT WOOD JOHNSON FOUNDATION'S HEALTH CARE FOR THE HOMELESS INITIATIVE. On a much larger scale and a secular version of "extending the mission," the Robert Wood Johnson Foundation partnered with Pew Charitable Trusts in 1985 to take the lead in addressing the urgent and unattended health problems of homeless men and women. Committing $25 million over five years to 19 pilot programs, the Health Care for the Homeless (HCH) initiative promoted active outreach, links between shelters and clinics or hospitals, and accessible clinics just for homeless individuals. Using vans as rolling clinics and making sidewalk "house visits," doctors and nurses took to the streets on behalf of HCH.

The extent of unmet need was visible and urgent, including wounds, leg ulcers, skin rashes, lice, lung infections, frostbite, hypothermia, and injuries. Lack of sanitation meant exposure to unclean water, rodents and pests, and garbage. Infectious diseases included hepatitis A and C, HIV/AIDS, pneumonia, and tuberculosis. Relying on "dumpster diving" and food handouts dramatically increased the risk of food poisoning. Dental care was rarely available, leading to painful infections, tooth loss, and difficulties in eating and speaking. A lack of eye care meant that vision problems went uncorrected. Hypertension, heart disease, and diabetes were common. These problems put homeless men and women at constant risk of health crises and left them little recourse beyond a public hospital's emergency room.

In a survey of 1,250 of New York City's shelter inhabitants in 1987, the frequency of injuries and victimizations was 30 times higher than that of the general U.S. population (Padgett, Struening, Andrews, & Pittman, 1995). Traumatic injuries were the number one reason for emergency room visits, with limb fractures, concussions, burns, and skull fractures (in that order) the most common. At the time of the survey, only one of the 26 city-run shelters had a medical clinic (Padgett et al., 1995).

The HCH program was pioneering in its national scope and ambition. From the initial 19 demonstration projects, the program expanded to all 50 states in the United States, with 130 local offices. It is also given credit for helping to spur Congress to pass the McKinney Homeless Services Act, which included authorization to fund HCH programs. HCH programs raised awareness about the health consequences of homelessness at a time when the focus was on emergency food and shelter and little more. The Robert Wood Johnson Foundation may seem an unlikely counterpart to local religious organizations, but both exemplify "extending the mission," that is, transforming private giving into public services, whether motivated by religion or philanthropy. Box 3.1 describes another RWJ Foundation initiative specifically for the needs of homeless persons with serious mental illness.

Lineage 2: Advocacy with Action

Although missions and foundations did not eschew advocacy, it was not their primary goal. This second lineage represents putting advocacy first. Raising public consciousness and arguing for the human right to housing was no small effort (Byrne & Culhane, 2011).

ORGANIZATIONS AND MOVEMENTS PROTESTING HOMELESSNESS. Protest tactics of social activists were well honed by the time of the homelessness crisis, drawing inspiration from a variety of causes from civil rights to feminism to opposition to the Vietnam War. In October 1989, over 250,000 homeless men and women and their supporters marched in Washington, DC at a Housing Now! rally. Newspaper accounts of homeless protests were reported in over 60 U.S. cities during the 1980s with more than 500 protest events in 17 of those cities (Cress & Snow, 2000). With the prominent exception of the AIDs response, no social movement at the time had as much draw as homeless advocacy.[2]

Movements by or on behalf of the poor are inherently under-resourced—the primary stakeholders have to expend precious energy on top of struggling to survive. Moreover, unlike other social movements such as AIDS advocacy, they rarely attract wealthy benefactors. Thus, it is all the more remarkable that hundreds of

BOX 3.1
THE ROBERT WOOD JOHNSON FOUNDATION PROGRAM
ON CHRONIC MENTAL ILLNESS

One notable early effort to address housing and services for the mentally ill was initiated by the Robert Wood Johnson Foundation (RWJ) with its Program on Chronic Mental Illness (Cohen & Somers, 1990). In 1986, RWJ in collaboration with the Department of Housing and Urban Development (HUD) provided more than $100 million in grants, loans, and rent subsidies to nine American cities that successfully proposed to create an effective intervention to address the problems of the mentally ill homeless. It was obvious that existing systems of care were failing the mentally ill among the homeless: most urban mental health systems were fragmented. Mental health centers and hospitals that were available operated in specific catchment areas but without any formal relationship to one another or to other relevant services, especially housing.

The RWJ initiative had the bold aim of coordinating services by developing several hundred units of housing over a five-year period in each of the nine cities that were funded. The cities all had populations of greater than 250,000 and included Austin, Texas, Baltimore, Maryland, Charlotte, North Carolina, Cincinnati, Ohio, Columbus, Ohio, Denver, Colorado, Honolulu, Hawaii, Philadelphia, Pennsylvania, and Toledo, Ohio (Cohen & Somers, 1990). The program was generally considered successful; housing production did not reach its goals, but those who were able to enter housing reported being satisfied with their case managers (Cohen & Somers, 1990).

All nine cities reported disappointment with their inability to coordinate with hospital inpatient services and community based services; the program's evaluators concluded that the initiative achieved positive outcomes in specific programs and for specific practices but that systems change was difficult to achieve (Shore & Cohen, 1992). Taken together with its earlier and successful Health Care for the Homeless Program, the RWJ Foundation's efforts have had a profound influence on how services for the homeless could be improved.

thousands turned out to protest homelessness, many of whom were drawn from the ranks of homeless men and women.

Washington, DC was by far the favored location for such protests—no surprise for a movement bent on changing U.S. housing policies and increasing public assistance to the poor. In a study of homeless protest movements, Snow, Soule, and Cress (2005) noted that Washington, DC had 83 protest events in the decade 1980 to 1990; New York City followed in distant second place with 55 events. The corner of D and 2nd Streets in Washington, now named Mitch Snyder Place, was the ground zero of homelessness protest. It was the site of the largest homeless shelter in the United States in the 1980s, a repurposed Federal City College building with 1,350 beds; it was also the birthplace of the Community for Creative Non-Violence (CCNV).

Founded by a peace-activist Catholic priest and a few George Washington University students, CCNV opened a soup kitchen in 1972 followed by drop-in centers and a health clinic. CCNV was, like the antiwar collectives that had sprung up across the country, a place for nonviolent but determined social action. It was here that the most prominent activist on behalf of the homeless found his calling. Born in Brooklyn and living a restless itinerant life interspersed with jail time (including a stint in Federal prison for auto theft), Mitch Snyder came to the CCNV in 1973.

From that home base, Snyder led the way to overt action, occupying an abandoned building (what became the Federal City College shelter), holding public funerals of the homeless who died on the street, engaging in nonviolent protests and hunger strikes. Snyder's longest hunger strike ended after 51 days when President Reagan agreed to allocate funds to renovate the City College shelter (a promise he did not keep). A fierce advocate, Snyder confronted affluent religious congregations in nearby Georgetown, adroitly handled the media and attracted sympathy (as well as dismay) with his tactics. Snyder's redemptive life narrative and his tireless efforts gave homeless advocacy a sympathetic persona and media attention that was unparalleled for the time. A documentary and feature film were made about his life, the latter starring actor Martin Sheen—newspaper photos from the time show Snyder standing and smiling next to Sheen, both surrounded by shelter residents. Mired in a difficult relationship and exhausted by declining interest in the cause, Mitch Snyder hung himself in his room at the CCNV shelter in 1990 at the age of 46.

Related protest groups were emerging in other parts of the country. The National Union of the Homeless (NUH), a federation of activist organizations dedicated to housing rights and economic justice, began in Philadelphia in 1985. Like the CCNV, the NUH pushed for change at many levels, from preventing police harassment to voting rights to affordable housing. At its peak, the NUH had 20 local affiliates and 15,000 members. Part of the New York City affiliate, the Tompkins Square Union of the Homeless, was centered in a gritty East Village park in downtown Manhattan long known for social tolerance and antiestablishment movements.

On the spectrum of activism, NUH was more confrontational than other homeless advocacy groups, aggressively engaging in civil disobedience and occupation of abandoned buildings and federally owned unoccupied houses. It also put the spotlight on homelessness as part of the much larger problem of poverty.

Following the lead of the much larger National Welfare Rights Organization, NUH called attention to growing income disparities and the need for jobs as well as housing. A cosponsor of the Housing Now! march in 1989, NUH rejected the organizers' insistence on a peaceful, legally sanctioned rally and organized separate protests that led to numerous arrests. With losses in leadership and momentum, the organization ceased being active in 1993.

The National Coalition for the Homeless (NCH) has managed to stay viable since its inception in 1982. Attorney and Coalition founder Robert Hayes was an early champion of the cause, successfully suing the city of New York in 1979 to enforce a "right to shelter" law (the *Callahan v. Carey* court decision). As a result, the number of shelter beds almost tripled in the early 1980s, reaching close to 10,000 (Houghton, 2001).

Beyond litigation and protecting civil rights, NCH's activities included legislative advocacy and public education. Spawning several separate state coalitions, NCH joined forces with the National Law Center on Homelessness and Poverty and other organizations to fight the growing trend of criminalizing homelessness.

The National Alliance to End Homelessness (NAEH) assumed a less confrontational but no less energetic stance. Begun in 1987, NAEH convenes national conferences attended by over 1,500 service providers and homeless advocates. Under the leadership of Nan Roman, NAEH has become a leading voice of homeless advocacy at the Federal level. NAEH's work reflects the change in tactics of a movement that began with civil disobedience then evolved to modern-day use of social media, press conferences, and Congressional briefings to raise awareness and increase the effectiveness of organizations and governments.

Advocacy groups depend upon private giving and public interest. This affords freedom for outspokenness, but it also imposes the burden of constantly appealing for donations amidst the highs and lows of public opinion. Organizations that strategically moved toward including programs and services garnered public funds and ensured greater longevity. Two examples of this transition are given below.

ELLEN BAXTER AND THE HEIGHTS IN MANHATTAN. One of the first advocates to also take action was Ellen Baxter of New York City. Baxter had partnered with anthropologist Kim Hopper to document the extent of homelessness at a time when few were taking notice and fewer were doing anything about it. Their report, *Private Lives/Public Spaces,* came out in 1981 and received media attention sufficient to prompt disclaimers by politicians concerned about bad publicity. As later noted by Hopper (2003), it was intended as a "bill of indictment" targeting a "scandal of major proportions" (p. 115).

In 1983, Baxter succeeded in transforming an SRO into a precursor of supportive housing. Founding her own nonprofit, The Committee for the Heights Inwood Homeless, Baxter and colleagues opened The Heights in a low-income neighborhood in upper Manhattan near the George Washington Bridge. Their ingenuity lay in taking advantage of a little-known source of funds: capital money from the State Division of Housing and Community Renewal (DHCR) through its Special Needs Housing Act program (Houghton, 2001).

The Heights took in not only homeless persons with mental illness but also men and women with addictions and AIDS. Residents were given their own leases (unheard of at the time) and a sense of community was encouraged. Services for residents—mental health treatment, rehabilitation, health care—were outsourced to what would later become a large-scale nonprofit in the city—the Center for Urban Community Services (CUCS), its executive director was Baxter's husband Tony Hannigan.

JOHN PARVENSKY AND THE COLORADO COALITION FOR THE HOMELESS (CCH). The founding of CCH in 1986 and its subsequent growth was due in no small part to a leading advocate for the homeless, John Parvensky. A law school graduate, Parvensky and other CCH founders were unwilling to stand by as downtown Denver's streets and parks were home to growing numbers of destitute men and women. Among the first recipients of a Robert Wood Johnson Health Care for the Homeless grant, CCH used the $1.6 million to open the Stout Street Clinic as a one-stop site for medical, mental, dental, and vision care.

CCH's pursuit of comprehensiveness and multisite development helped it grow to include transitional housing for families and individuals and to offer scatter-site as well as single-site buildings with in-house services. Fortunate to have access to land and vacant buildings, CCH developed properties, erecting new buildings and renovating old ones. Adept at lobbying and advocacy, CCH was able to get an extension of property tax exemptions to include these acquisitions. Parvensky was given the Ford Foundation's Leadership for a Changing World Award in 2002.

Of course, there have been many Ellen Baxters and John Parvenskys in cities around the United States, individuals who take it upon themselves to do more than protest the deplorable state of homelessness in their midst. Although they share in the spirit of giving that is common to mission-based charities, action-oriented service entrepreneurs are motivated by a deep dissatisfaction with the status quo more than they are with concern for individual redemption.

Lineage 3: The Advent of the Business Model

As homeless organizations expanded in size and scale, and as private donors and businesses became more influential, business practices were introduced and promoted as important to maintaining solvency. Although profits were not the goal, homeless organizations could presumably benefit from business practices such as monitoring productivity, maintaining quality assurance, and focusing on results. This also made public–private partnerships go more smoothly because both "sides" shared the same language.

THE CORPORATION FOR SUPPORTIVE HOUSING. The Corporation for Supportive Housing (CSH) began in 1991 as a "middleman" organization extending financial and technical assistance to nonprofits seeking funding to house homeless families and individuals with special needs, including mental illness, HIV/AIDS, and substance abuse. Its founder, Julie Sandorf, was an advocate for the homeless who became inspired by priests at Manhattan's St. Francis Residence who had managed to transform SRO services into full-scale programs including housing for mentally ill parishioners.

Sandorf's admiration for this "extending the mission" approach, combined with her strong ties to foundations, led to the founding of CSH. With grants from the Pew Charitable Trusts, Robert Wood Johnson Foundation and the Ford Foundation, CSH benefited from the surge in availability of funds—and from the need for technical assistance to obtain those funds. CSH filled a niche, acting as a broker to help nonprofits get their share of the pie.

Another entrepreneurial force behind CSH's growth was Carla Javits, daughter of the late U.S. Senator Jacob Javits. Spearheading the West Coast operations of CSH, Javits later became its national President and Chief Executive Officer (CEO), overseeing CSH offices in 10 states. Under Javits, CSH made its mark by targeting the shortage of affordable housing for people with special needs and by developing complex public–private financial packages to build supportive housing for them. Negotiating low-interest loans and managing budgets and project costs were skills CSH offered. Box 3.2 describes this process in greater detail.

COMMON GROUND/TIMES SQUARE HOTEL. The founding of Common Ground (CG) in 1991 was a watershed event for homeless services in both the magnitude of the effort and in its creative acquisition of public and private funds. CG made its mark by taking aging SROs, renovating them, and restoring their architectural amenities, including carved moldings, woodwork, chandeliers, and planters. In

BOX 3.2
THE PUBLIC–PRIVATE MIX: LEVERAGING GROWTH
IN HOUSING AND SERVICES

It is difficult to overestimate the impact of the creative funding schemes that brought public and private interests together to feed the homeless service industry's growth. In the United States, building new housing—or buying existing housing stock and renting it—is traditionally the province of private developers or individual owners/landlords. This became almost exclusively the case as the Federal government withdrew from its post-Depression role as a builder of public housing. The governmental substitute—housing vouchers and rental subsidies—essentially proved to be a boon for private landlords.

New York, with its relatively generous support for public services, was an optimal testing ground for the maneuvering needed to make nonprofit development succeed using capital funding. The Heights and other programs were made possible by state Division of Housing and Community Renewal (DHCR) grants that were leveraged to seek loans from the city's Department of Housing Preservation and Development (HPD). These, in turn, increased the ability to procure private bank loans, foundation grants, and grants from private investors such as partners at the banking giant Goldman, Sachs & Company (Houghton, 2001). This lucrative but unwieldy combination of Federal subsidies, state grants, city-sponsored loans, and private philanthropy presented a challenge to nonprofit leaders unaccustomed to negotiating multimillion-dollar deals with moving and contingent parts. Organizations like Corporation for Supportive Housing (CSH), helped channel millions in capital funding and became major players in the growing homeless industry.

fostering a sense of community, CG adopted the "social mix" or integrated housing approach pioneered by Ellen Baxter's The Heights. Central to the CG model was the inclusion of low-income (non-disabled) tenants.

Founded and led by civic entrepreneur Roseanne Haggerty, CG started out with a decrepit welfare hotel in the middle of New York's busy theater district and used a robust budget of $36 million to transform its 652 units into affordable housing. With 200 formerly homeless and mentally ill residents already living there, the Times Square Hotel kept this "one-third" ratio and opened the remaining units to low-income tenants such as the elderly and local artists, actors and musicians.

The Times Square Hotel became the largest supportive housing facility in the country and CG went on to do the same sorts of renovations with the rundown Prince George Hotel in Manhattan's midtown east, later expanding to new buildings in the outer boroughs and Connecticut. Support services were contracted to the Center for Urban Community Services (CUCS) at the Times Square Hotel and to other nonprofits at other locations.

CG epitomized the big-ticket ribbon-cutting projects favored by political leaders, the business community, and real estate developers (whose membership overlapped considerably). Rehabilitating buildings destined for demolition or lingering decrepitude, bringing together the formerly homeless with low-income tenants in the same building, forging private–public economic partnerships—all were distinguishing features of the CG approach.

Haggerty and CG gave homeless services visibility and civic respect by aligning them with business district improvements. Times Square, once the seedy home of peep shows, bars, pawn shops, and tattoo parlors, became gentrified in the 1990s; a family tourist attraction with chain restaurants, Broadway musicals, and overpriced souvenir shops. CG's Times Square Hotel project was hailed for reducing homelessness in the area and giving local "starving artists" affordable apartments in a majestic building and historical landmark.

It would be overly simplistic to portray CG as a pure example of the business model approach—it also pursued advocacy by leveraging its prominence on the New York homeless services scene (and later through national and international expansion). But the singular contribution of CG was its success in obtaining millions of dollars for massive (by homeless-services standards) building projects. It could take years to strike a deal that cobbled together the right mix of low-interest loans, tax credits, and rental subsidies. Rehabilitating a worn-down SRO hotel—architectural redesign, upgrading electrical and plumbing, meeting a host of fire and other safety code requirements—can take years. Furnishing the units, setting up staff offices on-site, screening tenants, and performing routine maintenance add to the time and effort needed. When the building is finally open for business, the ceremony is a feel-good moment for city officials, business district leaders, and others involved in the project.

Blurring the Boundaries between Non-profit and For-Profit: The Rise of Social Enterprise in Homeless Services

One variant of the business model approach brought a blending of nonprofit and for-profit within the same organization. The most common version of this involves starting a small business venture within a homeless services program to generate revenue and provide jobs for clients. Common Ground, for example, took advantage of its prime location to invite an ice cream franchise onto its ground floor, stipulating that the owners must hire tenants as workers. Denver's CCH opened pizza parlors where program residents found jobs. Coffee shops and copy centers are also favorite small business start-ups, run and staffed by nonprofits.

Embedding small businesses within a nonprofit organization is a minimalist version of boundary blurring, given that it does not change the essential function or daily operations of the parent organization. At the opposite end of the spectrum are the rare businesses (e.g., Paul Newman's line of salad dressings and food products) whose primary goal is turning over profits to charity. In the middle realm are organizations whose mission is charitable (not-for-profit) but whose operations follow business principles.

The term *social enterprise* is used to refer to this harnessing of business practices for social good as well as profits for shareholders. By drawing wealthy donors deeper into solving fundamental problems like poverty and food insecurity, social enterprises have become a favorite of business leaders seeking social and ethical relevance. Seen as filling gaps left by the heavily bureaucratic public sector and underfunded nonprofit sector, social enterprises are posited as smaller and more responsive to local problems. Initial funds and technical assistance come from wealthy investors; organizational recipients are expected to help the needy and thereby reap "profits" that benefit society. These organizations abide by (and succeed according to) business practices such as accountability and cost–benefit calculations.

Corporate social responsibility has become de rigueur at Harvard's and other business schools where a "double bottom line" is promoted (Cornelius, Todres, Janjuha-Jivraj, Woods, & Wallace, 2008). The rise of social enterprise supplies a more sophisticated and monetized version of the traditional philanthropic giving to charitable causes (recall Lineage #1). Box 3.3 spotlights one such foundation funded by corporate wealth.

Growing Convergence among the Lineages Over Time

The three lineages set forth in this chapter rested on different logics and philosophies, the oldest of these rooted in traditions of charitable giving, the second arriving on the heels of the protest movements of the 1960s, and the third a response to the surge in public funding as well as the corporatization of the nonprofit world. The lines became blurred, however, as homeless service organizations adapted to changing times and funding streams.

One prime mover of convergence arose from decisions on eligibility for funding. The emphasis on serious mental illness opened the door to state mental health dollars targeted to housing and services. Single adults constituted the most visible

---

BOX 3.3

SOCIAL ENTERPRISE AS PHILANTHROPY: THE ROBIN HOOD FOUNDATION

An excellent example of social enterprise as philanthropy is the Robin Hood Foundation (RHF) in New York City. Started in 1988 by hedge fund and financial managers in major firms like Goldman, Sachs & Company, Tudor Investments, and Maverick Capital, along with media giants such as Clear Channel and CNN, the RHF seeks to merge "R&D with TLC" (www.robinhood.org) in fighting poverty. RHF proudly asserts that all donations go directly to services—board members themselves pay the costs of administration and fundraising. Grants go to about 200 of what the RHF website states are 27,000 poverty-fighting organizations in New York City, disbursing $1.1 billion over the foundation's lifetime.

RHF practices what it calls "relentless monetization," using metrics to estimate the benefit–cost ratio that separates good programs from mediocre or bad ones. An after-school tutoring program, for example, might be monetized for its dollar value reaped from keeping at-risk adolescents in school and boosting future earnings. These added benefits (minus costs) comprise the net value of the program and its fundability.

Sponsored by the city's wealthiest elite whose charity galas grace the society pages of local newspapers, RHF's fundraising events are among the most glittery and celebrity-driven in a city known for the opulence of its private events. An August 2013 fundraiser, for example, was held at a private horse farm in Bridgehampton, New York, owned by a hedge fund manager. RHF executives hosted a polo game featuring top players in the sport. http://www.bloomberg.com/news/2013-08-13/hamptons-scene-polo-for-robin-hood-with-nacho-dimenna.html

---

group of homeless people. Families—rarely seen living on the streets—were typically placed in temporary hotels or shared apartments. Adolescents were referred to nonprofit organizations that specialized in youth services—specific needs beyond shelter included determining guardianship, ensuring school enrollment, and seeking family reunification.

Single homeless adults were more likely to be male and had a significantly higher incidence of mental illness and addiction than homeless families or youths. In most large U.S. cities, single adult homeless were primarily African American. These demographic characteristics did not inspire a groundswell of sympathy compared with the response to other disabled and impoverished groups (Hopper, 2003). Of three types of disability—developmental, physical, and psychiatric—the first two were given special status in housing and service provision dating back to the early 20th century. Relatively few individuals who were blind, physically handicapped, or had developmental disabilities became homeless given the safety net services available for them. This was far from true for the third group. Persons with a psychiatric disability had (and still have) to prove their eligibility to a psychiatrist–gatekeeper—with varying degrees of accommodation given a lack of diagnostic clarity. Those with addictions are at the bottom of the pecking order of sympathy and disability entitlements.

However, the sight of homeless people visibly suffering from mental illness prompted action at several levels. In New York State, funding for mental health—largely a state responsibility—was supplemented by Federal dollars channeled through SSI, McKinney funds, and rental subsidies from the Department of Housing and Urban Development (HUD). The rationale for seeking funds for housing was simple: a sizeable minority (about one third) of the homeless had a serious mental illness and their mental problems were unlikely to improve while homeless. Rather than "treat and retreat," mental health providers entered the housing business (Houghton, 2001).

And thus a "disability ethos" became one of the bonds reaching across the disparate array of homeless services, along the way cleaving family homelessness from single adult homelessness and adjudicated disability from nonadjudicated disability. By comparison, homeless families were not subject to the same demands for treatment and other demonstrations of housing worthiness, but they faced different obstacles in not having the same access to disability income and housing-plus-services programs.

At the same time, the disability ethos created a labeled class for whom access to services meant accepting a psychiatric diagnosis that held lifelong consequences. The decision to accept disability income and related entitlements along with the potential for stigma and social exclusion was one made with few other options (see Box 3.4).

National Campaigns to End Homelessness

In 2000, the National Alliance to End Homelessness (NAEH) announced a bold national campaign challenging communities to develop "ten-year plans" to end homelessness. By this point, the so-called epidemic was entering its third decade, and few would disagree that a new approach was needed. NAEH was prepared to lead the way and it had a key ally in Philip Mangano, President Bush's appointee to the U.S. Inter-Agency Council on Homelessness (USICH). A self-described homelessness abolitionist, Mangano arrived in Washington just as the research findings on Pathways Housing First (PHF) were becoming widely known. The Ten Year Plan and its successor (the 100,000 Homes Campaign) were valiant attempts to inject national advocacy and energy into the lumbering bureaucracy

BOX 3.4

FEDERAL DISABILITY: SOURCES OF INCOME FOR HOMELESS
SERVICES AND FOR THE POOR

The U.S. Social Security Administration (SSA)—which oversees Federal disability
income programs—instituted eligibility changes in 1986 that opened the door to
certifying more recipients with psychiatric disabilities. But the rate of increase
rose even higher after 1990 when the SSA made a rare move to increase outreach
in response to homelessness—the number of SSI recipients tripled between 1982
and 1992. Supplemental Security Income (SSI) is unlike its counterpart Social
Security Disability Insurance (SSDI) in that the latter is available only to individuals with a formal work history. The source of income for most persons with
serious mental illness, SSI requires that a person maintain minimal financial
resources ($2,000 in total value) and to have tapped any other sources of income
before applying.

SSI certifications dropped in 1996 when Congress eliminated addiction as a
basis for eligibility, but certifications then increased to become a primary source of
poverty relief, with a four-fold increase in the annual growth of SSI beneficiaries
between 1996 and 1998 and a 50% to 100% growth in the number of young adult
SSI beneficiaries (30–59 years old) by 2000 (Jans, Stoddard, & Kraus, 2004).

SSI benefits are rarely sufficient to cover basic living expenses, but SSI recipients are eligible for food stamps, a vital additional support. SSI is also tied to
receiving Medicaid coverage, which is critical for anyone receiving medical treatment or taking medication. And yet the security of SSI income—and the Medicaid
coverage and food stamps that SSI certification makes possible—can be a lifeline
for someone with few other options (Hansen, Bourgois, & Drucker, 2014). This
steady income can also enhance a homeless person's attractiveness to housing
programs. At Pathways to Housing and other HF organizations, the model dic-
tates that no more than 30% of this income is used to help pay the rent. In some
non-HF programs, the charge for program services may be the entire amount of
the SSI check.

surrounding homeless services. In a sign of the times, the 1980s protests and
hunger strikes had morphed into sophisticated media-driven campaigns.

As we will see in Chapter 7, the 100,000 (100K) Homes campaign was an ambitious project that galvanized local communities throughout the United States.
Ending in July 2014, 100K was featured on national television (the CBS news show
"60 Minutes") and garnered international attention. Organized by Community
Solutions, Inc. (founded by Rosanne Haggerty), the campaign depended on
sophisticated media outreach, coordinated assistance, and buy-in by local homeless providers (many of whom were eager to try something new to jump-start
flagging programs and morale).

Growing Convergence: Charity, Advocacy, and Business under One Roof

By the late 1990s, the converging of the three lineages had evolved such that the first two became small players in the larger industry. Rescue missions and soup kitchens continued to exist, but their assistance was stopgap and temporary. Similarly, advocacy groups continued to push for more funding and services, but the heavy lifting at the policy level was taken up by national organizations such as the NAEH and the National Coalition for the Homeless. Advocacy-only groups, dependent on private donations, also faced shortfalls in times of compassion fatigue. Many began to find a place as providers of services, taking advantage of public funds to offer direct services.

Between 1987 and 1993, Congress appropriated 4.2 billion dollars in McKinney-Vento funds for emergency food, shelter, and transitional housing programs as well as demonstration projects in mental health and job training (U.S. Government Accounting Office, 1994). In this climate of expansion, large multipurpose organizations were far more capable of securing grants and contracts for services and remaining self-sustaining via a mix of contracts, grants, donations, tax benefits, and low-interest loans. Enjoying the advantages of scale and diversification, they could produce sophisticated proposals for funding, oversee quality assurance, and assure donors large and small that the money would be responsibly spent.

What did such organizations look like? The bigger ones might have the staircase fully represented: drop-in center, emergency shelter, community residence (an entire building or portion of a building dedicated to congregate living for clients), scattered apartments where clients live two or three per unit, and single occupancy apartments (the ultimate step). Clients might enter at the bottom and work their way up or, if deemed higher functioning at the time of referral, enter at a higher step (only HF gave access to the highest step right away).

A more common approach for the larger-scale organization would be to stay with the middle steps, leaving the lowest to city authorities and private shelters and the highest to the individual's initiative.[3] Larger cities spawned several such organizations. In New York City, Project Renewal, The Bridge, Goddard-Riverside Community Center, Bowery Residents Committee, Common Ground, and Center for Urban Community Services (CUCS) coexisted and competed for city and state contracts. The primary advocacy organization in the city—the Coalition for the Homeless—continued to pursue litigation and produce policy briefs and press releases, but it also added service components such as scatter-site housing for persons with HIV/AIDS, summer camps and after-school programs for homeless children, and emergency rental assistance.

Conclusion: Lineages, Logics, and Paradigm Shifts

Despite diverse beginnings, homeless organizations serving single adults shared an institutional logic invested in the continuum or mainstream model and dependent on funding tied to disability. Homeless families with young children were given more immediate entrée to housing, typically short-term transitional housing that offered few support services.

The three lineages thus evolved. Charities that started out offering free meals or a bed for the night grew into multipurpose operations. Their much larger counterparts—philanthropic foundations—channeled private wealth toward public services. Advocacy groups shifted from protest marches to lawsuits and media campaigns; many also turned to government service contracts to stay solvent. The third lineage, the business model approach, came to subsume but not submerge the other two. Much of this evolution was a response to increases in funding for homeless services and the bureaucratization that accompanied growth and complexity. Close ties to the business community ensured greater access to wealthy donors as well as to expertise in management and accounting.[4]

Program founders and advocates mentioned in this chapter—Baxter, Haggerty, Parvensky, Snyder, Hayes, Sandor, and Javits—were successful institutional entrepreneurs, garnering support for their organizations and drawing attention to the cause of ending homelessness. All of these individuals and organizations depended upon public funds and private partnerships and all were severely constrained by a level of demand that far exceeded the supply. To the extent that service providers were wedded to the mainstream model, a significant portion of the "demand" was unhappy with the "supply."

Where does this leave Pathways to Housing and Housing First? Among the three lineages, PHF most likely fits under "advocacy with action." It was never intended to be an advocacy-only organization and it does not fit the model of a charity—program tenets such as harm reduction and consumer choice were a poor fit with the religious values motivating many charities. Nor was PHF amenable to large-scale business development, given that it was decentralized in services and housing (no large buildings to attract philanthropists and political leaders). Soon, however, PHF became known beyond its local origins and outside the bounds of the U.S. homeless services "industry" or "institutional complex." What elevated it from small start-up to international role model was no doubt a combination of things. Research findings probably helped to move the needle but motives for adoption or rejection were varied and not always predictable.

Notes

1. Skid Row Housing Trust (SRHT) is one of the largest HF providers in Los Angeles, operating 24 buildings with over 1,600 units. SRHT opted for the "mixed-use" housing approach, buying new or rehabilitated buildings in which to house disabled tenants as well as tenants paying market-rate rent. In 2007, SRHT was part of LA's Project 50, whose goal was to adopt HF for 50 of Skid Row's most chronic, high-service-using homeless adults (Willse, 2010). Organized by Common Ground staff (using the model developed in New York), Project 50 used a single-site or abridged version of HF to place those found most vulnerable (but also most costly). Most recently, United Way in LA launched the "Home for Good" program to end chronic and veterans' homelessness by 2016 (Parvini, 2014).

2. AIDs activism differed in more ways than the size and scope of effort. The visible suffering and untimely deaths that afflicted gay men, intravenous (IV) drug users, hemophilia patients, and sex workers were omnipresent, with no apparent end in sight. Attracting the attention of celebrities, patrons of the arts, and wealthy donors as well as medical researchers competing to be the first to find the cause (and then a cure), the AIDs epidemic had an attraction for powerful elites that homelessness did not bring to bear.

3. As funding for permanent supportive housing became more readily available after 2007, larger programs might add the top step, thereby allowing clients to traverse the full staircase to earning their own apartment while in the same program.

4. A lesser-told part of this story: businesses profited directly from homeless and disability funding. Landlords, for example, have made millions in New York City by renting SRO-type rooms and apartments to the city at daily rates that rival Manhattan's luxury hotels.

4 Housing First Gets its Evidence Base and Momentum Builds

BY THE START OF the millennium in 2000, homeless services were, for good or ill, booming. Arrayed along a continuum ranging from drop-in centers to shelters to transitional housing, this vast network of private and government-run programs was intended to work with hospitals, clinics, rehabilitation centers, and entitlement programs. Sometimes coordination happened, at other times, disjointed services left much to be desired.

Advocacy and service organizations were well established, including the National Alliance to End Homelessness (NAEH), the Corporation for Supportive Housing (CSH), and the National Coalition for the Homeless (NCH). Many other groups had a vested interest in how the homeless were treated; the National Alliance for the Mentally Ill (NAMI), the Bazelon Center for Mental Health Law, and the National Conference of Mayors, to name a few. The Veterans Administration (VA) had its own homeless population stretching back to the Vietnam War era, as soldiers returned from tours abroad with posttraumatic symptoms and substance abuse, many unable to find a home or job. Newer cohorts of veterans from the wars in Iraq and Afghanistan were returning after 2005 with their own problems in adjustment, some ending up homeless.

Although vast networks of services provided a necessary safety net, the number of homeless persons did not decline. Generations of Americans were growing up assuming homelessness to be a fact of life rather than a shocking but "temporary"epidemic of the 1980s (Hopper, 2003). Like many homeless organizations, Pathways was founded by an institutional entrepreneur. As noted in Chapter 1, successful entrepreneurs frame issues convincingly and mobilize support, drawing on new or revised cultural logics to advance their cause (Lockett, Currie, Waring, Finn, & Martin, 2012). Unlike economic entrepreneurs who take risks to reap profits, institutional entrepreneurs are more often driven by ideology. Of course, that ideology may be presented as an unquestionable article of faith or as a testable work in progress.

Pathways's ideology arose from the frustration of seeing homeless adults refuse repeated offers of help, preferring an apartment to a psychiatric ward and a park bench to a shelter bed. The core tenets of Housing First (HF) promulgated by Pathways were a "package deal," but that package was considered fallible enough to subject to rigorous evaluation. This chapter will discuss how, beginning in 1997, Pathways embarked on an experiment in self-evaluation that laid the groundwork for greater national then international impact (Stanhope & Dunn, 2011).

Building an Evidence Base: Research and Business Practices

Science has a strong allegiance to the "pyramid of evidence" with randomized controlled trials (RCTs) at its pinnacle (i.e., the gold standard against which all other study designs are judged). Unlike clinical trials testing the efficacy of a new drug or medical procedure, RCTs of social service interventions are less frequent and feasible. Working outside of the relative sterility and controlled environments of medical RCTs, researchers contend with real-world "noise" generated by a lack of control inherent to naturalistic community settings (Hohmann & Shear, 2002).

The idea that untested programs and interventions may do more harm than good is hardly novel. But the answer to this problem—designing and conducting a study—requires the program to accommodate systematic data collection (and perhaps even random assignment). It also requires a willingness to accept the results even if less than positive. Concurrent with the move toward evidence-based practice has been the adoption of business management practices such as performance measures and monetizing results. Although they are two very distinct activities, research and business practices can be conflated as an unwelcome intrusion into social services provision, emphasizing, as they do, accountability and oversight to the detriment of humane concerns.

Self-evaluation: Letting the Chips Fall

The previous discussion sets the stage for the decision by Tsemberis and others at Pathways to pursue research on the model. Anyone appraising Pathways's effectiveness, having little or no precedent to go by, could be forgiven for assuming that clients were as likely to fail as to succeed. How could homeless men and women with complex problems be expected to live on their own, maintain an apartment, and adjust to a new neighborhood? In the early days, Pathways staff witnessed it happening, again and again: men and women leaving the streets and entering into their own apartment in a matter of days, living there as if they had never been homeless in the first place. The few who had problems maintaining their tenancy—and there were a few—were the exceptions that proved this new "rule."

Still, anecdotal observations of staff and consumers did not constitute research evidence. The first evaluation of the program's effectiveness was made possible through collaboration between Pathways, New York State's Nathan Kline Institute, and New York City's Human Resources Administration (HRA). HRA had been compiling residential outcome data for several thousand participants residing in the New York City/New York State (NY/NY) programs. Analyses of the data compared continuum of care programs and Pathways HF over a five-year period. They controlled for differences in client characteristics before program entry because these differences might otherwise explain the outcome. Results showed that that 88% of HF consumers remained housed as compared to 47% of consumers in the traditional programs (Tsemberis & Eisenberg, 2000).

This was a very strong finding but the gold standard—a randomized trial—was needed to test the model fully. For such an experiment, homeless individuals would have to be found eligible, consent to participate in the study, and then be randomly assigned to Pathways HF or the alternative (usual care) and followed for a period of years to ensure sufficient numbers of observations. In a fortuitous circumstance, in 1996, the Federal government agency most interested in mental illness and homelessness—the Substance Abuse and Mental Health Services Administration (SAMHSA)—issued a request for proposals. There were a large number of applicants and Pathways was awarded one of six available grants. As a condition of awarding the grant, SAMHSA specified that all grantees agree to use a common set of outcome measures for comparability across sites. Among the grantees, Pathways was the only program testing HF and using an RCT.

Design and Conduct of the New York Housing Study

With Tsemberis as its principal investigator, Dr. Sara Asmussen as the project director, and Dr. Mary Beth Shinn as the project evaluator, the New York Housing

Study (NYHS) began in 1997 as a four-year experiment in which homeless mentally ill persons in New York City were randomly assigned to the Pathways Housing First (PHF) model or to "treatment as usual." The NYHS team, graduate students in psychology and the social sciences, worked together in a long-term effort (four years). For HF tenants, interviews were conducted in their apartments or in offices rented for the study. The latter were also used for the non-HF participants, but interviews were also conducted in parks, coffee shops, jail and prison cells, and shelters; interviewers sometimes traveled to other cities and other states. Their allegiance to the study participants—wherever they might be—required flexibility and tenacity. Study participants often noted that having this regular contact was one of the few social constants in their lives (Stefancic, Schaefer-McDaniel, Davis, & Tsemberis, 2004).

Although this is a seemingly unusual scenario—a program founder heading up the evaluation of his program's impact and reporting on the findings—it is often how complex psychosocial interventions are tested. The study's experimental design, the impartiality and reputation of the evaluator (Dr. Shinn), close oversight by SAMHSA project officers, and transparent data collection procedures shared across all six sites helped to counteract insider bias.

The study's participants were recruited from safe havens, drop-in centers, psychiatric hospitals, and via New York Housing Study (NYHS) outreach on the streets. They were asked for their consent to join a longitudinal study, with the understanding that, based on a lottery system, they would be referred to different housing programs in the city. Inclusion criteria for the study required that participants: (1) spent 15 of the last 30 days on the street or in other public places; (2) had a history of homelessness during the past 6 months; and (3) had a psychiatric diagnosis of severe mental illness (e.g., schizophrenia, bipolar disorder, or major depression).

Although substance abuse was not an eligibility requirement, meeting the study's inclusion criteria virtually guaranteed a history of alcohol or drug disorders (90% of those enrolled in the study). Recruitment, which lasted from November 1997 to January 1999, produced a sample of 225 people (99 in the experimental PHF group and 126 in the control group) who would be followed for four years (see Box 4.1 for more information on the study).

The 99 people assigned to the experimental PHF condition were provided immediate access to independent apartments (studio or one-bedroom) in affordable areas of New York City, mostly in Harlem and the Bronx but also in Brooklyn and Queens. Participants received services through Assertive Community Treatment (ACT) teams, which included 24/7 on-call response intended to support the newly housed tenants in the evenings and on weekends. ACT teams have a well-documented research record for providing effective support and treatment to individuals with

BOX 4.1
A RANDOMIZED CONTROLLED TRIAL HITS THE STREETS:
ETHICAL QUANDARIES

For the New York Housing Study (NYHS), outreach workers were critical to finding potential subjects for recruitment. At the outset, these workers were reluctant to comply, arguing that it was irresponsible to recruit someone into the HF arm of the study, tantamount to setting them up for failure. It was only when an outreach worker was invited to dinner at the apartment of the client he had reluctantly referred to the study that he was able to grasp that success was possible (Tsemberis, 2010). "Seeing is believing" had its merits.

As the NYHS proceeded, the ethical quandaries soon reversed direction—the lottery or coin toss analogy used to convince subjects to accept random assignment discomfited outreach workers and research staff who balked at assigning subjects to the control group. This dilemma was settled to the staff's satisfaction only after a promise was made that all participants still homeless at the study's end would be given the option of a HF apartment right away.

severe mental illness in the community (Stein & Test, 1980). An important philosophical modification in PHF ACT required the teams to change their approach from clinician-driven to consumer-driven (Salyers & Tsemberis, 2007).

The Pathways HF program came with two requirements. First, tenants had to pay 30% of their income—typically SSI benefits—toward their rent. In most cases, they had to allow Pathways to become their representative payee (manage their money) to ensure this portion of the rent was paid. The remainder of the rent (or all of the rent if the participant was not receiving SSI) was paid by the program.[1] Second, tenants had to allow the support services team to make a weekly visit to their apartments.

The 126 individuals assigned to the control group were referred to "usual care" or "treatment first" (TF) as the mainstream approach was also called. For those able to find a place, this was typically a group home, shelter, or single-room occupancy residence in which clients were expected to attend day treatment and other therapeutic groups (preceded by detoxification and rehabilitation for substance abuse if needed). Residents were expected to remain drug and alcohol free and follow prescribed medication regimens as supervised by on-site staff. Sleeping, cooking, and bathing facilities were shared and house rules governed curfews, visitors, and on-site behavior. In keeping with the ethos of the mainstream approach, having a place of one's own was positioned as a goal, the ultimate reward pending cooperation with program requirements.

Participants in the NYHS experiment were interviewed every six months over a four-year period. Along with the other SAMHSA-funded projects, the study used a battery of standardized measures focused on housing stability, alcohol and drug use, participation in treatment, psychiatric symptoms, and perceptions of consumer choice.

The demands of a prospective design—in particular when applied to this population—raise obvious concerns about retaining participants over such a long period of time. Having lived almost constantly on the move, these men and women were expected to stay in the study for four years and be available every six months for extensive interviews. In order to maintain contact and reduce attrition, participants received a $25 incentive payment for each interview and were asked to call in on a monthly basis for a five-minute interview that provided an additional $5 payment.

The NYHS investigators knew that serious attrition could cause the experiment to break down, introducing bias and reducing the sample size below the level needed to assess group differences statistically. Incentive payments were one means of enticing participants to stay enrolled, but NYHS staff also spent many hours staying in touch with the enrollees, tracking them down if they left their program for a hospital, jail, or the streets. Using the telephone numbers of contacts volunteered by the participants at the baseline interview, NYHS staffers reached out to find missing persons; they visited hospitals, drove to upstate prisons, and went to fast food outlets to get their interviews completed. The consistency of repeated contacts, along with the friendly tenacity of the research team, helped explain the study's high retention rate of 94% at 12 months and 87% at its end (Stefancic, Schaefer-McDaniel, Davis, & Tsemberis, 2004).

Findings from the New York Housing Study

Early reports from the NYHS study included a description of the program and logic model (Tsemberis & Asmussen, 1999), one-year findings (Tsemberis, Moran, Shinn, Asmussen, & Shern, 2003), and two-year outcomes (Gulcur, Stefancic, Shinn, Tsemberis, & Fischer, 2003)[2]. To check on whether randomization had produced equivalency between the two groups, they were statistically examined for differences in composition by race, gender, psychiatric diagnosis, education, and marital status; none were found (Gulcur et al., 2003). Reflecting the larger homeless population in New York City, the sample was predominantly male (77%) and never married (69%). Forty percent were African American, followed by 28% Caucasian, 15% Hispanic, and the remainder self-identified as "other, or mixed ethnicity."

Two years into the NYHS, PHF clients were significantly less likely to spend time homeless and hospitalized for psychiatric problems (Gulcur et al., 2003). The greatest impact of the study undoubtedly came from the publication of findings in the *American Journal of Public Health* (Tsemberis et al., 2004). The primary outcome of interest—housing stability versus homelessness—showed that individuals assigned to the Housing First group spent approximately 80% of their time stably housed compared with only 30% for participants assigned to TF after two years.

This striking difference between the two groups became even more remarkable when one considered what and who were being compared. With regard to who was being compared, the experimental design dispelled the notion that HF only worked by "creaming" higher functioning consumers. (This concern was linked to the earlier archival study at Pathways, although the opposite of creaming was more likely because Pathways accepted clients rejected by the mainstream programs.) Both arms of the experiment received roughly the same group of individuals coming from the streets, hospitals, and drop-in centers.

The "what" being compared was more than just immediate access to independent housing. The comparison became one of voluntary compliance and permanent housing versus required compliance and temporary housing. To appreciate the significance of this, one need only recall a guiding principle of providers and organizations working in mainstream services: Taking psychotropic medication and abstaining from substances are fundamental to getting back on one's feet. Critics of harm reduction see it as enabling, ceding control to a person who is diagnostically labeled as out of control.

Nevertheless, one might reasonably assume an increase in substance use given the absence of prohibitions and the privacy of an apartment in which to partake. Yet, using the prevailing measure approved by SAMHSA, (Sobell, Sobell, Leo, & Cancella,1988) an expected increase in substance use among PHF tenants proved unfounded. As one article noted, ". . . individuals who use substances or engage in disruptive behaviors may be more easily housed in private apartments than in congregate settings where their behavior directly impinges on others" (Gulcur et al., 2003, p. 182).

Similarly, the higher rates of substance abuse treatment found in the control group were to be expected given program mandates. Yet this traditional abstinence approach was not more effective at reducing rates of substance use (see Box 4.2 for more on this subject). Similarly, an absence of demands that PHF participants take psychiatric medications did not result in an increase in psychiatric symptoms.

Table 4.1 shows a summary of the NYHS findings for its major outcomes and includes the measures used and their reliability coefficients. Statistically significant group differences favoring PHF were observed for housing stability, time spent homeless, and perceived choice. Nonsignificant group differences were

BOX 4.2
EVALUATING HOUSING FIRST: THE DEBATE OVER SUBSTANCE
USE OUTCOMES

As the New York Housing Study and other studies of Housing First gained momentum, questions arose regarding which outcomes were the most significant indicators of HF's effectiveness (or ineffectiveness) and how they should be calculated. One in particular proved to be a flashpoint in discussions of HF's impact: use of drugs and alcohol. As discussed in this chapter, findings from the NYHS were overall positive toward HF when juxtaposing harm reduction versus abstinence as the relevant practices. But the results were not unequivocal (Padgett et al., 2006; Tsemberis et al., 2004). Critics of HF have pointed this out, arguing that HF clients were likely in remission at program entry or had been misclassified as substance users (Kertesz, Crouch, Milby, Cusimano, & Schumacher, 2009).

PHF was not intended to end addiction, so this charge of ineffectiveness is not entirely fair. Yet once housing stability is so clearly in evidence, it seems obvious to look for other positives if they exist. The NYHS itself examined an array of outcomes (see Table 4.1) and it is a logical move for other researchers to pose similar questions and test them in different settings and with different populations. Weighing in with their own research, HF critics at the University of Alabama conducted a study of housing as an intervention for heavy cocaine users (Kertesz, Mullins, Schumacher, Wallace, Kirk, & Milby, 2007; Milby, Schumacher, Wallace, Freedman, & Vuchinich, 2005).

Kertesz et al. (2007) tested an abstinence-contingent model in which cocaine users are given a furnished apartment that is retained through weekly drug-negative urine tests (positive tests result in shelter transfer with a return predicated on a negative test). Clients spend 6–8 hours per day in behavioral treatment and employment training. Comparison groups included clients whose housing was not abstinence-contingent and those who received only the day treatment without housing assistance. After six months, the abstinence group showed more housing stability than the other groups, although this was not statistically significant.

Criticism by Kertesz et al., published in major journals, received attention. However, later research showed a strong effect on substance use with HF clients over 3 times less likely to use illicit drugs or abuse alcohol in the year after being housed compared to non-HF clients (Padgett, Stanhope, Henwood & Stefancic, 2011). This study also controlled for group differences in baseline substance use (to address the 'misclassification' bias asserted earlier). A recent implementation study by a group of researchers at Columbia University's National Center on Addiction and Substance Abuse found that fidelity to HF principles was significantly related to housing retention (75% remained housed after two years) and lower use of stimulants and opiates (Davidson, Neighbors, Hall, Hogue, Cho, Kutner, & Morgenstern, 2014).

TABLE 4.1

RESULTS OF THE NEW YORK HOUSING STUDY: COMPARING HOUSING FIRST
AND TREATMENT FIRST

Outcome Variable	Measure	Reliability	Results
Housing retention rate	Residential Follow-back Calendar	Test-retest .84–.92	HF more time stably housed**
Proportion of time homeless	Residential Follow-back Calendar	Test-retest .84–.92	HF less time homeless**
Use of alcohol and drugs	Six Month Follow-back Calendar	Test-retest .78–.98	No significant difference
Participation in substance abuse treatment	Modified Treatment Review	Test-retest .84–.94	TF higher use**
Participation in mental health treatment	Modified Treatment Review	Test-retest .84–.94	TF higher use**
Psychiatric symptoms	Colorado Symptom Index	Internal Consistency .90	No significant difference
Consumer choice	Consumer Choice	Internal Consistency .92	HF more perceived choice***

Note: Results reported for 6, 12, 18, 24, 36, or 48 months.
**p < .005 (Bonferroni corrected value), ***p < .0005.

found in psychiatric symptoms or in use of alcohol and drugs. TF participants were higher users of mental health services and substance abuse treatment. This is not altogether surprising. In these programs, treatment is required, not chosen. Of course, it is possible that PHF participants had unmet need or were avoiding services.

By any metric, these findings are remarkable. If similar results were found in a pharmaceutical trial, investigators could be ethically obliged to stop the experiment and provide everyone with the experimental medication—a phenomenon known as *equipoise*. These results did get attention, particularly the success of PHF in residential stability when prevailing beliefs would have predicted the opposite. Table 4.2 shows the results of these and six other studies with rates of housing stability falling between 77% and 85%. As discussed in

TABLE 4.2.

STUDIES REPORTING ON HOUSING RETENTION AND STABILITY RATES WITHIN
HOUSING FIRST PROGRAMS

Research Report	Location	Housing Retention/ Stability Rate	Duration
Tsemberis & Eisenberg, 2000	New York, New York	88%	5 years
Tsemberis, Gulcur, & Nakae, 2004	New York, New York	80%	2 years
Perlman & Parvensky, 2006	Denver, Colorado	80%	6 months
Stefancic & Tsemberis, 2007	Westchester County, New York	78%	4 years
Pearson, Montgomery, & Locke, 2009	New York, New York; Seattle, Washington; San Diego, California	84%	1 year
Tsemberis, Kent, & Respress, 2012	Washington, DC	84%	2 years
Stefancic & Tsemberis, 2013	Vermont	85%	1 year
Collins, Malone, & Clifasefi, 2013	Seattle, Washington	77%	2 years

Box 4.3, these findings remained surprisingly consistent across the studies and over the ensuing years.

Spotlight on the Chronically Homeless: The Case of Million Dollar Murray

Malcolm Gladwell's essay on "Million Dollar Murray" in *The New Yorker* in 2006 drew public attention to the costs of homelessness as no statistics-laden research report could. Murray, a former Marine with psychiatric problems and an intense fondness for vodka, ran up nearly one million dollars in public costs over a 10-year period in his hometown of Reno, Nevada. In and out of jail cells, shelters, emergency rooms, and rehabilitation clinics, Murray remained likable, incorrigible, and unable or unwilling to stop drinking. His costly ways came to a halt when he was given housing without the usual contingency requirement that he quit drinking (Murray later died of intestinal bleeding).

BOX 4.3
A SURPRISING CONSISTENCY

One of the more interesting phenomena emerging from controlled comparisons of Housing First and Treatment First has been the consistency in reports on housing stability. Hovering around 75% to 88% and favoring HF, these studies, beginning with the New York Housing Study (NYHS), show markedly lower stability rates for the TF group. In 2004, two years after the NYHS ended, the U. S. Interagency Council on Homelessness (USICH) launched a national Initiative to Help End Chronic Homelessness with Federal funding to support demonstration projects. Seven of the 11 cities funded by the initiative used the HF model and achieved 85% housing retention rates after 12 months (Mares & Rosenheck, 2007). Two years later, HUD published the outcomes of a three-city, 12-month study of HF programs with a reported 84% housing retention rate for 12 months (Pearson, Montgomery, & Locke, 2009). Somewhat lower but still statistically significant rates were found for long-term shelter dwellers. In that study, approximately 78% of HF participants remained stably housed over a four-year period (Stefancic & Tsemberis, 2007). Table 4.2 summaries these consistent findings.

Housing stability was central to what HF was about, but it has rarely been examined more closely for what it represents. In the NYHS and elsewhere, it is typically measured by the number of days housed within a specified period (the latter determined by the timing of follow-up and subject to wide variation). Being unhoused is defined as spending time in shelters or on the streets. By this definition, "number of days housed" obscures "housed where" and "how many times re-housed." The HF model provides for rehousing and such programs often have to move clients due to substance use, landlord evictions for tenant violations, or incarceration. Programs also have to move clients due to landlords not maintaining their buildings, tenants becoming targets of victimization, or tenants' special needs. Having housing stability does not mean continuous occupancy nor does it mean one's life is stable.

Gladwell's article popularized the notion that homelessness is "easier to solve than to manage." More importantly, the solution that Gladwell highlighted—Housing First—could save public monies and rationalize the distribution of a valued commodity such as housing. The cost of a shelter cot— $24,000 per year in New York City—was astounding given that this came with minimal services and overcrowded and custodial (at best) conditions. Jail and hospital stays, not to mention emergency room visits, were far more expensive; men like Murray could accumulate 80 or more ER visits in a year. At per capita costs running far less, HF offered a solution to homelessness that appealed to local governments weary of spending on homeless services. Indeed, by the late 1990s, shelters had become de facto housing for too many.

Chronically homeless adults thus achieved notoriety and a benighted status, the reason for disproportionately high rates of jail and hospital stays, not to mention emergency room visits, and other expensive acute care services. The health consequences of severe alcoholism are dire—liver disease, intestinal bleeding, lung abscesses, and pneumonia from aspirating vomit. It also brings a high risk of falling, getting hit by traffic, beaten up or mugged. Head injuries, including subdural hematomas, which can be fatal, are common. The cumulative costs of treatment and jail time (typically the default option to force sobering up) can be staggering.

Cheap and legal, beer and liquor have a definite attraction. But marijuana, heroin, and crack cocaine had their attractions as well, overshadowing alcohol as the substances of choice among the chronically homeless. Their health consequences, short of death from a heroin overdose, came largely from personal neglect and the exposure to harm (usually to self) that came from the desperation needed to feed a drug habit. Ultimately, the Murrays of the world were anomalies among the homeless, replaced in public opprobrium by the crack addict (Hopper, 2003).

Growing Impetus for Housing First: The Costs of Chronic Homelessness

Gladwell's writing was inspired by the research of Dennis Culhane and colleagues at the University of Pennsylvania and by the success of Philip Mangano in promulgating HF as a means of ending homelessness. Culhane, Metraux, and Hadley (2002) looked at administrative data for 4,679 individuals who gained access to housing between 1989 and 1997 through the NY/NY agreement. Through accessing a variety of city and state data sources including shelters, jails, and prisons, as well as health records (including the Veterans Administration), the researchers had a bird's-eye view of service use and the homeless service industry's operations.

Their findings showed that leaving people on the streets cost, on average, over $40,000 per person annually in jail and hospital stays, emergency room visits, and the like. Culhane et al. (2002) also showed that a small minority of the homeless was responsible for a disproportionate use of resources—about 10% of the homeless responsible for 50% of overall costs. This subgroup, labeled the "chronically homeless," became the new focus of attention.[3] Distinguishing this group from other homeless groups (e.g., families, youths, nonchronic homeless adults) were characteristics that further solidified their problem status (i.e., they were more likely to have serious problems with drugs or alcohol and to be male and African American) (Hopper, 2003).

This seeming paradox—singling out a group for special treatment that has not enjoyed much sympathy in American society—deserves further scrutiny. The obvious rationale—to save money—was provided by Culhane et al. (2002), but the rapid shift to focusing on the chronically homeless seemed more than a matter of economic calculus. Willse (2010) points to this change of direction as a saving grace for the "non-profit industrial complex" (p. 174). Channeling and triaging resources for the chronically homeless appealed to the fiscally conservative, but it also served a neoliberal agenda of narrowing government responsibility and diverting attention from wider discussions of poverty, housing insecurity, and increasing inequality (Willse, 2010). That the service recipients were not the most sympathetic group could be overlooked if a greater good plus cost savings were achieved. The spotlight on the chronically homeless infused new life and purpose into the homeless services institutional complex. It also helped propel HF to greater heights of recognition.

Conclusion: New Questions for HF

Returning to neo-institutional theory, HF had its origins in institutional entrepreneurship and a larger context of dominant but not impenetrable structures surrounding homeless services. It introduced an opposing cultural logic that gained legitimacy through rigorous research and the co-occurring evidence-based practice (EBP) movement sweeping through health services in the United States. Many homeless programs, including HF, were aided by a disability ethos that defined the worthiness of clients and gave access to steady funding streams in mental health. The disability ethos also reinforced and expanded a process of labeling (and potentially stigmatizing) serious mental illness as the entree to housing and services.

HF's flying the banner of evidence-based practice is unusual for two reasons. First, by emphasizing individualized support and flexibility, HF is far from a standardized treatment. Its claim to legitimacy via EBP belies a messy iterative process of abiding by client choice and working toward mutually agreed-upon goals. The second reason relates to the explicit-values premise of HF. In the comparatively sterile world of EBP (a world where values are dangerous sources of bias), HF stands virtually alone in leading with a rights-based stance.

The chronically homeless adults Culhane and Gladwell called attention to were the people PHF had focused on from the beginning—individuals that other programs rejected because of their seeming recalcitrance, multiple problems, high service use, or histories of violence. Culhane and colleagues' findings gave further empirical support to arguments that the current system was very expensive and ineffective (i.e., a smarter investment would be to provide homeless people with housing [first]).[4]

Such a convergence of research evidence established an unprecedented bottom line by the early 2000s: Providing immediate access to an apartment and support services to someone with mental illness and addiction was not only humane but cost effective. PHF received recognition from establishment organizations such as the American Psychiatric Association.[5] Of course, it was not unanimously embraced. For example, some critics focused on the absence of differences in substance use in the NYHS as a cause for concern (Kertesz et al., 2009; Milby et al., 2005). Such criticisms, combined with a widening positive regard for HF in the wake of the NYHS, opened the door to new questions:

- For which populations does HF work (or not work)?
- What outcomes besides housing stability does HF affect positively (or negatively)?
- Is HF peculiar to New York City funding streams and housing markets?
- How transferable is HF to other countries where service systems, socio-political philosophies, and cultural norms differ?

These questions are addressed in the remainder of this book. In the next chapter, we examine the impact of HF (and non-HF) programs as seen from the inside.

Notes

1. This requirement of having the program manage money and pay the rent was later revised to allow some tenants to make their own rental payments.

2. The six studies funded by SAMHSA and their common protocols are described in Volume 17, Issue 1–2 of the *Alcoholism Treatment Quarterly* (1999).

3. Defined as ". . . an unaccompanied homeless individual with a disabling condition who has either been continuously homeless for a year or more or has had at least four episodes of homelessness in the past three years" (U.S. Department of Housing and Urban Development [HUD], 2008, p. iii).

4. As discussed in later chapters, cost-savings proved to be a major focus of studies of HF in the U.S. and abroad (Keller et al., 2013; Larimer et al, 2009; Thomas et al., 2014).

5. Pathways to Housing received the American Psychiatric Association's Gold Award in the category of community-based programs in 2005.

5 Housing First From the Inside
QUALITATIVE RESEARCH WITH CLIENTS

QUALITATIVE STUDIES OF Pathways Housing First (PHF) complement the plethora of statistics found in reports from the New York Housing Study (NYHS), among many others.[1] In addition to addressing the same outcomes from a different perspective, qualitative studies emphasize less tangible or measurable workings of the model viewed through the subjective experiences of clients and staff. Whether part of mixed-method (quantitative and qualitative) or stand-alone (qualitative only) designs, these studies have focused on how individual lives are affected by Housing First (HF), including intended and unintended effects. In this chapter we focus on the client experience as a means of expanding our understanding of HF beyond what the numbers have shown.

We begin by describing the major qualitative studies of HF then move to summarizing their collective findings organized around salient themes. (When the program being studied is not a direct or replicated version of PHF[2] we use HF as the connotation.) Qualitative researchers are known for practicing alternative styles of inquiry, that is, for posing questions rather than hypotheses; using narratives rather than numbers; rejecting traditional notions of reliability, validity, and generalizability; and emphasizing the researcher-as-instrument, accepting rather than apologizing for the reflexivity this entails. This chapter features the

products of these inquiries, including brief vignettes and quotes from participants using pseudonyms.

Large-scale Qualitative Studies: Contexts and Methods

THE NEW YORK SERVICES STUDY (2004–2008). Two multi-year qualitative studies, both funded by the U.S. National Institute of Mental Health (NIMH), were
headquartered at New York University's Silver School of Social Work and led by
the first author (Padgett).[3] The first of these, the New York Services Study (NYSS),
began in 2004 a few years after the end of the NYHS. Bridging these two projects,
Padgett collaborated on a quantitative analysis of the NYHS data to report on
drug and alcohol use (Padgett, Gulcur, & Tsemberis, 2006).

As described in Chapter 4, the NYHS and other quantitative studies produced
robust findings but also left some questions unanswered or unresolved. It was a
natural segue to go beyond the distancing effects of statistical analyses to examine the PHF experience from insiders' perspectives expressed in their own words.
Qualitative studies can lead to better understanding of quantitative findings,
help clarify the less-than-robust or nonsignificant findings and, more importantly, address deeper questions of "how" and "why" the program works when it
does (and when it does not).

In the NYSS, the choice of central outcome—engagement and retention in
care—was a strategic decision because high dropout rates were (and continue to
be) among the most persistent problems in services for the homeless. Why so
many men and women walked out on (or were terminated from) their programs
was remarkable, given that these services were designed to stabilize their lives at
little or no financial cost to the client. Box 5.1 offers a vignette description of one
such individual who "dropped out".

Focusing on improving rates of engagement and retention was no doubt pivotal
to success in obtaining funding for the NYSS, but there were also safeguards built
prominently into the grant proposal to disarm quantitative reviewers and others
skeptical about the value of qualitative methods. Thus, the NYSS included several
"strategies for rigor" (Padgett, 2012) that enhanced the study's trustworthiness.[4]

The NYSS had two complementary but distinct dimensions: program comparisons (PHF and non-HF) and individual change over time (which might
or might not be compared according to program enrollment). Cooperating
sites for the study included Pathways to Housing (PTH) and three continuum
(non-HF) programs in New York City (not difficult to find since PTH was the
only HF program in the city). Phase 1 was devoted to collecting "life histories

BOX 5.1
DROPPING OUT AND IN AND OUT AGAIN

Felipe entered the New York Services Study (NYSS) as a resident of a transitional housing (non-HF) program in New York City's midtown area. A month after his baseline interview, he discharged himself and returned to the streets, blaming crowding and "feeling trapped." He remained a day client of the program over the next year, availing himself of its food, laundry, and showers, but the program ceased prescribing his medications and other services because he was no longer in residence. Felipe spent the rest of his time in the study sleeping in a Harlem truck depot, a railway tunnel, emergency shelter, hospital psychiatric ward, jail cell, and his mother's apartment. Public assistance, food stamps, and food pantries gave him a meager living on the streets. Felipe argued frequently with his mother, and his threats against her led to his arrest, jail time, and a restraining order taken out against him. A heavy drinker and sporadic marijuana smoker, Felipe said he drank "when things are going bad." Worried about side effects, Felipe did not take psychiatric medications until the last two months of the study despite seeing a psychiatrist at a local hospital walk-in clinic and complaining of hearing voices. Living in an emergency shelter at his final 12-month study interview, Felipe was trying to get into a detoxification program to get treatment, housing, and meals. This was his fourth detox/rehabilitation stint in six years of being homeless. He was on the wait list for the Street to Home program and hoped to get his own Section 8 rental assistance voucher in the future.

with a purpose," that is, asking program clients about what services had worked (or had not) as they made their way through psychiatric hospitalizations, rehabilitation, shelters, and other stops on the "institutional circuit" (Hopper et al., 1997). Phase 2 was a 12-month series of three interviews with new enrollees in the programs to observe in real time what services they used, what services they avoided, and what providers helped (or hindered) them. Relying on in-depth interviews of clients and their case managers, the NYSS had 39 participants in Phase 1 (21 HF and 18 TF [treatment first]) and 75 in Phase 2 (27 HF and 48 TF).

THE NEW YORK RECOVERY STUDY (2010–2015). The findings of the NYSS added to a rapidly growing body of research on homelessness and serious mental illness, including research on HF. Together, this work laid the foundation for the next all-qualitative NIMH-funded study examining PHF. The New York Recovery Study (NYRS), also originating at New York University,[5] extended earlier findings about poverty, cumulative adversity, and the benefits and challenges of independent living. Figure 5.1 shows the areas of focus for the NYSS and NYRS respectively.

The NYRS was a direct response to the mental health recovery movement. Clinicians expressed concerns about raised expectations and dashed hopes, but the "rhetorical consensus" surrounding mental health recovery (Slade, Amering, & Oades, 2008, p. 128) solidified over time. The jumping-off point for the NYRS was to take the recovery promise at its word, especially its applicability to persons for whom mental illness was not their only problem or even their worst problem. The recovery movement's spokespersons were almost exclusively from white middle-class backgrounds. Their success stories—graduate school, marriage, authored books, blogs, research careers—are moving and inspirational. However, such levels of achievement are rare for any group and cannot fairly be expected of all persons living in and with mental illness.

The NYRS was designed to explore mental health recovery from the perspectives of the same group studied in the NYSS: formerly homeless persons with serious mental illnesses. Repeating the NYSS design, the NYRS had two comparison groups (PHF and a non-PHF program) and two phases, the first consisting of interviews with clients nominated by their programs as having positive recovery

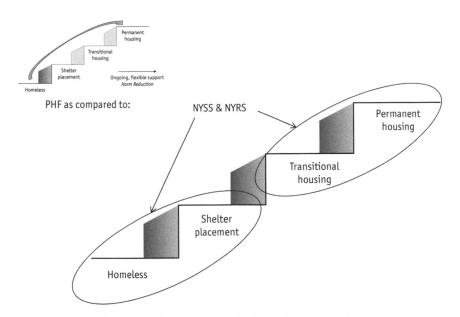

FIGURE 5.1 Qualitative Studies Comparing Pathways Housing First to the Staircase Approach.

trajectories and the second an 18-month follow-up of new enrollees' recovery trajectories. The role of housing and services was important, but we remained open to any factors—personal, organizational, or otherwise—that might help us understand recovery "from the inside" and over time.

Understanding mental health recovery required probing yet sensitive questions about mental illness, use of drugs and alcohol, social relationships, and other aspects of participants' lives that moved them forward or held them back. Ending in 2015, the NYRS accumulated both interview and observational data to be analyzed using case study analyses (of individual lives over time) and grounded theory coding and thematic development. As described in Box 5.2, the study included a photo-elicitation interview component that proved to be valuable in several ways.

BOX 5.2

PHOTO-ELICITATION INTERVIEWING IN THE NEW YORK RECOVERY STUDY

The NYRS was designed to take advantage of observation to complement the interview data that are the hallmark of qualitative studies. In addition to ethnographic observation of clients (shadowing or go-along interviews during their daily activities) and their programs (site visits during program activities), we incorporated a technique from anthropology—photo-elicitation interviewing. This method involves giving participants cameras and asking them to take photographs depicting their lives and narrate their meaning (Harper, 2002).

Reasoning that study participants might find photographic portrayals a creative means of expression, we purchased low-cost digital cameras and asked 17 men and women to portray both positive and negative aspects of their lives (Padgett, Smith, Derejko, Henwood, & Tiderington, 2013). The results were impressive for a few reasons. First, several brought photographs and described life events that they had not mentioned in earlier interviews, for example, the young man who brought his seemingly innocuous photo of an apartment building and explained that this was where his girlfriend lived before her death from a heroin overdose. Second, participants celebrated having a home—taking photos of their apartment keys, their apartment interiors, their neighborhood, and visiting friends and family.

But they also showed a degree of civic spirit and self-awareness that had been missing from the verbal-only interviews. Thus, they showed photographs of community gardens along with photos of community murals in Harlem and scenic urban neighborhoods. Their narrations revealed the murals to be sources of racial and ethnic pride. Other urban scenes, for example, a colorful street in Chinatown, were invoked as examples of "seeing the world with new eyes" after years of substance abuse and homelessness.

Cross-cutting Themes in Qualitative Research on Housing First

In reviewing qualitative research on HF, five broad themes can be identified. The first is concerned with the deeper meaning of housing and living independently, the second with trauma and adversity over the life course, the third captures the dual valence (negative and positive) of social relationships, and the fourth is about dealing with substance abuse. The fifth theme is related to service engagement—what helped and what hindered. Each of these is described below.

LIVING INDEPENDENTLY: THE IMPORTANCE OF A HOME. Whether by celebrating its presence or bemoaning its absence, the idea of living on one's own loomed large in participants' narratives (see Box 5.3 for a description of one person's experience). By this we refer to that exalted state easily taken for granted: Having a home is where one can lock the door, drink a beer, invite friends over, or simply enjoy being without supervision. Stories abounded of the horrors of life on the streets or in shelters, of the constant struggle to hold onto one's belongings and bodily safety, and of the frustrations of having to prove one's housing worthiness to harried and overworked program staff.

BOX 5.3
NO PLACE LIKE A HOME

Nina, a Pathways tenant who lives in upper Manhattan, is a recovering heroin addict on methadone who is taking medication for severe depression and anxiety. She has a 30-year-old son who lives out of state. Nina's boyfriend Lorenzo visits daily, but she is adamant that she does not want to live with him at his place. "I told him, 'I'm not leaving my apartment.' He has his and I got mine, but I like my space." Nina refers to her coming to Pathways as a close call, having first been referred to a single-room occupancy (SRO) "So when they took me to the SROs, oh thank God I didn't take them. You can't have visitors. Your boyfriend cannot go there. He could only go visit you on a Saturday. . . . I felt like I was in prison. I have more freedom in prison. You can't have friends over. The rent was 650 [dollars]. Thank God Pathways stepped in." This amount, virtually her entire monthly SSI income for a single room in an SRO, was far more than the 30% taken by Pathways for rent.

Although not always happy with her Pathways case managers—and assertive enough to let their supervisors know—Nina's satisfaction with her living situation has not wavered. "I'm just excited that right now I just want to be the way I am. I don't want to have nobody controlling me and nobody telling me what to do and when to come. I just want to live my life the way I am now. I'm very happy and stabilized, thank God. I don't want it no other way."

Paraphrasing Charmaz (2006), this theme had a lot of "grab" in the data, a reference point for something readily appreciated or frustratingly out of reach. It also mapped almost perfectly onto a rather obscure concept from the literature: "ontological security." With origins in R.D. Laing's (1965) writings about the "ontological insecurity" induced by psychosis, the term was further developed by modernist sociologist Anthony Giddens (1990) as conveying a sense of constancy in one's social and material environment, which, in turn, provides a secure platform for identity development and self-actualization. As described in greater detail in Chapter 6, evidence of ontological security emerges in sharp relief when a person gets a home for the first time after years of life on the street.

THE TOLL OF ADVERSITY AND TRAUMA. Participants' accounts of trauma and loss, much of it stemming from childhood and continuing steadily into adulthood, were threaded through their life narratives. Most had grown up poor, exposed to childhood neglect and abuse, to easy availability of drugs and alcohol, and to neighborhood violence. The adversity this brought cast mental illness and homelessness in the unlikely position of not necessarily being the worst thing to have happened in their lives.

Not all participants had turbulent or traumatic early lives, but by virtue of the study's inclusion criteria all had been exposed to the trials of street life (see Box 5.4 for more on this topic). Beyond acute stressors were the cumulative effects of chronic and often unrelenting deprivation—poor health, depression, and physical disability. The milestones in life taken for granted by middle-class Americans—college, marriage, parenting, a career—were missed entirely, cut short, or troubled. Feeling "out of sync" with the larger society (Shibusawa & Padgett, 2009), participants had to cope with a lack of education and job skills that might have kept them from becoming homeless. These deficits in human capital created an undertow, a drag on efforts to recover.

THE DEPLETION AND DUAL VALENCE OF SOCIAL RELATIONSHIPS. The literature on homeless persons with serious mental illness paints a portrait of social isolation, largely the result of estrangement caused by mental symptoms, substance abuse, and hitting bottom economically. There are also longstanding accumulations of social losses, termed "disappearing acts" by Hawkins & Abrams (2007). This depletion of social networks was exacerbated by strained relationships, but it was also due to more definitive forms of separation: premature death, incarceration, and abandonment.

The common thread here is, once again, poverty and its dense web of disadvantage. The ranks of family members, neighbors, and friends are thinned by

BOX 5.4

TRAUMA AS TOLD

Despite having diagnoses of schizophrenia, bipolar disorder, and severe depression, and despite taking powerful antipsychotic medications such as Haldol, Seroquel, and Risperdal, study participants spent far less time talking about their diagnosis than about other challenges in their lives (a few denied having the diagnosis at all). One participant preferred to name her mental problem "despair" resulting from homelessness, saying she goes along with the diagnosis because it is the only way to get services, especially housing.

It is impossible to disentangle the effects of a psychiatric diagnosis from those of trauma—being raped as a child; sexually assaulted while homeless; brutally beaten by family members, boyfriends, or strangers; or losing family and friends to violence, early death, and accidents. Add to this the effects of psychiatric hospitalizations with physical and chemical restraints, as well as the effects of jail or prison terms (with all the latter implies, including long periods in the "box," or solitary confinement). Then there are the more quotidian experiences of gnawing hunger, sleeping outside on freezing winter nights, and having nowhere to relieve one's self or bathe.

The New York Services Study team decided early on not to probe for traumatic events out of respect for privacy and to create a climate of trust for such revelations to come out voluntarily. What we heard, then, was volunteered information. Not everyone reported childhood or adult trauma, but what *was* reported made us wonder what could have been left out. The temporal depth, multiplicity, and cumulative nature of exposure to adversity were striking (Padgett, Smith, Henwood, & Tiderington, 2012).

violence, accidents, prison stints, and substance abuse, along with a host of diseases undertreated and under-recognized: asthma, cardiac problems, diabetes, and cancer. Common life scenarios included unemployed or absentee fathers, blended stepfamilies with many children and few supervising adults, and neighborhoods with easy access to drugs, gangs, guns, and alcohol. Whether victim or perpetrator (or both), participants were often mired in networks where violence was the default means of settling arguments and illegal activities brought income (Padgett, Henwood, Abrams, & Drake, 2008; Stefancic, 2014).

Programs using the TF approach tend to discourage clients from social connections until they become stable on their medications and in their sobriety. Visitation is curtailed or prohibited and weekend furloughs are given as rewards for good behavior. Drug-using friends and family can be trouble and are often the reason for eviction of HF tenants by landlords. In addition, the congregate living arrangements in TF programs, at times including organized social outings, have been cast as ready-made (yet more supervised) opportunities for social relationships.

Meanwhile, clients are frequently asked to provide names of family or others who can help out in a crisis or if they are discharged from the program. Aside from the marked absence of supportive others is the lingering trauma associated with those losses, many due to violence or accidents. One NYSS participant witnessed his younger brother hit and beheaded by a speeding car, another had lost several family members to AIDS within a short time.

Participants had experienced social rejection whether for having a mental illness, being addicted, being homeless, or a combination of all of these (Padgett, Henwood, Abrams, & Drake, 2008). Interviewers' questions about whether they wished to meet a romantic partner or make new friends were typically met with "yes, but" or "not yet" responses. Men talked about an inability to please women who expected expensive dates or the pitfalls of being lured into paying for sex and drugs. For their part, women gave voice to a deep distrust of men rooted in fears (and previous experiences) of sexual aggression, exploitation, and abandonment. The give-and-take of an intimate relationship, coupled with emotional destabilization if it failed, made avoidance the safer course of action. Box 5.5 further describes the dual valence inherent in social relationships.

More than simply avoiding risk, the men and women of the NYSS voiced "loner talk," a professed desire for solitude or time to stabilize before embarking on new relationships—a yearning that was both protective and self-aware (Padgett, Henwood, Abrams, & Drake, 2008). Participants would assert that they were not ready; they had too much else going on in their lives. This "something else" included unstable housing, struggles with addiction, frayed family ties, and parole restrictions. Finding sober friends and avoiding negative influences was a delicate balance. Erring on the side of caution, cherishing privacy, and deferring the risks of failed romances tipped that balance away from seeking new relationships (Stefancic, 2014).

Qualitative analyses give nuanced takes on critiques that PHF isolates individuals and dampens social integration (Hopper, 2012). Feelings of belonging or of loneliness are deeply subjective and situational (e.g., holidays can be lonely but at other times having one's privacy is cherished). To be sure, living solo can be lonely—and many Pathways clients complained of this. As importantly, however, the alternative—congregate living and institutional care—does not necessarily provide a sense of community and no Pathways clients expressed an interest in that alternative.

Qualitative analyses revealed that feelings of loneliness were balanced by a desire for solitude and emotional consolidation. HF participants report having

BOX 5.5
SOCIAL RELATIONSHIPS: GOOD NEWS AND BAD NEWS

Participants spoke of how social ties could alternate between positive and negative depending upon the context, timing, and nature of the relationship. Felipe (see Box 5.1) had only his mother to help him—she took him in for two months during the study—but their violent arguments cut short his stays and led to arrest and jailing. Carl was estranged from his sister and had tenuous relationships with his sons' mothers (one of whom was living in a shelter with their two sons). On parole after being imprisoned for selling heroin, he tried to spend time with his sons and court a new girlfriend. "That's one thing I don't like, having a girlfriend when you ain't even got a job. Because you don't want nobody to see you going through that, but she understands. At the same time, I push her away, but she's still around. ... My other sons' moms know that, but they don't think it will last because I'm just coming home [from prison]." Letitia went AWOL from her program, relapsed into drugs and homelessness, and was referred to an adult home where she was charged $450 per month for a room shared with three other women. Letitia's two young daughters lived with her mother down South and her brother was in jail. Letitia missed seeing her daughters and regretted having no money to visit them, but she was committed to taking her medications and working on her recovery. "People I used to get high with, I try to stay away from," she said. "All they're gonna do is try to suck me back into it. You know what I mean? That's like going to the barber shop. You keep going, you're gonna get a haircut once in a while."

a secure platform from which to reconnect or restore broken relationships, but they were often wary of closer relationships for fear of being exploited due to their newly acquired apartments. They also feared the emotional instability of rejection or insecure attachments to others (Stefancic, 2014). TF participants echoed the latter fear of destabilization but with added concerns that relationships were more difficult due to the time-limited nature of their programs, as well as program restrictions on having visitors or furloughs to visit friends and family. Indeed, TF participants expressed repeated concerns about their roommates. Though some had friendly relations, these were the exception. More common were complaints about poor hygiene, theft, and rule-breaking (Padgett et al., 2008).

GENDER ROLES: OUTCASTS AND OUTLAWS. Gender was tacitly but deeply influential in how homeless persons were perceived and in the options available to them. As maligned as homeless men are, they benefit from a degree of societal tolerance for their masculine choices and (mis)behaviors, especially in the poor neighborhoods where most grew up (Anderson, 2000; Duneier, 1999). Surviving at the lowest rungs of society, homeless men nevertheless share with their non-homeless brethren access to male activities—whether in the underground economy of drug trading, street peddling, pimping, and day labor or in the tolerance of unruly public behaviors—drinking alcohol, hanging out on street corners, gambling, pick-up basketball games, and the like. This "code of the street" (Anderson, 2000) also sanctioned violence as necessary for defending one's self and honor.

Such tolerance was not accorded women who were excoriated for neglecting or abandoning their children, excluded from many street economies (recycling bottles and cans and sex work being among the few options available to them) and all-too-often on the receiving end of violence—both domestic and street-level, sexual and physical. Behaviors shared with their male counterparts—poor hygiene, hoarding, and indecent exposure prompted by needing to relieve one's self or bathe outdoors—were more egregious violations and were considered "unfeminine" (Padgett, Hawkins, Abrams, & Davis, 2006). Thus, while men identified with "outlaws" from movies and rap music, women were more likely to be treated as "outcasts" by their families and society.

Not every man neglected his children or beat his wife/girlfriend, and plenty of men had suffered the same abusive childhoods as women. Also, plenty of women used violence to exact revenge or fight back against an aggressor. But the advantages of male gender still accrued in fewer recriminations for antisocial behavior and more opportunities to earn income in the underground economy. Off-the-books work is vital to many who have no other means to make money.

DEALING WITH SUBSTANCE ABUSE. This theme expanded considerably upon what had been learned from the NYHS and other quantitative studies. Substance use and abuse is pervasive in the lives of homeless adults. Beer, malt liquor, whisky, marijuana, crack cocaine, and heroin are common, and methamphetamine, painkillers, and tranquilizers ("benzos") are easily obtained on the streets. Getting high brings feel-good moments and social belonging, but it also exacts a well known toll in lost income and increasing criminal activity to support a habit. Substance abuse is episodic and follows an unpredictable course in a person's life. For researchers, it is often the subject of omission, obfuscation, or outright deception.

In the NYSS, we were interested in how (if at all) the programs influenced the decision to abstain (or use) and the contexts of substance use when it happened. One of the earlier publications from the study focused on participants' comments about why they used drugs and alcohol in the first place (Henwood & Padgett, 2007). Responding to a popular notion that people with schizophrenia and other major mental disorders drink and use drugs to "self-medicate" their psychotic symptoms, a different picture emerged from the NYSS data. In the first place, substance use almost always pre-dated the onset of mental illness, extending back to childhood and early adolescent experiences living in a home and neighborhood with easy access. This almost constant exposure continued into adulthood in the neighborhoods where the programs placed their clients.

Life history interviews in Phase 1 of the NYSS provided retrospective accounts of participant's struggles with drugs or alcohol that were analyzed using cross-case analyses (Patton, 2002) to ensure individual trajectories were retained. A total of 27 out of 31 had achieved long-term abstinence and the remaining 4 were occasional users. In the interviews, stopping was explained as either a gradual thing (sometimes facilitated by time spent in jail or prison) or a discrete decision prompted by a health crisis or deliberation about the consequences of abuse (Henwood, Padgett, Smith, & Tiderington, 2012). Harold, a 55-year-old African American man, had been clean and sober for six years after his eldest daughter pleaded with him to stop. "I've been sober since then . . . no 12 Steps, no AA, none of that bullshit. Just a promise to my child." The gradual approach was described by Jim (a 46-year-old African American man). "I stopped for long periods and you'd think about it and you might have a drink or you might smoke a joint, but as time went on it, it just wasn't a factor anymore."

Thematic case analyses also revealed different but overlapping attributions for achieving versus maintaining recovery (Henwood et al., 2012). The transition to housing was often a reason to contemplate the consequences of using. Terence explained that he had something to lose now that he had his own apartment. ". . . This is a head start right here. I got an apartment, and if I go backwards, I lose everything." Participants were divided over the benefits of 12-Step programs such as Alcoholics Anonymous. For some, these group meetings were welcome support, but for others they were reminders of a past from which they preferred to move away. John said he stayed away from 12-Step groups because ". . . I could not bring myself to say . . . 'My name is [x] and I'm an alcoholic' . . . I would say, 'I'm an ex–drug addict or I'm an ex-alcoholic,' but that was something in the past." The 12-Step slogan urging members to avoid "people, places, and things' begs the question of how to make that happen when living in neighborhoods with active drug markets, numerous liquor stores, and few wholesome distractions (Henwood et al., 2012).

ENGAGEMENT AND RETENTION IN SERVICES: WHAT HELPED, WHAT HINDERED. Explorations of the subjective experiences of clients revealed the service sector left much to be desired. Among the findings from the NYSS, one publication directly answered the "engagement and retention" question central to the study (Padgett, Henwood, Abrams, & Davis, 2008). From analysis of life history interviews, a grounded theory model (Charmaz, 2006) was developed focusing on participants' experiences in and out of services—medical, mental health, detoxification, rehabilitation—as well as institutional experiences such as long-term hospitalizations and incarcerations.

This model revealed some expected and unexpected themes. Study participants readily acknowledged that their mental problems and substance abuse could work against service use, especially when the terms of engagement dictated sobriety and supervised congregate living. Negative aspects of their service experiences included the absence of "one-on-one" therapy and the omnipresence of rules and restrictions. An "in vivo" or participant-generated theme, the desire for "one-on-one" talk therapy was a reflection of the need for trusted confidence in a practitioner with whom traumatic experiences could be shared and worked through. Far more common were group therapy sessions where breaches of confidentiality could turn into neighborhood gossip (Padgett, Henwood, Abrams, & Davis, 2008).

The "rules and restrictions" theme was part and parcel of the TF approach. Mostly men in their 40s or older, study participants bridled under the watchful eyes of younger (mostly female) case managers, most of whom were poorly trained and poorly paid. Both client and case manager operated under a program philosophy dependent on waiting for months and years at a time—and compliance with program rules in the meantime.

Incentives to engagement were less commonly experienced but deeply appreciated nonetheless. Three themes—pleasant surroundings, acts of kindness, and rapid access to housing—were developed from the data. Pleasant surroundings and acts of kindness referred to the rare occasions when the setting, for example, a garden-like private psychiatric hospital, or the provider, perhaps a kindly and understanding psychiatrist or social worker, stood out in stark contrast to the noisy, crowded wards and harried staff to which they were accustomed (Padgett, Henwood, Abrams, & Davis, 2008). The last theme in the findings—access to permanent housing—was confined to the HF study participants. Engagement and retention were by no means easy at Pathways, but they were enhanced when consumers lived in their own apartment (Stanhope, Henwood, & Padgett, 2009).

Staying Open to Hear All Sides

The NYSS findings dug deeper into explaining the positive aspects of HF, but we also stayed open to negative consequences, as well as to the counterintuitive and unanticipated. Not all PHF tenants were happy, and some expressed concerns about the lack of structure (more on behalf of others than on behalf of themselves). Some case managers (and landlords) were less responsive than others and left tenants feeling disrespected. Other complaints encountered: Pathways should do more to find jobs for tenants, to help them get more education, or to help them relocate to a better apartment or neighborhood. Despite these complaints, however, PHF participants did not want to leave the program to go to a non-HF program.

One of the more poignant findings from the NYSS concerned the "what's next" worries coming mostly from PHF tenants (Padgett, 2007). Reminiscent of Maslow's hierarchy of needs, having a secure home and access to services sets the stage for new needs to rise to the surface (Henwood, Derejko, Couture, & Padgett, 2014). These might include repairing relationships with one's children, getting a job, becoming involved in the community (however defined), or taking steps to improve one's health. The poignancy came from tenants knowing that their life spans were not likely to be long—so many others in their lives were already gone—and that the losses and poor health they had sustained would be hard to overcome.

The profound effects of cumulative adversity and premature mortality could not be "treated" out of existence nor would they disappear upon settling into an apartment after months or years of waiting. The daily struggle to survive on the streets may have mercifully postponed the reckoning that awaited them—a struggle that, ironically, hastened that reckoning.

Conclusion: Rounding Out the Picture

When analyzed via first-person accounts rendered in tenants' own words, HF's benefits and limitations are revealed in greater depth, and the same is true of the TF programs. Beyond program effects, these studies explored the intricate webs of people's lives, where the cumulative effects of poverty take their toll in depleted social networks and repeated exposure to trauma. The synergism of substance abuse and mental illness created hardships, but individual resilience was also present to counter these effects. The dual valence of social relationships was notable; some friends and family members were supportive, others were missing, unhelpful, or worse.

Though properly grounded in the minutiae of consumers' lives, qualitative research also draws in the bigger picture through situating meaning in larger contexts. Although not spoken about directly, the role of gender was nevertheless powerfully evident in the nature and extent of life adversity as well as the street-level activities available to men but not women. Formerly homeless adults, even when securely housed, contend with "what's next" questions that speak to larger structural problems—stigma and social exclusion, a lack of jobs and job training, premature mortality, and lingering poor health.

This interplay of individual adversity and socioenvironmental context underscores the importance of what happens in-between—the place where nonprofit organizations are entrusted with public funds to meet unmet needs. Though hardly a panacea—more than a few PHF tenants expressed dissatisfaction with their case managers or their neighborhood—the qualitative findings underscored the benefits of having a home and choices about treatment. Although not likely to have the same policy impact as the results of an experiment, these findings rounded out the picture, supplying depth and greater understanding. As we will see in the next chapter, qualitative studies uniquely lend themselves to in-depth case studies of individual stories. The reductive benefits of coding and thematic development "pull the thread," but they also obscure individual stories—the subject matter of the next chapter. As with this chapter, the framework for Chapter 6 is one of comparing HF with TF (non-HF) clients.

Notes

1. Most of the qualitative research reviewed in this chapter was conducted on Pathways to Housing in New York City, but recent years have witnessed a growing body of qualitative and quantitative work emerging from other cities and Canada's At Home/Chez Soi project (see Chapter 8).

2. To clarify regarding use of PHF or HF: PHF refers to Pathways to Housing, Inc. affiliated programs that share a national governing board (currently in New York City, Philadelphia, Washington DC, and Vermont). When another program closely follows the PHF model, we also use PHF to refer to it (e.g., the Chez Soi/At Home projects in Canada). Many programs now use HF without adhering to the PHF version.

3. Members of the NYSS study team besides Padgett included Andrew Davis, Courtney Abrams, Ben Henwood, Ana Stefancic, and Robert Hawkins.

4. Six strategies for rigor culled from the literature on qualitative methods include (1) prolonged engagement, (2) triangulation of data, (3) auditing, (4) peer debriefing and support, (5) member checking, and (6) negative case analysis (Padgett, 2012). Of these, the first four were used in the NYSS.

5. Members of the NYRS study team besides Padgett include Victoria Stanhope, Bikki Tran Smith, Ben Henwood, Emmy Tiderington, Katie-Sue Derejko, Mimi Choy-Brown, and Stacey Berrenger.

6 In Their Own Words
CONSUMERS SHARE THEIR STORIES

IF YOU COULD take a moment to think about your typical activities of daily life, they would most likely include sleeping in a bed, taking a shower, getting the mail, watching television, preparing a meal, inviting friends over, and locking the door as you leave (or go to bed). Take away all of these mundane activities—add bad weather, traffic noise and pollution, strangers' stares, and the threat of violence—and that is life on the street. Individual journeys into this lamentable state of existence are invariably obscured by the statistics of research and government reports.

In this chapter, we offer first-person accounts in a more holistic fashion. These stories were handpicked from interviews with nearly 200 individuals who have been gracious enough to share their lives as part of the New York Services Study (NYSS) or the New York Recovery Study (NYRS). We acknowledge that we are the ultimate arbiters, or "storytellers," because we are appropriating and excerpting these lives for our purposes.

Our goal is to report on the lived experience of being homeless and, more importantly, on what happens after being housed in a Housing First (HF) or a non-Housing First (non-HF) program. Complementing the previous chapter's overarching themes, this chapter takes what individuals told us and maintains the dynamism and depth that characterize their lives.

Although these types of narratives are often rehearsed accounts, formulated to please the teller or the listener, the prolonged engagement and trust that comes with qualitative methods helps to offset any such tendency. From the first open-ended question, interviewees are alerted to the fact that this is not business as usual. Nor is the interviewer a clinician or entitlement specialist who must ask pointed questions and get pointed answers—psychiatric consumers are accustomed to giving repeated recitations as they share their treatment history, diagnoses, medication needs, emergency contacts, and other linchpins of a service plan.

Qualitative interviews may also elicit such factual information, but it is embedded within an extended and flowing format of the teller's choosing. These men and women have endured horrendous things, but they have also experienced good times and personal triumphs. The losses are great, but the hopes and dreams are still there.

The individuals featured in this chapter have all received diagnoses of serious mental illness—schizophrenia, bipolar disorder, major depression—and have experienced homelessness and substance abuse. For them, moving into a supportive housing program—whether transitional or permanent—is a new beginning even if it is on the heels of earlier less successful "new beginnings." This is the starting point around which the following stories unfold—with occasional retrospective life history review.

Some enter a program that offers permanence and services while living alone (HF) and others enter a program that offers transitional living and the hope of permanence contingent upon displaying "housing readiness" (TF). Symptoms of mental illness may still be troubling and recovery from addiction[1] tenuous, but at least they are no longer homeless.

Themes of the previous chapter—living independently, cumulative adversity, depleted social relationships, gender differences, and recovery from substance abuse—become personified in this chapter. Given the premise of this book, we are obviously interested in Housing First—the role it plays in altering the course of individual lives as well as its limitations. For comparison, we also describe the lives of individuals in transitional (i.e., TF) housing, whether dormitory-style quarters or shared apartments. To help frame this experience, we first re-introduce the concept of "ontological security."

Ontological Security and the Meaning of Home

At the outset of the New York Services Study (NYSS) in 2004, HF was making headway but not yet in the news or receiving national endorsements. Nevertheless, the

New York Housing Study (NYHS) randomized trial had been completed and the quantitative results were starting to emerge and attract attention. Three years later, the NYSS and its qualitative findings also were finding their way into print. From this immersion in the interview data, a deeper understanding of the meaning of "home" began to take shape. Enter the concept of ontological security.

Ontology, or the nature of being, became the basis for the concept of "ontological security" through the writings of psychoanalyst D.W. Winnicott on infant attachment and the trust it engendered (1964). Around the same time, Scottish psychiatrist R.D. Laing wrote of the "ontological insecurity" induced by schizophrenia, wherein patients lost their sense of identity and place in the world (1965). Several decades later, British sociologist Anthony Giddens brought the phrase into wider usage in referring to life in a fast-paced yet homogenizing modern world (1990). To Giddens, ontological security is "a sense of continuity and order in events" (p. 5) (i.e., the feeling of well-being that arises from a sense of constancy in one's social and material environment). This, in turn, provides a secure platform for identity development and self-actualization. The absence of ontological security, a state of uncertainty in one's sense of self and place, is a risk inherent in modern 20th century life (Giddens, 1990).

The phrase has been put to use in various ways, none more fundamental (or reflective of middle-class Western values) than studies of the psychological benefits of home ownership (Dupuis & Thorns, 1998; Hiscock, Macintyre, Kearns, & Ellaway, 2003). If owning rather than renting confers ontological security, imagine what might happen when one comes indoors after months or years of living on the street.

Having a roof over one's head is clearly one of life's necessities, but shelter from the elements is not the same as having a "home"—and here is where the meaning of ontological security plumbs greater depths, especially for homeless individuals coping with mental illness. It is ironic that Laing wrote about a group of people who so often lack access to the housing that would help ease their ontological insecurity.

In referring to the benefits of one's own housing in general (not after being homeless), Dupuis and Thorns cite four "markers" or conditions of ontological security that are met when home is: (1) a place of constancy in the material and social environment; (2) a place in which the day-to-day routines of human existence are performed; (3) where people feel in control of their lives because they feel free from the surveillance that characterizes life elsewhere; and, (4) a secure base around which identities are constructed (1998, p. 29). Building on this previous work, analyses of NYSS data produced a report in which these markers mapped onto participants' experiences remarkably well (Padgett, 2007). The last marker—identity construction—was less evident, but primarily because this was not a focus of the NYSS.

The case vignettes that follow will shed light on ontological security as it relates to housing. Of course, they also portray much more, but the four markers of ontological security represent a schema for understanding the role of housing—its benefits and its limitations. To protect confidentiality, we use pseudonyms and alter minor facts. To maximize giving "voice," we use quotes as much as possible.

Alfred: "I was that guy . . ."

Alfred, a 49-year-old African American man, started his interview by saying he was nervous and had slept poorly the night before. Soon, however, he relaxed and talked without holding back.

> I was that guy that society would probably write off, you know. All I've ever heard was stuff like "you'd be better off dead," or "they should just lock you up for life," and "you'll never amount to anything," "this guy he's just fucking crazy." Sorry, I didn't mean to curse.

Alfred started having hallucinations (both auditory and visual) when he was 16 years old, shortly after his mother's death. This loss haunts him and Alfred says that his troubles continued thereafter for over two decades.

> I was a drug user or abuser for well over 20 years. Mostly crack cocaine, I've never done heroin, not that that makes a difference. But it kind of slowed down the voices and helped with the pain. I, as a teenager and all through my twenties, I was extremely delusional, extremely violent, and I had no understanding of my mental illness, who I was or why I was even the way that I was. And the only thing that seemed to work was the drugs. Unfortunately, they made things worse when you came down. And before you know it, you kinda just needed the drugs more than you needed anything. And I lived like that for many years.

A key turning point for Alfred happened at the age of 40 when an organization that helps prisoners with mental illness known as CASES (Center for Alternative Sentencing and Employment) reached out to Alfred while he was in jail on Rikers Island. CASES had contacted him twice earlier and Alfred had turned them down.

"I just thought it would be easier to stay the way I was than to try to work on anything."

But this time he accepted their offer and was placed in the YMCA and in halfway houses while awaiting housing. Alfred grew impatient. *"I was starting to lose faith in their ability to help me and resorted back to drugs and all this whole other stuff."* Alfred explains that his failures in drug treatment were because, *"I'm easily distracted by women."* When not institutionalized, Alfred lived with one or another girlfriend and there were usually drugs involved.

When CASES found a men's residential drug treatment program for him, Alfred got a new start toward recovering from addiction without his usual distraction of being around women.

[Laughing]I had no choice but to pay attention! . . . And it literally worked for me. It literally, literally worked for me. And I don't know, I guess over the years of all the therapy, you know you don't think you pay attention, but these things somehow just stick in the back of your brain. And I always had tools; I guess I just never really tapped into 'em. The more I learned, the more I remembered, then I was just able to start putting things together.

Alfred credits his CASES service coordinator with standing by him through thick and thin. And she was ultimately able to connect him with Pathways to Housing. *"I got my very own apartment for the first time ever. I fell in love with this apartment."* He explains the attraction:

It was the only place that I ever had that was mine. That had my name on it . . . I've always lived with some woman. If it wasn't living with a woman, I was in a state facility. I was passed through a lot of different programs and promised a lot of stuff. It was my apartment. My name was on the lease. I had my keys. There was a lot of reasons why I fell in love with it. It was home (his emphasis).

For Alfred, having his own place for the first time in his life was a revelation:

And you know, after sleeping in shelters and halfway houses, it's amazing how just to be able to wake up in the middle of the night and smoke a cigarette without somebody yelling at you. You know, little things, being able to take a bath, things that people take for granted, are just so much. I truly enjoy these things. I don't share this with people, but I enjoy taking bubble baths. You know, just something I never was able to do. You know, so to be able to smoke a cigarette in my own bedroom, take a bath, or cook, you know, It's mine. And it's been almost nine years, and I still have that feeling every time I stick my key in the door.

Another turning point in Alfred's life came when he attended the Howie the Harp (HTH) training program and began working part-time at Pathways. *"CASES and Pathways were the only programs that ever delivered on anything that they said. And which is one of the reasons I hopped on the opportunity to work for them."* Alfred trained to become a peer support worker because *"with everything else that I've gained through my own personal experience, just made it seem like it was something that I could do."* The HTH training also gave him a chance for personal growth through his work:

> *And I kind of liked the work, and one thing led to another, I started becoming more insightful about my own mental illness, and the more I learned the more I wanted to learn. And the better I started getting. For some crazy reason I wanted to be able to share that with other people. It's something that sorta came natural. I'm a much better person at work than I am in my personal life.*

Alfred's personal life had its share of turmoil. At age 18, he fathered a daughter and, *"my psychosis has got in the way of my fatherhood. My substance abuse also got in the way of my fatherhood. There's a lot of things I coulda did better."* At the time of the interview, however, Alfred felt strong enough to withstand future adversity:

> *I've been lonely. I've been homeless. I've been emotionally hurt and broke for so long, that I have a chance to literally live and breathe. And if I lost this job today, life would still be okay. You know, I guess I have a purpose, you know? And freedom.*

Mitch: "I just didn't have the means"

Mitch is a 56-year-old white divorced man living in a Pathways apartment in East Harlem. He has two grown sons and a longtime girlfriend, Diane, who is struggling with mental illness and addiction. The daughter of affluent parents, Diane met Mitch at an AA meeting. While he was homeless, Mitch slept in a park near the upscale building where Diane's family lived—she sometimes joined him sleeping there.

Mitch was frequently abused by his stepmother while growing up in a public housing project. He missed school due to asthma but still made high grades and loved science courses. Nevertheless, Mitch started drinking at age 10 and was trying drugs—marijuana, pills, LSD—in his teens. By the time he was 16 years old, Mitch had started shooting heroin and cocaine. This drug abuse continued into his forties.

At the time of the interview, Mitch was taking antidepressant and antipsychotic medications and attending day treatment programs. Experiencing an enormous weight gain of 150 pounds after beginning the medications, Mitch has managed to lose most of the excess weight and to get his medication dosages reduced. Mitch is vague about his psychiatric diagnosis but mentions several times that he was committed to an upstate psychiatric hospital for over a year. He spent five years homeless, committing petty crimes to support his drug habit. In terms that can only be described as mystical, Mitch related how he finally stopped using heroin after being hospitalized for a severe infection in his hand. He feared losing his hand to amputation after the infection had spread to the bone.

. . . this was November 4, 1986. The doctor who was performing the operation came into my room and said to me, "We're cutting off your hand and we're going to cut at the wrist and maybe that's all." And I said "OK." And when he left the room I started crying, and crying, and crying. And that was something I hadn't done. . . . It was probably when I was a kid, but it was a very long period of time. Then this India doctor came into my room and started talking to me, really didn't say that there was any change in plans. Talked to me for probably half an hour or more . . . I believe that doctor for whatever reason took an interest in doing the work to save my hand. The other doctor's attitude to me was, "Fucking junkie cut off his hand" and "Get him the fuck out of here. Get him out of my life."

Mitch had the surgery and woke up assuming he had lost his hand.

I woke up from the surgery . . . I kept looking out the window . . . .and then I heard a voice and it was as clear as hearing you talk to me or any voice, it was clearer. . . . and it said to me "You don't have to do that anymore." And for whatever reason I knew exactly what they were talking about. . . . no more drugs. Then the voice said "Go ahead take a look at your hand." And when I looked I saw this finger, the tip of it, sticking out of the foam rubber cast, and I was thinking if my hand is gone why is that finger there, you know? And I cried again and whatever work that doctor did to save my hand.

The end of drug abuse for Mitch also began a period of healing for him.

It was like somebody took a switch and . . . .it just stopped. For the first time in my lifetime ever I was at peace. There was this incredible quiet and peace, which has continued to this day . . . I don't know what that voice was about, but I'll tell you this, it allowed me to have a life.

Mitch volunteers teaching science classes at a local hospital and would like to find a job, but then he would be held liable for $50,000 in unpaid child support from his ex-wife. Still, he reflects on how much better life has become:

I wake up every day and you know something, there's not a day that I wake up that I don't realize how blessed I have been to be put in a position where I am because if someone left it up to me to find an apartment and get a security deposit. . . . [then] I'm still homeless. I just didn't have the means. I didn't have the means mentally to work and I don't even know if I ever had the financial means to afford an apartment on my own.

He worries about Diane's emotional fragility and her drug dependence, and he also hopes to deepen his relationships with his sons, *"All of my hopes and dreams are tied up in the boys."* The older son had a few problems in school, joined the military, and recently returned from a tour in Afghanistan. The younger son is a model teen holding a steady job and making good grades in school. Mitch jokingly questions how this could happen, *"So I tell him 'steal a car so I know you're my kid.' And he says 'You're just crazy, dad.'"*

Mitch has few friends. *"Most have died of AIDS or overdose, . . ."* he says, but he is proud to have made a friend under rather unusual circumstances, Judith, a widowed mother of five he met at a rural convenience store in upstate New York. Mitch was buying coffee at the store while on one of his walking treks through the countryside around the state psychiatric hospital where he was residing. (The hospital allowed him to leave the grounds.) Judith, an executive at a large company, made friends with Mitch that day.

And then we were leaving and she was like, "Where's your car?" and I was like, "I don't have a car." So she says "You don't have a car! You can't walk around here! Like everything is far!" I used to walk like this 'cause I was homeless . . . I would walk 10, 20, 30 miles a day. . . . So she says to me, "Do you need a ride?" So I said 'Sure, I'll take a ride." . . . And she says "Well, where do you live?" I said, "state hospital." And then she starts looking at me [demonstrates look of shock and fear, then laughs]. And I said, "Judith, I'm not chopping your head off . . . you can leave me here if you want. I walked here, I'll walk home."

Unperturbed by his explanation, Judith invited him to her home to visit her family and later on for holidays. In return for her generosity, Mitch did yard work and house repairs while still living at the hospital. At the time of the study interview, Mitch said that Diane would be spending the upcoming Christmas holiday with her mother, his sons with their mother, and he would go to see Judith and her family. "*And you know [I will spend the] holidays there and um, she's just a really, . . . I have so much respect for this lady. She has raised five children, put them all through college. . . . She cannot ask me something that I would not do.*"

Pathways was not Mitch's first experience with a housing program; the two previous programs had not worked out. The first sent him to drug rehabilitation for having a positive urine test. "*That place was a nightmare.*" The second discharged him in the middle of winter. By then, Mitch had already given up hope "*. . . so the bottom line is they weren't supplying anyone to apartments. There was one guy who got an apartment that I saw in the year that I was there, and he was having a [sexual] relationship with the director.*"

Mitch stayed away from shelters after a bad experience at the city men's shelter on Ward's Island. "*I mean there's rampant drugs, there's fights, it's like being in jail, the same environment, the same people, you get everything stolen from you, but in any case, every experience I've had with every other agency in the city—and there were several—it's just been, like, horrendous.*"

Mitch was offered entrée to Pathways while in the upstate psychiatric hospital and greeted it with disbelief:

Well, the last thing I was thinking of when I was in _____ Hospital for the past year was that somebody was going to walk through that door, a complete stranger . . . and say "Hey . . . we don't know you from Adam and we're just going to hand you a fully furnished apartment. And we really don't have any hoops for you to jump through. You don't have to go to drug treatment." If I said that, my counselor would have freakin' put me back in a locked ward or something.

Mitch is deeply grateful to Pathways, saying, "*They are nothing short of magnificent.*" He has sometimes "bumped heads" with his case manager over missed appointments but is thankful to have an apartment after being homeless:

I mean, it has exacted a toll and you know, I wouldn't recommend it. If you had to choose something, I'll say this, don't choose that one. That's probably, it's worse than a drug problem. It's worse than anything I ever experienced in my life. It's worse than being in jail. In jail you have shelter and food, in the street you have zero.

Walter: "There's more to life than the way I'm living"

A 48-year-old African American man, Walter is living in a non-HF program apartment with a roommate. He has stopped using hard drugs and is in a methadone program, but he says he needs to smoke marijuana daily, although the program could discharge him or require him to go to drug rehabilitation if this was found out.

> I still smoke weed. But I don't consider that as getting high. I consider that as a relaxer ... when I got it in me, I'm cool, calm, collected. And I'm motivated. But when I don't have it, I'm not motivated. I don't wanna do shit. That's the attitude I have. But once I got it in my system? All right, let's go, fight the world, I'm ready!

Walter is relieved to have housing and believes that his current lifestyle (including smoking marijuana) is a great improvement over his earlier life:

> See the way I am now I got a roof over my head. I keep a couple dollars in my pocket. I still work. I still go to my groups. I do everything I'm supposed to do. I'm like what they call a functional addict, and I been doing it like this for eleven years. I don't harm nobody, I'm not robbin' nobody, I'm not killin' nobody. These are the main things I used to do. I used to love doing that shit. I used to rob the drug dealer. Get high off all of his drugs. Use his money to buy more drugs, and then go take them from him again ... I had no sense. I don't have no school education. Everything I learned, I learned from the streets and in jail.

At age 14, a stray bullet meant for someone else hit Walter, and he spent months in the hospital recuperating from his wound. Walter has a long history of fighting ("*I love fighting.*") and getting into trouble for physical attacks on others. Since being hospitalized for schizophrenia, he has developed an unusual strategy for containing the consequences:

> I got a thing where if I don't have a fight in a certain amount of time, I get frustrated. Whether I lose or win, I have to have a fight. So what I do is I go to any one of the psych wards and sneak [up on] one of the security guards, because I know their job is not to hurt me, but to subdue me. Interviewer: You sneak up? *Walter: By punching them in the face. They grab me, then we get to wrestling and tussling and stuff like that there. Then after it's all over with, I'm gone. I'm good. I don't get in trouble. That's how I get my fighting ability off without getting in trouble.*

Walter has a deep distrust of others, including family members and friends who he feels have betrayed him. "*When I talk to people I try to talk to them from a distance. You know? Because I don't want to extend myself to them and then they hurt me. And that's been going on a lot lately.*" He stays clear of his current roommate:

Cause when we in the house, we don't talk. Only time we talk is when, say like if he's in the kitchen and I come out my room . . . But that's it. You know, it ain't no real heart to heart or nothing like that . . . The category I got my roommate in is easy to be replaced. And that's the category I'm gonna keep him in. You know, until he grow on me or I grow on him.

Walter goes on to assert his approach to relationships and the exception he makes for his adult children: "*. . . I am not trying to make new friends that I don't have to. And I'm not trying to babysit nobody, 'cause my kids is grown. They take care of their damn selves. They don't need me, but I need them. Ain't that something? (pause) Eh, but life goes on.*"

A turning point for Walter came in 2002 when he finally began taking psychiatric medications after a suicide attempt in a shelter. "*Depakote, Risperdal . . . I mean they was giving me so much different medication I forgot the names of it . . . They was to help me sleep—'cause I was having real bad nightmares . . . waking up screaming—I woke up one time in the shelter, I had a knife in my hand.*"

The youngest of eight siblings, Walter says he is the only one left alive. "*They died of natural causes, AIDS, car crash, murdered.*" During the interview, Walter expresses frustration with his program, saying that he has lost 30 pounds in the six months since entering because he is stressed and cannot eat. "*If a strong wind go by, I'm scared if I ain't got no rocks in my pocket I'm gonna fly.*" Given all he has been through, Walter would like more counseling but has not received it:

I never got a chance to talk to nobody. And I explained it to them. Didn't get no answers. Because they never got back to me. And they tell me they got a psych [psychiatrist], but this is a psych for medication. This is not a psych to talk about your problems. That's the type of psych I need, a type that I can talk to about my problems. And [the program] don't offer that. I mean they might offer it, but they haven't offered it to me yet. 'Cause it's like they wanna talk to you just to know what's going on and give you the business. They don't wanna talk to you to try to figure out what's going on so that they can help you find a solution and straighten it out . . . I can't do that.

Walter works part-time in maintenance to earn extra money. Otherwise, he is biding his time and trying to stay out of trouble:

If I'm home, you can best believe I'm not outside . . . Not unless I'm going to visit somebody. . . . all you gotta do is come to my house and in my room is where I'll be. And once I go in, I close my door. And I be in my room like just being there, watching TV, listening to music, or just laying in my bed looking at the ceiling. Though unhappy with his living situation, Walter takes responsibility. "*. . . There's more to life than the way I'm living. So what I gotta do is figure out a better way to live my life.*

Dolores: "They said I died but I came back"

Dolores is a 55-year-old woman of mixed ethnic background, including Native American ancestry. Dolores recalls a happy childhood until family life abruptly ended with the psychiatric hospitalization of her mother and her father's serious injury from a car accident. Placed in foster care, Dolores and her sister were physically and sexually abused by their foster mother.

A heavy drinker from a young age, Dolores was able to hold a cleaning job for a few years before losing her housing and spending the next five years homeless and transiting among women's shelters in Brooklyn. During this time, she was brutally raped and beaten and left for dead while sleeping in an abandoned building.

> *I didn't know the person that raped me. All I know was that he was trying to kill me. He tried to throw me out the window three times . . . but he couldn't lift me up and I know I didn't weigh that much, and I believe it was God's will that he couldn't pick me up . . . But he was trying to throw me out an apartment building. It was a real awful feeling . . . that's another reason why I see a psychiatrist. Because after those things you're not well. Mentally you're not well. You think you are, but you're not because then you have to deal with the emotional trauma.*

Dolores explained her strategy for survival in the shelters:

> *I acted like I was a man so they didn't want to bother me . . . because I was afraid of these [shelter] people. I better act worse than them otherwise I'd be beat up because the first time I went I got beat up. They stole my chain off. They ripped it off my neck. Then they beat me up, so I said now I know what I have to do. If I have to stay out in these streets then I have to act like they do. So I started acting like they do. I became nuttier than a fruitcake (laughs).*

In addition to these tribulations, Dolores had two horrific accidents that changed her life. The first was a near-fatal fire ignited by smoking in bed after a drinking bout that left her with severe burns and a year's hospitalization with numerous skin grafts. "*I did almost die twice during the surgery. And one of the surgeries they said I died but I came back. I don't remember that but that's what I was told.*" Early in her hospital stay, Dolores tried to commit suicide to escape the pain and a sweltering room when the public hospital's air conditioning broke down. She made her way to the roof.

And I was going to jump off . . . I had taken the IVs off and everything so you know I was bleeding all over the place, and I said "Okay, let's do this." And then I hear somebody go, "What are you doing?" I said "Nothing, I'm not doing anything. Does it look like I'm doing something?" . . . I was lying my behind off because I didn't want to go to the mental hospital, but behind that I did end up going.

Dolores was next committed to a state psychiatric hospital for three months.

It was a nut farm (laughs), *but for some reason I had a good time. . . . They was giving me all this medicine, and if you don't learn to speak up for yourself, you'll be walking around like a zombie 'cause I say, "You're giving me too much medicine. I can't stand this." So they said, "No, you need this medicine," and I said, "I don't need Thorazine." . . . We used to call it the Thorazine shuffle. . . . I say, "Oh god this is terrible." And then I ran into my aunt, and she worked in the hospital, and that's who got me out of the hospital and into [current program].*

The program Dolores's aunt got her placed in was a TF program that required she first undergo detoxification for alcohol abuse. She had stopped smoking after the fire but continued to drink heavily even while in the state hospital:

But then I had to go to detox because they didn't want me, you know all that medicine that I was on. Plus I was getting liquor I was, heck yeah, somebody was bringing me liquor from the outside. I said, "Oh god, now I'm getting ruined 'cause now I can't get my alcohol the way I want it," so I was mad.

However, Dolores' drinking did not stop until after her second horrific accident, in which she fell in the shower and broke her neck and back. Her account of the incident—which had occurred five years before the study interview, began with showing the interviewer some pill bottles:

This is Percocet. That's for my neck. And I take this, morphine. That's for my neck because I have a bar, whatever they call that thing in there . . . It can never come out of my neck . . . I knew my neck was broke. I didn't know my back was broke. My back was broke, too. I'm lucky I'm not dead . . . And I was talking to him [surgeon] like I'm talking to you. And he said, "Have you been drinking?" And I said, "No, I don't drink." (laughs) I did, I told him I don't drink, and he said, "Um, you sure?" And you know what, that's what saved my life. Me drinking. Because they said if I had not been drinking, I wouldn't have been so relaxed. I would have been in a state of shock or whatever.

Dolores spent four months in a nursing home in rehabilitation, learning to walk again. She has a metal rod bracing her neck (she showed the scars from incisions) and suffered seizures as a result of the injury.

And it still hurts. That's why I take those [pain medications]. This will hurt me until I die because the bar is six and half inches long. I saw it on the X-ray . . . They don't like the patients to see, but they had me in the room and I saw it. And I said, "What's that? Whose X-ray is that?" 'Cause I didn't know what it was. It looked like something out of a horror movie. And they said, . . . "That's yours." They had the bars and they had little screws in them so every time them screws come out they have to go back in and put the screws back in again, so I've been lucky so far, I've had seizures but none of the screws have come out . . . I have a walker . . . When I came home, I couldn't walk. I'm glad it happened, otherwise I'd still be drinking.

When asked what she thought of her program, Dolores said, *"You know I had already been in __ State Hospital so . . . I said oh god I'm with the same type of people. But then you realize you all came from the same background but some people are stronger than others."*

Dolores feels that program staff do not help much. *"Because in this job you have to really like people and people that don't like people are sometimes in this job. They just do it for the money. And that's what I believe is happening right now. I don't think they really like the people so much. It's just about the money."* Money was also a sore point because the program took clients' SSI checks (about 800 dollars per month) as their representative payee and doled out only $10 per week in spending money. *". . . We was complaining because we didn't get our money.* Interviewer: What did they tell you? *Dolores: Oh, they was paying for this and they was paying for that. . . . They was paying a lot of bills they said . . . Just what bills are you payin', please! If you are, let us see. Let me see what I'm signing my signature for then. I never saw it."*

By the time of the study interview, Dolores had obtained a Section 8 rental voucher (of her own doing) and was no longer dependent on the program as her representative payee. Her health problems were diverse and debilitating—diabetes, lifelong deafness in one ear, a neck brace, and daily pain medications. Visiting nurses and a home health aide come to assist her. Dolores enjoys warm relations with her neighbors, her sister, and volunteers at a burn treatment center. A lively woman with a dry sense of humor, Dolores explained her survival as a form of spiritual salvation:

At one point in time I didn't believe in anything, just drink, you know, just drink my life away and be happy. But when I had these accidents happen then I started believing, because I think no one in their right mind should be alive through all of this.

Rob: "My life is going pretty good"

Rob is a 52-year-old African American man living in a Pathways apartment. He greets the interviewer's opening question with a ready reply, *"Right now my life is, my life is going, pretty good, um, I have some form of control, if you will. I pay my bills. I don't like to, but I pay my bills* (laughs). *I have my own place. I have my children back in my life and my grandchildren . . . I'm in church. I find myself wanting to know more and more about me each day. So yeah, my life is, going pretty well, doing pretty well right now."*

Rob is one of a few study participants who decided to stop taking psychiatric medications. This was not an isolated decision but a move reflecting a larger sense of self-determination and personal choice. Asked when he thought things started to change for the better, Rob replied:

When I was able to share why I stayed out there so long. When I was able to come to grips with why I stayed in that circle and why I didn't feel that I was worthy with anything better than the situation that I was in at the time. When I was able to take control and say, "No more, I'm tired." You know I don't need being told I need this medication for this, that medication for that. I need to see what I'm truly made of. But understand it's gonna hurt, 'cause you're no longer medicated, so you're gonna feel what you been medicating for in reality, the real deal. And I realized then . . . I believe I began to take control with what I should do with those feelings instead of stuffing them, and I began to take a look at the part that I played and all those wasted years doing what I was doing not to deal with reality in my life.

Rob is reluctant to say much about the bad years, referring to a particular drug scene in Harlem as his "Babylon." But he admits to neglecting his children (now adults).

Don't get me wrong now, I have, what's it called, instant gratification defect. I want what I want last year" (laughs). He also had some difficult times early on in Pathways. *"At the time, I was taking medication. I let the doctor tell me I had anxiety and depression, and I, if he said take two, I'd take four and sleep through the weekend. Now that's comatose . . . that's sick. 'Cause I didn't want to feel anything . . . I just didn't want to be part of nothing but my little world, which was nothing going on but eye-witness news.*

Rob equates psychiatric medication with illegal drugs, and said he weaned himself from all of them three years earlier.

And then one day I decided enough is enough. And this is what helped: I came off that addictive medication without any other addictive medication. My philosophy was why get off one, to get on another? Methadone was involved, antidepressants, and six months of detox. It took six months and it took me two years to detox of all medications. Cold turkey. And I went through, it wasn't the physical part, please don't misunderstand me that was rough, it was the psychological part. . . . there were moments I cried like a little boy.

Rob says that he was resistant to a case manager's challenge that he aim higher and get more involved with Pathways programs. Once he began to attend, Rob realized, *"I may think different but I'm not any different than anyone here that would like to reach out."* Though shy and reserved, Rob's determination produced positive results—he was hired by Pathways to help other eligible clients transition away from ACT (Assertive Community Treatment) to less intensive case management services within the program. *"Then I really got involved. Hey, I'm an important person. What? Me? And I said, 'I could do this. I can share and all I have to do is be me."*

In hindsight, Rob gives that case manager credit.

She called me on my stuff and I was uncomfortable. And I could have poof! disappeared. How dare you ask me, why am I still here. Don't you know I don't know! And I couldn't give an answer. I blamed it on a marriage that went bad. I blamed it on everything I could . . . I didn't like her at that moment.

Rob still keeps to himself when not working.

People say, "Why?" and I say, "If I want to sit in a tub all day I don't have to answer to nobody, "Why you in the bathroom so long?" If I want watch that program on TV, I don't hear, "Why you always watchin that?" I don't have to explain anything, excuse my reasoning, besides still today I move around by myself. . . . I would go home, watch the news, sports, and maybe a movie, and when it's time to go to sleep, I'm turnin' the lights out. I love the solitude in the dark and I think. And today I'm not afraid to do that.

Shirley: "That shows independency"

Shirley is a 51-year-old well-dressed African American woman who takes pride in her beauty regimen. Shirley has a boyfriend (Devon) of almost 10 years, who stays at a men's shelter nearby. Her Pathways apartment is immaculate and decorated with personal items—stuffed animals, dried flowers, and arrangements of her cosmetics on a bedroom chest.

Shirley has spent most of her adult life in and out of jail for theft and drug dealing, her longest incarceration lasting three years. She was never street homeless, but, aside from jail, spent 18 years living in shelters and doubling up with friends, including five years at a women's shelter in Brooklyn. Her drug use included crack, pills, and heroin.

I got tired of going to jail, losing all my belongings, having to start all over, you know? And, the shelter was stealing my clothes, my cosmetics, things I build up and I wind up losing. And one day I just say, "God please." I just prayed, prayed, prayed, and I asked him to remove the drugs from me, remove the stealing part from me, work on me please . . .

Shirley's childhood and adulthood were—to put it mildly—difficult. She never knew her father's identity and fled to her grandmother's care after being sexually molested by her mother's boyfriend. When speaking of her four children (ages 9, 13, 14, and 20 years of age), Shirley tears up. She left the father of her three younger children to escape domestic violence. He was a drug dealer often jailed and absent from the family. The eldest son's father was shot and killed on the street. While Shirley was in jail, she lost custody to the younger children's father. She worries about her teenage sons and the crowd they are hanging out with.

When I see him, his eyes are real red and small, and I know the guys he be with, they smoke weed . . . and then two of the guys, they are bad, they stole a car, and I am like saying, "Oh my God, what kind of people is he dealing with?" But my fiancé [Devon] told me, "They're boys. They got to be men one day . . . They got to go through just like we got to go through. They have to learn. There is nothing you can do. You can't sit here worrying yourself."... And I understand what he is saying, and he is right. But you know, being a mother, you worry that is your kids....., but he don't wanna see me worry so bad to where I make myself sick and then he says "What good is that going to be to me?"

Shirley is close to her siblings but has a strained relationship with her mother dating back to the molesting boyfriend. While Shirley and Devon were living in separate shelters, they would go visit her mother to cook meals. Tension came when Shirley got her own apartment and stopped going to her mother's place to cook.

I would come and cook for her and us, and the food, there would be enough food to last for three days ... and I would clean up and we would go over there to keep warm, for a couple of hours. And then we would leave around 7 o'clock to go back to the shelter. So we was doing that for a while, so I think she is mad because I have an apartment so I don't have to go to her house no more.

Mobility is difficult for Shirley because she has severe arthritis and knee pain that she blames on years sleeping in cold overcrowded shelters. Moving into her Pathways apartment was an experience she had not thought possible.

I have been getting my blessings ... When I first came, they [Pathways staff] took me shopping and they bought me the comforter and some pots and stuff. You know, to get you started? And they took me, bought me some food. So the food ran out fast, so I was like, "Wow."... She [Pathways case manager] went down for me on my behalf and those food stamps, one day I just happened to call to see if I had any food stamps and it was it was 277 something dollars ... So I went and bought a lot of food, and I was like, "Thank you God. Thank you.".... Every month I get $200 in food stamps to go food shopping. And my boyfriend, he gets, even though he lives in a shelter, he still gets $200. So he puts food in the house, too. You know, because he comes here and eats. Then when my son comes by he eats, and my son can eat! Boys can eat!

Living on her own for the first time, Shirley described with pride how she learned to budget the 70% of her SSI check left over after Pathways takes 30% of her check to help pay the rent:

... My [part of the] rent is only 211 dollars a month. I got to pay light and gas but we have controlled heating. That knob on the wall there? That's control heating ...

So when I first moved here, I didn't understand it so I used to turn it on, you know make it nice and cozy in here and stuff, and watch TV. And so when the first bill came, I was like, "WHAT?" (laughs). I said, "That thing is staying off!" . . . Next winter I will be prepared . . .

Shirley describes the advantages of having SSI and control over her budget: "*SSI is not like welfare, thank God! They don't pester you at all with a bunch of face-to-face interviews . . . Once a year they want to see you. That's it. . . . So I got direct deposit. so I got a bank card. I just go to the ATM and swipe and take out what I need. I pay all my bills myself.*"

With financial independence and her own apartment, Shirley is proud, noting, "*That shows independency. That means I can do this. I want my apartment.*" She also does not want to risk anyone causing trouble.

I got a blessing. And you think I want to lose this? . . . The only one who has been here is my son, my sister, you [interviewer], and Devon. And that's it. I don't have no company. You're not tearing up my house. I don't want any of those people to know where I live at . . . People I know, I speak to. But really, somebody I know for a long time that's drug-free like me, not getting high. They are welcome to come to my house . . . and a lot of people I know still smoke crack. You are not coming in my house. You are not casing out my joint. You are not stealing from me . . . my cosmetics, my bedroom. You are not stealing from me.

Shirley spends a good portion of every day traveling to her methadone program in the Bronx—a one and a half hour trip each way by subway then bus.

I was raised in a church by my grandparents . . . You know, I go to church every now and then, but I'm looking forward to getting back into the church. Not hard hard core, but just going in there for a peace of mind, and my way of showing God I that appreciate what He done for me.

A Few Threads: The Importance of Housing and the Limits of Housing

These personal accounts by no means capture the myriad experiences of individuals who enter housing programs after bouts of homelessness and mental illness. The traumatic incidents related in these life stories might seem extreme, but they were far closer to the norm than outlying. Chronic pain and disability, social betrayal and estrangement, decades-long struggles with drugs and alcohol, and violence—both suffered and perpetrated—were all-too-common themes. And yet, these individuals—Rob, Walter, Mitch, Shirley, Alfred, and Dolores—took stock of their troubled lives with the candor and wit that made them excellent interlocutors.

For Pathways tenants, having their own apartment was almost always a first-time life experience. With troubles starting early on, their places of residence alternated among foster homes, detention centers, jails, shelters, hospitals, and the occasional family member or friend whose patience had not yet run out. Given this history, the ability to adjust to apartment living could by no means be assumed. (Indeed, transitional programs do not make this assumption.)

Revisiting ontological security, "constancy in the material and social environment" is a marked departure from the inconstancy of street life. The daily rhythms of life carried out in the privacy of one's own home are mundane yet elevated by their long-dreaacprof-of circumstances. One can leave home to go shopping, to visit relatives, or to see a movie, and know that it will be there, unsupervised and welcoming as only a home can be. Small but meaningful indicators of personal routines can be found in Alfred's secret love of bubble baths, Shirley's rows of cosmetics carefully displayed, and Rob's embrace of his solitude after he turns out the lights at night. Alfred's use of romantic terms to describe his apartment ("I fell in love . . .") speaks for itself.

Walter has access to these daily routines but must share them with a stranger. Dolores has them without hindrance because she persevered in obtaining a Section 8 rental voucher that gave her greater independence. Otherwise, apartment inspections, curfews, rules against personal decorations and bulletin boards pinned with program rules convey the message of, "Do not consider this permanent or separate from the program requirements."

That having a home of one's own confers ontological security seems unassailable by now. However, the indicator of "secure platform for identity construction" (Giddens, 1990) raises the ante and muddies the waters (forgive the mixing of metaphors). Forging a new or revised identity means foregrounding positive self-images and suppressing bad identities (e.g., mental patient, criminal, addict, vagabond).

Moreover, the power of the new has to overcome the undertow of the old "spoiled" identities (Goffman, 1963). Shirley's pride in managing her household shows a sense of mastery, budgeting her expenses and cooking for her fiancé when he visits her from his shelter. Alfred's employment as a peer support worker endows him with a sense of purpose and "giving back." Defying the odds (and providers' skepticism), Rob stopped taking his psychiatric medications, came out of his shell, and became an exemplary representative of Pathways in public presentations. In contrast, Walter was still finding his way, frustrated by his lack of independence and access to therapy to help him overcome a life of violence and inner torment. Dolores endured unimaginable horrors and survived to overcome alcoholism and achieve independent housing.

Having a home is a necessary platform for identity development, but it is not sufficient. Critics of HF rightfully have pointed out how lonely a person can feel after years or even decades of tumultuous cohabitation in hospital wards, jail cells, shelters, and overcrowded apartments comes to an abrupt halt. This is a vulnerable time, and some newly housed clients fall prey to drug associates and dealers seeking a base for distribution, as Shirley wisely foresaw. The social environment is often dictated by avoiding the wrong people as much as finding the right people and here again having one's own apartment affords the option.

Beyond four walls are neighborhoods, communities, and larger social forces, and here is where some of the most intransigent barriers to a recovered life are found. Urban neighborhoods with affordable housing may also offer temptations and bad influences—drug markets, cheap liquor, and distance from parks and other amenities.[2] Study participants often found themselves housed in the same communities where they had grown up or run into trouble.

The effects of decades of poor health, of hypertension and diabetes, disabling injuries, and poor nutrition are not easily negated. Nor are the lingering effects of deep and horrific traumas, both sexual and physical. Missing out on major rites of passage—high school or college graduation, parenting, a job or career—appears as much due to deep poverty as to personal crises. Evidence of this can be found in data on low-income communities, as well as in reports by study participants of impoverished peers who met similar or worse fates—incarceration, addiction, and premature death from AIDS, overdoses, and violence.

The limits of housing and the surmounting effects of structural barriers arise from this "fundamental cause," namely, poverty (Link & Phelan, 1995). Following the capabilities approach pioneered by Martha Nussbaum and Amartya Sen (Nussbaum & Sen, 1993), individuals may have resources or skills but still be unable to realize their potential. Like being poor, having a psychiatric disability can be a "capabilities deprivation" (Hopper, 2007, p. 874). Reducing the impact of symptoms can increase one's capacity to function, but success comes only when valued social roles are available to be carried out as a result of such an improvement (Hopper, 2007). Quality of life requires more than abilities or resources, it also depends on commensurate opportunities and options.

The classic way of illustrating the meaning of capabilities—teaching a person to read is meaningless if there are no books or libraries—expands the discourse on disability to hold the surrounding environment accountable. For persons emerging from homelessness, improvements in job skills, sobriety, and mental health rarely result in acquiring living wage jobs or social acceptance. A hostile or minimally accommodating environment withholds access—and the means of gaining access.

The gratitude expressed by Rob and Alfred when hired by Pathways was genuine, although the job was predicated on their status as "peers," or psychiatric consumers. Such conditional employment, typically one of few job options available, provides job skills but rarely leads to "outside" jobs at a living wage.

Social acceptance is a more nuanced problem, given that stigma and exclusion can be countered with personal agency, which may manifest as a desire for solitude or a well-deserved distrust of the motives of others (Padgett et al., 2008). Such distrust does not preclude finding "strength in weak ties" (Granovetter, 1973). Indeed, as intimate and familial relationships are lost, broken, or estranged, one could arguably be more open to new contacts where the risks are lower and emotional investments less fraught (Townley, Miller, & Kloos, 2013). Acquaintances rather than close friends are also a more effective bridge to the outside world and the opportunities to be found there (Granovetter, 1973).

Weak ties are not easily exploited when the individual is isolated. For members of our study population, one arena was the 12-Step meeting—AA, NA, and the like—where differences in social class, race, and gender are trumped by the common denominator of addiction and the search for absolution. Mitch met his affluent girlfriend, Diane, at an AA meeting and enjoyed her ability to pay for meals or cigarettes. He also met a close friend who became his ready-made family (Judith) in a chance encounter at a convenience store. Rob's off the cuff conversation with a staffer at Pathways brought him to act on an inchoate desire to become involved in the program's activities.

Wanting a romantic partner, close friends, and loving family relationships is also commonly expressed, and some individuals we studied (such as Shirley and Mitch) made significant progress. But the circumstances of their lives—living in a program defined by the "disability ethos," a limited income, long-standing estrangements, and social exclusion—put barriers in place that are not easily overcome.

Conclusion: The Power of Personal Stories

This chapter was intended to build on but also depart from previous chapters by featuring in-depth individual experiences. Selected in order to better understand Housing First through the lived experience as-told, these personal stories reveal the deep gratifications of home, a benefit taken for granted until taken away, and even more celebrated when never having been had in the first place. The stories limned the meaning of ontological security, the quotidian acts made possible by the security and constancy of having a home without being watched and supervised. To illustrate this point visually, we introduce in the next few pages a series of photos taken of Pathways's Philadelphia tenants engaged in a participatory action project examining how one's health outlook changes after transitioning from homelessness to having a home (Henwood et al., 2013).[3]

The forging of new identities and a new life is made possible by having ontological security, but it is hardly a foregone conclusion. Many a HF study participant talked about the ultimate freedom of living outside of any program's purview, of being fully independent and able to work, pay bills, and save for a rainy day. They longed to interact with their children and grandchildren from a position of self-sufficiency rather than dependency. Their dreams were tempered more by the realities of a lifetime than the exigencies of the present.

We sought to include the story of a "HF failure" in this chapter—one of the 15% to 20% of participants in the quantitative studies who were unable to live on their own despite having support services. However, in the NYSS and NYRS studies—where we recruited 85 and 53 participants for the longitudinal phases of the studies—only three persons left Pathways because of an inability to live independently. One was a man with serious delusions who discharged himself to go live with his family in Chicago. Another man had close ties to drug dealing, was in and out of jail, and went AWOL from the program. The other was a mentally impaired woman with serious incontinence and poor hygiene who could not maintain tenancy due to neighbors' complaints and landlord objections.

The converse—individuals in a TF program who are successes—is more difficult to report given that "success" consists of staying with the program as opposed to dropping out because of relapse, a return to the street, and/or institutionalization. In TF, this means accepting the terms of engagement and trusting that compliance will reap rewards. Here, the reviews are mixed. In the NYSS, where TF programs were at the lower end of the staircase—dormitory-style supervised living—53% went "AWOL" (via self- or program-discharge) within the 12 months of study follow-up. Relapse was a common outcome, but AWOL clients (who still remained in the study) spoke most commonly of impatience with the requirements of curfews, random urine tests, close-quarter living, etc.

In the NYRS, the TF program offered a "higher up the staircase" option of shared apartment living with off-site supervision. In this study, TF program discharges involved a relapse (alcohol), a psychiatric hospitalization, an imprisonment, and a self-discharge to move to another state. During the 18 months of study follow-up, none graduated to a higher level of independent housing.

In neither study did we encounter a TF client who preferred transitional over permanent apartment living. A few endorsed it for others ("some people need this structure") but not for themselves ("I'm not one of those people"). To be fair, we heard from TF clients who were satisfied with the program and their living situation. Just as Pathways clients expressed hope to live free of any program (especially one targeted to persons with mental illness), TF clients expressed hope to move into independent housing of their own eventually.

In the final chapters of this book, we zoom back out to the bigger picture to describe the expansion of HF beyond its humble (albeit heavily researched) origins.[4] The next chapter is devoted to its dissemination in the United States and the inevitable challenges of fidelity that came with expanding into new cities, new populations, and with new institutional entrepreneurs.

Notes

1. Histories of poly-drug use as well as alcohol abuse render the use of any single term for recovery from substance abuse problematic. Though less than optimal, we use the term "sobriety" to refer to abstaining (or near-abstaining) from the use of drugs as well as alcohol. Alternative terms such as "abstinence" or "clean" are too absolutist. Thus, "sobriety" refers to a state of control over substance use but not necessarily total cessation.

2. As mentioned in the previous chapter, we conducted photo-elicitation interviews in the NYRS in which participants were given cameras and asked to take photographs of both positive and negative aspects of their lives (Padgett et al., 2013). We were struck by their propensity to go to "friendly neighborhoods" in lower Manhattan, such as Greenwich Village and Union Square Park in particular. These were areas with parks and open spaces, as well as nonjudgmental populations—all amenities that participants appreciated.

3. This participatory action project (also known as community-based participatory research, or CBPR) was led by coauthor Henwood while working at Pathways Philadelphia. The resulting video production is available at: http://www.youtube.com/watch?v=3VNZGEpuKBY

4. While the dissemination of any innovative program is unpredictable in its outcome, HF carried the "baggage" of its origins in New York City. This meant that opponents could (and did) argue that New York was too generous in funding and too saturated in services to be the basis for realistic adoption of HF elsewhere. Proponents, on the other hand, could (and did) argue that to succeed in the intensely competitive service system of New York—and to succeed with clients who had been rejected even in this service-rich environment—was hardly an accomplishment to ignore.

7 Growth of Housing First in the United States
CHALLENGES OF EXPANSION AND FIDELITY

THE EVIDENCE AND recognition of Pathways Housing First (PHF) expanded with each passing year. In 2007, PHF was added to the Substance Abuse and Mental Health Services Administration's National Registry of Evidence-based Programs and Practices (SAMHSA, 2007). The National Alliance to End Homelessness published a manual on how to adopt Housing First (HF) to foster organizational change (NAEH, 2009). Two resolutions by the U.S. Conference of Mayors endorsed it, and Housing First was the only intervention identified by the Conference as an evidence-based practice. Major newspapers carried stories about local HF successes and Malcolm Gladwell's (2006) *New Yorker* article lent unusual cache to an organization serving homeless adults.

To be sure, there were some who resisted joining the bandwagon. Professional evaluators working for Abt Associates, Inc. conducted a review of housing models and concluded that "debate continues over the effectiveness of the housing and service approaches associated with housing first and which elements of the model are most important ... [There is] interest in identifying which housing and services approaches work best for whom, but so far [this interest] has not resulted in a commensurate level of rigorous research to provide answers to these questions" (Locke, Khadduri, & O'Hara, 2007, p. 9).

Yet the proven effectiveness of HF attracted an unusual endorsement from President George Bush's conservative Republican administration—unusual in that HF's institutional logic was based on a liberal, harm-reduction, rights-based perspective. The U.S. Interagency Council on Homelessness (USICH) promoted HF on its website (as a "central antidote" to homelessness; www.usich.gov). Philip Mangano, who breathed life into the moribund USICH after his appointment by President Bush in 2002, began traveling across the United States to preach this new gospel of abolishing chronic homelessness.

Building on the groundwork laid earlier by the NAEH, Mangano challenged communities to shift from "managing" homelessness to "ending" it. Mangano himself was a "quick study," and he realized that an evidence-based, cost-saving approach would be most effective in ending chronic homelessness. Meeting with mayors, governors, city councils, chambers of commerce, and anyone who would listen, Mangano introduced a new institutional logic with equal measures of passion and facts. As a Republican Presidential appointee, he was able to gain access to business and civic leaders that other advocates for the homeless could not match.

Mangano's skill in highlighting HF as a results-oriented fiscally sound approach created an unusual opportunity for bipartisan political agreement on a complex social problem (Stanhope & Dunn, 2011). Among his most successful achievements, Mangano was able to forge an unprecedented agreement to provide $35 million in Federal funding for a national initiative to end chronic homelessness. With the combined efforts of the USICH, the NAEH, and others, over 400 communities developed 10-year plans to end homelessness, and more than 70% of those plans included a Housing First program. Four USICH members—the Department of Housing and Urban Development (HUD), SAMHSA, the Department of Health and Human Services (HHS), and the Veterans Administration (VA)—joined forces to provide three years of funding to start HF programs. Over 100 applications were reviewed and 11 cities ultimately funded: New York, New York; Philadelphia, Pennsylvania; Chattanooga, Tennessee; Miami, Florida; Los Angeles, California; San Francisco, California; Denver, Colorado; Columbus, Ohio; Portland, Oregon; Seattle, Washington; and Louisville, Kentucky. Among cities that did not receive funding, many started their own HF programs using local dollars.

With such widespread dissemination, various and differing versions of HF began to appear across the United States. Those opting for a faithful replication of PHF usually sought direct advice and consultation from Tsemberis. Pathways to Housing in New York also expanded to other cities and developed a training and consultation program. (We use the acronym PHF for spin-offs of Pathways or programs that faithfully adhered to its core tenets.) Spin-off programs, begun at

Pathways to Housing's instigation and having a shared governance structure, are also referred to as "affiliates." These are located in Washington DC, Philadelphia, and Vermont.

In the span of a few years, a hallmark of HF—independent scatter-site housing—was becoming more commonly offered by programs to their homeless clients. A study of 1,000 persons with severe mental illness presenting for outpatient treatment in five regionally disparate U.S. cities (Tampa, Florida; Worcester, Massachusetts; San Francisco, California; Durham, North Carolina; and Chicago, Illinois) found that living in an independent apartment was the predominant type of housing for 50% or more of the sample at four of the sites (Robbins, Callahan, & Monahan, 2009). Data from New York City showed that the number of mental health consumers living in independent scatter-site housing with support services almost doubled between 1999 and 2003, going from 2,359 to 4,207, a proportionate increase from 31% to 38% (New York State Office of Mental Health, 2006).

The Recovery Movement Momentum

Another coinciding paradigm shift gave HF added legitimacy and forward motion—the recovery movement in mental health. Sharing roots in consumer empowerment and psychiatric rehabilitation (Anthony, 1993; New Freedom Commission, 2003), HF and the recovery movement emerged on the scene at about the same time, tapping overlapping but distinct constituencies. Their fit—philosophically and practically—made HF and recovery complementary and synergistic in their effects. In a sense, HF was the programmatic embodiment of recovery as applied to the needs of homeless consumers. Coinciding with this was an unprecedented and comprehensive shift in mental health treatment that challenged many of the fundamental beliefs about serious mental illnesses such as schizophrenia.

The recovery movement had its origins in research findings that had been around for some time (Harding, Zubin, & Strauss, 1987) but gained far greater traction due to a small but vocal and eloquent group of consumers. Judi Chamberlain, Patrick Corrigan, Patricia Deegan, Dan Fisher, Ed Knight, Howie the Harp, and Elyn Saks are a few of the leading voices of recovery who gave personal testimonies of their struggles with mental illness and described how they moved on to lead productive meaningful lives. These candid and uplifting accounts, bolstered by research covering decades of follow-up in longitudinal studies of psychiatric patients in Vermont (Harding, Brooks, Ashikaga, Strauss, & Breier, 1987) give the lie to beliefs regarding the intransigence of mental illness and progressive disability (Corrigan & Boyle, 2003).

The recovery movement has been transformative in the United States and has spawned thousands of articles, books, online blogs, and media reports. Although the movement's impact on day-to-day treatment of patients and among staff working in psychiatric hospitals and clinics is far from clear, recovery-oriented practices have been widely endorsed and have prompted researchers to develop measures and practice guidelines (Anthony, Cohen, & Farkas, 1982; Corrigan, Salzer, Ralph, Sangster, & Keck, 2004; Davidson & Roe, 2007; O'Connell, Tondora, Croog, Evans, & Davidson, 2005).

Just as HF brings a profound shift in understanding the relationship between housing and treatment, recovery in and beyond mental illness requires practitioners to set aside traditional assumptions and training. Although HF is used with non-mentally ill homeless persons and recovery applies to all persons with a serious mental illness, their overlap in values is substantial. These convergent values—person-centeredness, optimistic thinking (hope), self-determination, risk taking, and giving opportunities—and the coincidental timing of the recovery movement gave legitimacy to HF from the consumer perspective.

Implementation Science: Understanding Uptake or the Lack Thereof

Expansion and growth in HF—though relatively rapid—was by no means a simple matter of producing positive experimental results and waiting for "inevitable" uptake by eager adopters (see Box 7.1 for discussion of Rogers' theory of innovation). Many laboratory-tested interventions have resulted in massive failure when removed from the controlled conditions in which they were developed. HF started out with "real world" implementation in the highly competitive crucible of New York City services but the outcome of its adoption elsewhere was unknown.

In the past 10 or so years, the field of *implementation science* has taken off, its growth stimulated by the need to address the what, how, and why of effective changes in service delivery (Greenhalgh, Robert, Bate, Macfarlane, & Kyriakidou, 2004). Barriers and incentives to uptake can originate at a number of levels: patients or clients, providers, organizations, and policies (Damschroder et al., 2009). Individuals and organizations can reject or champion novel approaches, and those with greater power and authority can affect the outcome, positive or negative. Policies such as funding restrictions may inhibit adoption. A program may absorb an intervention intact, tug it away from its original application, or

BOX 7.1
ROGER'S DIFFUSION OF INNOVATION THEORY

Long before implementation science gained prominence, broader concerns with the spread of innovation were explored by Everett Rogers (1962). Rogers's theory of diffusion remains a frequently cited resource in market research and organizational studies; the phrase "early adopter" is now common parlance. Rogers presented five stages of diffusion: awareness, interest, evaluation, trial, and adoption—with a tipping point reached toward the final stage. Adoption is frequently influenced by opinion leaders and authority figures; its origins may be top–down or bottom–up.

Diffusion theorists also have distinguished between *adopting* and *adapting* innovations (Ansari, Fiss, & Zajac, 2010). For adoption to succeed, innovative practices may require customization or reconfiguration to fit local contexts. This process of adaptation is a point of contention for advocates of evidence-based practices who insist on program fidelity to ensure reliability. Others argue that adaptation is the rule, rather than the exception, and should be understood and managed rather than prohibited (Ansari et al., 2010). Adaptations can bring innovation, but they can also dilute the model or distort it to conform to existing practices.

The story of HF's dissemination is replete with this tension between maintaining fidelity (adopting rather than adapting) and altering the model (adapting rather than adopting). And, once adaptation of HF is pursued, the question arises: Is this a means of subverting the model or operating on "adaptable peripheries" while maintaining allegiance to core tenets?

alter it beyond all recognition. The fidelity of the adoption is always in contention, its success hinging on the fit between the new host and the innovation being introduced.

Damschroder and colleagues (2009) reviewed the extensive literature and proposed a CFIR (Consolidated Framework for Implementation Research) with five domains mapping the terrain of implementation: the *intervention, inner setting, outer setting, individuals involved,* and the *process* of the implementation. Variability in any of these domains can enhance or prevent implementation. Interventions may be rigid or they may have "adaptable peripheries," inner and outer settings may foster change or inhibit it through availability of funding and resources. Individuals have the ability to accept, alter, or reject innovation; the implementation process may be straightforward, non-linear, stop-and-start, or it may stall out and fail.

New interventions may come equipped with a robust evidence base that attracts or repels stakeholders (depending on their appraisal of the methods and findings). Interventions may be relatively simple or complex, easily incorporated into ongoing program functions, or multifaceted endeavors that require major adjustments. Cost savings calculated in one application may not carry over into another. A new approach may not be a good fit with local social norms, values, and cultural beliefs.

The vocabulary of implementation science is conceptual, but because it is impossible to map all possible iterations of the process, it is also conjectural. The CFIR and similar frameworks perform a necessary function in focusing on the poorly understood borderland between well-tested innovations and their applications under novel circumstances.

Pathways to Housing's First Expansions

PATHWAYS'S FIRST VENTURE INTO A SUBURBAN COUNTY: 1999. The first expansion of Pathways began in Westchester County just north of New York City. It was a difficult move, though not for the reasons that might first come to mind. Westchester County is a wealthy urban and suburban area with wide income disparities ranging from horse farms and lavish estates to poor and working-class neighborhoods. Concerned about the growing number of people who were homeless and cycling in and out of their shelter system, Westchester county social service officials sought to replicate the Pathways model.

Not long after the $1.3 million contract was signed with Pathways, opposition began and snowballed. Beginning with a newspaper editorial and letters to the editor and extending into the county's Board of Legislators, objections centered on the presumed irresponsibility of giving apartments to those who were drug-addicted and mentally ill, without first requiring that prospective tenants attain sobriety and stability. The leading organizers and representatives of this opposition came from a church that ran a large shelter in the county.

On a warm May evening in 2001, Pathways founder (Tsemberis), officials from the Westchester County Department of Social Services, and the church's minister sat uneasily on the stage of a large meeting hall located in the White Plains Public Library. The public meeting, attended by several hundred people, was a two-hour venting of emotion replete with jeers, cheers, and boos amidst testimonials of support for and opposition to HF. Those opposed made accusations of secret deals in contractual procurement and voiced stern warnings of the dangers of HF to law-abiding neighbors. As the evening wore on, it became clear that, with the exception of a few concerned citizens (both pro-HF and con), the majority of those in attendance were employees of local shelters, in particular the church-run shelter whose minister and staff psychologist spoke out at the meeting. County officials defended their decision and their process of securing the contract, and Tsemberis explained that many of the audience concerns could be effectively addressed by the program. This event was surprising both for its intensity and the boisterous audience that showed up.

In an intriguing case study, Felton (2003) conducted a post hoc analysis of the Westchester implementation of HF, interpreting it from the perspectives of multiple stakeholders. As Felton notes, things got "ugly" (p. 312) because local providers resented outsiders (especially from the big city) and thought they themselves should have been given a chance at the contract. Not everyone was opposed; some program administrators told Felton in confidence that the Pathways approach was a "paradigm shift" (p. 316) and an improvement on the "Elizabethan" requirements (p. 317) of local programs.

In what would prove to be a common objection as Pathways dissemination gathered steam in later years, several providers argued that they were "already doing it." In any event, they said, existing programs could learn to use the model without having an outside program come in. Felton (2003) points out that the expected NIMBY ("not in my backyard") response by residents and community organizations did not materialize, perhaps due to the use of scatter-site living as opposed to a single-site building that would have attracted attention. After what one official summed up as "a little street fight" (p. 318), opposition eased up, officials forged ahead with the contract, and Pathways settled into its Yonkers offices and began housing clients. A year later, the contract was renewed and the program declared successful with 54 chronically homeless men and women housed. The church shelter also remained in existence. (Box 7.2 offers more information on common objections to Housing First.)

PATHWAYS'S CONTINUED EXPANSION: WASHINGTON, DC IN 2004. Although Westchester County ultimately proved to be a successful replication, it was still carried out in New York State. In 2004, a combination of right people, right place, and right time occurred when Nan Roman (Director of the NAEH) introduced Tsemberis to Marti Knisley, then Director of the Department of Mental Health in Washington DC. That meeting resulted in a plan to bring the Pathways program to Washington to serve the same population as in New York City: people with severe psychiatric disabilities and multiple co-occurring conditions who were living on the streets.

The expansion did not begin well. The problems were primarily financial, with too little in the budget to support a full start-up of the program. Had it not been for the contribution of staff time and resources by the New York Pathways program and a grant from the William S. Abel Foundation, the nascent Pathways DC would not have survived. Even with an adequate budget, there were no professionals in

BOX 7.2
COMMON OBJECTIONS TO HOUSING FIRST

Beginning in the early 2000s, Pathways founder Tsemberis traveled extensively, appearing at conferences and meetings to speak about Housing First (HF) and consult with programs interested in the model. Audience reactions ranged from enthusiasm to mild skepticism to hostility. Three of the most common objections were: "HF can only work in New York City," "the housing market in our city has a very low vacancy rate," and "this will never work with *our* clients" (implying their clients were more mentally ill, more addicted, or both).

The first of these was disproven fairly quickly as HF spread to other cities with positive results. Low vacancy rates can be an obstacle, although the numbers of homeless persons needing housing are more often in the tens or hundreds than in the thousands. The rise of single-site HF, a response to different population needs (active substance abuse) or program philosophies (integrated housing including low-income tenants) could be seen as a way around low vacancy rates. The final objection is difficult to take seriously as one can imagine few if any cities with greater numbers or concentrations of such persons than New York City.

A later argument against HF, namely, that it is "not for everyone," has had more traction. Such an assertion also underscored the turnabout in perceptions wrought by the research evidence, given that early rejections of HF were more along the lines of "not for anyone." Few programs are "for everyone" and HF is hardly a panacea. More to the point is the question: Is HF beneficial for significant portions of the homeless population?

the Washington, DC area with experience operating the model, and this created significant management and supervision problems. Approximately two years into the program, Christy Respress, a social worker and seasoned staff member at Pathways New York, moved to Washington to assume operational responsibility for the program. Thereafter, the program became stabilized and grew to serve over 500 clients (Tsemberis, Kent, & Respress, 2012).

In 2010, there was a significant tipping point for HF in Washington DC. Newly elected Mayor Adrian Fenty reviewed the city's services for the homeless and pronounced HF to be the city's primary homeless policy. Acting on this change, and as a way to kick-start the other agencies, the city declared that it would close a 300-bed shelter in the downtown area. It enlisted the help of Pathways DC and other willing agencies to accept contracts to place the shelter residents into apartments of their own with support services.

PATHWAYS IN PHILADELPHIA IN 2008. The replication of Pathways in Philadelphia, four years after the challenges experienced in Washington DC, was very different. In the first place, it began with an enthusiastic invitation by Mayor Ray Nutter.[1] Having learned the lessons of the Pathways DC experience, the Philadelphia program negotiated a contract that included full start-up costs and hired an experienced Pathways New York staffer as its clinical director right from the start (coauthor Henwood). A social worker who had worked on the Brooklyn Pathways Assertive Community Treatment (ACT) team and gone on to pursue a doctorate in social work, Henwood was charged with hiring and training staff to ensure a high fidelity replication for the Philadelphia program. He was joined by Christine Smiriglia, an experienced administrator with deep knowledge of the city's social services.

The city's welcome embrace made for a rapid yet smooth transition. The presence of a skilled team, affordable apartments, and cooperative landlords in Philadelphia made the scatter-site part of the HF model easier to achieve. Six months after being asked to engage 125 chronically homeless adults considered the most difficult to house, Pathways PA had its first tenant. By 2010, the program had reached capacity with housing retention rates exceeding 90% according to an evaluation conducted by the Scattergood Foundation (Fairmount Ventures, 2011).

One of the more interesting reactions to the Philadelphia program came from the business community. Not long after Mayor Nutter's election, the president of the Downtown Business Improvement District noticed—from his office overlooking Center City—that the number of homeless people in the city's downtown parks had dropped. Curious, and believing that the newly elected city administration, like many others across the country, was removing them to improve the city's quality of life, he instead found that most were living in their own apartments, stably housed and receiving services from Pathways PA.

Pathways PA emerged as a successful replication of the PHF model and has expanded to serve over 400 individuals, with one of the teams working with the local VA to house and provide treatment and support for veterans. See Figures 7.1, 7.2, and 7.3, for photos of individuals who transitioned from homelessness to permanent housing through the Pathways PA program. These photos (used with permission) were part of a project in which consumers were encouraged to take photographs to document their life changes.

PATHWAYS VERMONT: RURAL EXPANSION. In December 2009, Pathways opened a program in Burlington, Vermont and soon expanded to other areas within the state. Funded through a federal demonstration grant from SAMHSA, this marked the first attempt at implementing HF in a rural setting, and alterations would be needed (Cloke, Milbourne, & Wiedowfield, 2002). Consistent with the formula used to ensure high fidelity to the PHF model, the Vermont Pathways program was led

FIGURE 7.1 Pathways PA—The Keys to Home

by Hilary Melton, who had been part of the original start-up team for the Pathways program in New York City. The expansive geographical boundaries of service delivery, along with limited public transportation and workforce shortages, necessitated program adaptation as well as innovation. To address these challenges, the program organized geographically based caseloads with regional staff and local service coordinators, using a hybrid Assertive Community Treatment–Intensive Case Management (ACT-ICM) model (adaptation) (Henwood, Melekis, Stefancic,

FIGURE 7.2 Pathways PA—Relaxing at Home

FIGURE 7.3 Pathways PA—At the Door

& York, 2014). Innovation came in the form of technology, including personal computers for staff and consumers (Stefancic et al., 2013).

Computer-mediated care and communication streamlined teamwork and permitted program staff to respond to consumers more efficiently. For consumers, in-home computers (purchased affordably or donated) and Internet access (at negotiated reduced rates) allowed for "video visits" with staff and for Internet access to connect with others (only two clients broke agency rules and sold their computers). Team members in different cities met on Google Groups (an online meeting platform) to discuss clients' needs and plan interventions. Shared calendars and contacts allowed team members to keep up to date with appointments, manage crises, and cover for one another when necessary. One-year outcomes for 170 clients showed 85% housing stability (Stefancic et al., 2013), a finding similar to the New York experience despite clients who originated from a very different population (mostly rural and white, with a disproportionate number recently released from jail).

Compared with Felton's (2003) study of the suburban extension of Pathways, Vermont Pathways met with little or no resistance at the outset. But opposition did become public in 2014 when the program—faced with an end to its SAMHSA funding—sought certification to bill Medicaid to pay for support services. In response, mental health providers argued that Pathways's services were not needed, and that they could supply services instead (Henwood et al., 2014).

But the prospect of Pathways closing produced a strong reaction from those most affected. A public hearing organized by the state's Mental Health Department in April 2014 attracted over 50 attendees. In emotional testimony, Pathways clients related previous negative experiences with services. "Pathways's approach is to meet you where you're at," said one 42-year-old man. A peer advocate testified that Pathways ". . . is really on that journey with the people they serve." http://vtdigger.org/2014/04/14/supporters-turn-hearing-pathways-vermont-funding-application/. In response, the Vermont Legislature passed a bill that approved Pathways Vermont as a state Medicaid provider, the first new Medicaid provider approved in 20 years.

Variation in Housing First: High Fidelity, Low Fidelity, No Fidelity?

Whatever the origin or nature of local objections, the institutional logic of homeless services was inexorably shifting toward HF in the United States and elsewhere (see Greenwood, Stefancic, & Tsemberis, 2013; Johnson, Parkinson, & Parsell, 2012; Stanhope & Dunn, 2011; USICH, 2013). In 2010, the U.S. Federal government declared HF the "clear solution" to chronic homelessness in its first ever comprehensive plan to end homelessness (USICH, 2010).

Not surprisingly, rapid growth in HF prompted new and different versions to appear. Also not surprisingly, Pathways researchers worked with other experts in the field to develop a fidelity measure for use with programs seeking to adopt the PHF model (Stefancic, Tsemberis, Messeri, Drake, & Goering, 2013). The measure has five domains—housing choice and structure, separation of housing and treatment, service philosophy, service array, and program structure—and it may be used independently or as part of program site visits by experienced Pathways staff (Stefancic et al., 2013). Detailed instruction on how to implement Pathways Housing First can be found in Tsemberis (2010). With notable exceptions discussed below and in the following chapter (especially Canada's national HF implementation), research on HF adaptations is just beginning to appear in the literature (Gilmer, Stefancic, Katz, Sklar, Tsemberis, & Palinkas, 2014).

DENVER'S HOUSING FIRST INITIATIVE: EARLY ADOPTION. The Colorado Coalition for the Homeless (CCH) in Denver was one of the organizations funded by the USICH initiative to end chronic homelessness. Already established as a homeless service provider, John Parvensky and his colleagues seized on this new funding opportunity and CCH became part of the Denver Housing First Collaborative (DHFC) in 2003. The DHFC, initially funded for three years, transformed an old YMCA building into apartments for some clients and placed the others in scatter-site apartments with rental assistance, a total of 150 clients in all.

The Denver experience provided a unique opportunity to test consumer preference because the DHFC gave clients the option of choosing between a single-site building or a scatter-site apartment. Contrary to expectations, most chose a modest apartment of their own in the community over the newly renovated downtown YMCA. After the apartments were filled, participants accepted the YMCA over life on the streets.

Parvensky's efforts stood out for doing something still rare in the world of nonprofits—conducting research on his program's effectiveness. In line with growing interest in the costs of chronic homelessness, the DHFC study focused on outcomes of residential stability, improving health, and cost effectiveness of the model (Perlman & Parvensky, 2006). The resulting cost benefit analysis tracked clients' service utilization two years before and two years after entering the Denver HF program. Service use and costs dropped dramatically after program entry, including such services as detox treatment, emergency room visits, jail nights, and emergency shelter stays, which resulted in savings that averaged $31,545 per person. The net savings after program costs were $4,745 per person. When extrapolated to the over 500 chronic homeless adults in the Denver area, the savings ran into the millions. Although not a randomized trial with a comparison non-HF program, the study garnered national attention for its meticulous documentation as well as its cost-savings findings.

SEATTLE'S DOWNTOWN EMERGENCY SERVICE CENTER: SINGLE-SITE HOUSING FIRST Having its origins in 1979 as an emergency shelter, Seattle's Downtown Emergency Service Center (DESC) has become one of the best-known homeless service providers in the United States. Owing much to an institutional entrepreneur—Bill Hobson—DESC was an early adopter of HF, albeit with significant modifications. Formerly a political science professor, Hobson's journey to homeless advocacy included working at a shelter before becoming director of the DESC. In a *Seattle Weekly* article, the outspoken Hobson explained how his left-leaning years of "blaming capitalism" gave way to a realization that home-less individuals have serious problems that require behavior change as well as low-threshold access to services.

With authorization from King County in 2005, DESC began to house the heaviest service users identified from jails, hospitals, and sobering units—a total of 75 out of 79 individuals who were approached accepted the offer. Criticized by a local news-paper as supplying free "bunks for drunks," DESC practiced harm reduction and the "no strings attached" approach of HF, that is, they assured clients that they could continue to drink without loss of their housing. Rejected by local shelters and con-demned for public urination and drunkenness, this population drew far less sympa-thy than homeless families or the mentally ill. In Seattle, they were almost all males, middle-aged, and predominantly White or American Indian/Alaska Native—a clear difference from HF clients in New York and other Northeastern cities.

DESC's most significant departure from HF praxis was its reliance on single-site facilities for housing. The first building, known by its address as 1811 Eastlake, was located in a commercially zoned area near downtown Seattle, distant from residential neighborhoods and schools. In a radio interview, Hobson explained this choice not as one of safety (the men were hardly a risk to anyone but them-selves) but of avoiding the unpleasant aspects of their behavior. (http://www.npr.org/templates/story/story.php?storyId=5567184)

That the DESC experience has received considerable acclaim is due in no small part to its investment in outcomes research that earned its way into leading medical journals such as *the Journal of the American Medical Association* and the *American Journal of Public Health* (Collins, Malone, & Clifasefi, 2013; Larimer et al., 2009). Using a quasi-experimental design with wait-list controls, researchers assessed cost-offset benefits, the latter calculated by subtracting program costs from total public sector service-use costs. At six months into the program's exis-tence, these benefits were already favoring the HF group at savings of $2,449 per person per month (Larimer et al., 2009).

HF participants also showed a significant decline in drinking to intoxication compared with the controls, despite having no program requirements to reduce or end their alcohol intake (Larimer et al., 2009). Two-year follow-up of the 1811 Eastlake group showed housing retention at 77% with one fourth of the dropouts eventually returning to the facility (Collins et al., 2013). The authors note these findings defy the conventional wisdom that heavy drinkers are poor candidates for HF. "This risk [of homelessness] might depend less on the affected individuals' behavior and more on the fit between individuals' needs and available models of housing" (Larimer et al., 2009, p. e5).

COMMON GROUND'S STREET TO HOME PROGRAM. A more independent take on HF was started by Common Ground (CG) with its Street to Home (S2H) program in 2003, a program inspired by England's Rough Sleeper Initiative (RSI). Similar to the RSI, S2H teams would cover a defined geographic area, identify and keep a registry of the street homeless, then seek to engage these individuals and get them into transitional or permanent housing. In line with HF tenets, consumers were not required to demonstrate sobriety or treatment compliance to obtain and stay in housing. S2H's use of transitional housing was a deviation from HF, but it did skip some of the lower steps on the staircase (shelters or drop-in centers).

Unlike PHF, S2H reached out to street homeless individuals whether or not they had a serious mental illness. (S2H was funded by private foundations and thus did not need to abide by the psychiatric disability requirement). Services, which included financial management, mental health counseling, and advice on how to maintain housing, were offered but not required, and S2H case managers served clients until they helped them find permanent housing (Jost, Levitt, & Porcu, 2011).

S2H began in CG's home territory—the 250 square blocks surrounding Times Square. Set in the middle of Manhattan's business core, the area had long been a destination for homeless adults, many of whom slept in the vast shadowy corridors of the nearby Port Authority bus terminal. According to Jost et al. (2011), by 2008, "S2H had 'housed' (defined as remaining housed for at least 30 of the first 45 days after placement) over 400 unsheltered homeless individuals, nearly 100 of whom have been placed into permanent housing, and 96% remain housed" (p. 248). CG proudly announced on its website that the program brought an 87% reduction in street homelessness in the Times Square business district.

The S2H project was a "modified continuum with relaxed entry requirements" (Jost et al., 2011, p. 248). As with its progenitor the RSI, S2H's focus was on getting homeless people off the street and into whatever programs were available to house them right away. The added layer of case management by S2H staff contributed to smoother follow-up and transition through the continuum. In addition, the easing of requirements helped engage clients as they waited their turn at obtaining permanent housing. To keep clients engaged while living in transitional settings, S2H staff attended to their permanent housing applications (of which about 25% were successful) (Jost et al., 2011).

THE 100,000 HOMES CAMPAIGN. Responding to the reframing of the problem of homelessness as ending chronic homelessness rather than managing it, the

100,000 Homes (100K) campaign was a laudable and ambitious move to transform homeless services in the United States. With HF prominent in its manifesto (http://100khomes.org/read-the-manifesto), 100K began in 2011 under the auspices of a nonprofit organization, Community Solutions, Inc. (CSI), established by Common Ground's founder Rosanne Haggerty. Becky Kanis served as the 100K field coordinator.

The goal was a simple one: house 100,000 chronically homeless individuals across the United States.[2] A small team of 13 CSI employees worked from a national field office offering technical assistance and on-site consultations. Recalling the RSI and S2H models of engagement, the 100K Campaign provided a toolkit and instructions for locating and assessing homeless individuals' needs and linking them to existing programs.

What distinguished 100K was its strategy of identifying those most vulnerable due to physical illness and the likelihood of death. Influenced by Boston's Health Care for the Homeless program headed by Drs. Jim O'Connell and Stephan Hwang, 100K outreach workers used a brief survey—the Vulnerability Index—to ascertain mortality risk. Administering the survey and taking a photograph of the individual provided documentation that set in motion a triage-style expediting of access to housing for those suffering from life-threatening illnesses such as renal failure or those who were "frequent flyers" at local emergency rooms.

100K's national influence came from a public relations apparatus well honed from the CG experience and Haggerty's prominence in policy circles. The campaign's far-reaching goals required a sophisticated media platform that included online information and interactive websites. Social media such as Facebook and YouTube were used to create virtual communities where homeless advocates could pose questions and share success stories. YouTube videos depicted moving personal accounts of individuals rescued from the streets. Websites replete with maps and resources spurred national fervor to reach the 100K goal. Over 237 communities joined the campaign from around the United States. The deadline was reached and exceeded on June 11, 2014. Earlier in 2014, Becky Kanis appeared on the national television show "60 Minutes" to speak about 100K's success.

An obvious criterion of 100K's success was whether it could bring about the cooperation among local service providers necessary to follow through on its commitment to housing and services, especially medical care. 100K proudly flew the banner of HF, but local homeless organizations were frequently dominated by continuum programs. By focusing solely on physical health, the campaign also relied on services less tied to psychiatric disability (i.e., shelters and transitional housing designated for the "general population" of homeless adults).

As a result, the population served by 100K was older and more likely to be male and substance abusers. Following a triage model designed to save those at highest risk of death was humane and imminently defensible, but it was a strategic decision nonetheless. It was also a strategy that gave unprecedented discretionary power to outreach workers as they ventured out to engage chronically homeless adults. This was the same group that homeless programs had failed to engage (or who preferred homelessness to abstinence-only housing). Having no wherewithal to ensure HF's principles, 100K found success but fell short in realizing its full manifesto.

THE HUD-VASH PROGRAM: ENDING HOMELESSNESS FOR VETERANS. In 2008, troubled by a report from the Department of Housing and Urban Development's (HUD) annual Point in Time (PIT) count estimating over 70,000 homeless veterans, the Department of Veterans Affairs (VA) and HUD announced a joint venture to end homelessness among veterans by 2015. This initiative, called HUD/VASH (the latter an acronym for VA Supportive Housing) provided ongoing rental assistance through Section 8 or Housing Choice vouchers and support services through the VA. In its first two years, some 30,000 vouchers and support services were allocated to the HUD-VASH initiative, yet HUD's annual PIT count did not show a decrease in homelessness among veterans. In 2010, the National Center on Homelessness among Veterans decided to implement the Pathways Housing First approach for HUD-VASH.

This initiative represented the largest implementation of HF by an organization in the United States. At its outset, the National Center selected 14 cities with the largest number of homeless veterans. This 14-city demonstration project consisted of several initiatives designed to drive down the number of veterans on the streets. It required the VA medical centers to have the HUD-VASH programs create HF teams charged with identifying veterans who were chronically homeless and had complex needs. The teams were also provided with additional clinical and support services anticipating the need for lower caseloads and additional support for the target population.

Early findings from the HUD-VASH Housing First Demonstration Project were positive and improved significantly from there. The results showed improved outreach to chronically homeless veterans, housing retention rates between 84% and 92%, and reduced use of costly inpatient hospitalizations. The 2013 PIT count showed an 8% decline from 2012, and a 24% decline from 2010. In early 2014, Salt Lake City, Utah announced that it had reached zero for homeless veterans and Phoenix, Arizona made the same announcement shortly thereafter.

BOX 7.3

HOUSING FIRST AND HOMELESS VETERANS

The persistence of homelessness among U.S. veterans in 2010 was old news but remained alarming news. The homeless veteran population mostly comprised older men (typically Vietnam War era) whose mental problems intermingled with substance abuse. Some lived in rural encampments; others were denizens of urban business districts. These men were hardy survivors, immune to the usual outreach techniques. All of this changed with the HUD-VASH Housing First Demonstration Project.

In January 2014, the *New York Times* reported that Phoenix, Arizona had housed all 222 of its chronically homeless veterans (Santos, 2014). Robert Stone, a typical client, had lived on Phoenix streets on and off for 15 years, until he moved into his apartment in a remodeled building named Victory Place in March 2013. Suffering from heart disease and the effects of long-term alcoholism, Mr. Stone said, "I'm coming up on nine months sober, and a big part of it is because I have a roof over my head."

HUD-VASH's success was undoubtedly assisted by Housing Choice vouchers subsidized by HUD (totaling $913 million in the first four years). In Phoenix, the local United Way also funded "navigators," peer counselors who assist housed veterans in applying for benefits and obtaining needed services. A sure sign of the newness of HF was the lack of planning and budgeting for expenses such as rental deposits and furnishings—creative local providers obtained private donations to fill the gaps. The Phoenix success story was featured on the official White House website and in a speech by First Lady Michelle Obama.

Building on these successes, the VA announced in 2014 that Housing First, as developed by Pathways, was the official policy and program approach for all HUD/VASH programs. Given this directive for large-scale system change, the VA expanded its partnership with Pathways to help train VA staff to implement and effectively operate the model in an additional 25 cities and eventually across all 135 VA Medical Centers (VAMC). An April 2014 report on cost savings showed that veterans in the HUD-VASH program had substantially reduced their use of costly medical and behavioral health services; the drop in inpatient care was "especially steep" (Byrne, Roberts, Culhane, & Kane, 2014, p. 5). Box 7.3 describes this success in greater detail.

HOUSING FIRST IN SALT LAKE CITY, UTAH AND CHARLOTTE, NORTH CAROLINA. From 2006 to 2015, the state of Utah reduced chronic homelessness by a remarkable 91%. In 2005, Tsemberis was invited to Salt Lake City by Lloyd Pendleton, the Director of Utah's Homeless Task Force, to work with a

BOX 7.4

In May 2003, Lloyd Pendleton traveled to Chicago as part of Utah's delegation to a national meeting to promote the Ten-Year Plan to End Homelessness. At the time, Pendleton was an employee of The Church of Jesus Christ of Latter-day Saints (LDS), commonly known as the Mormon Church. He had been "loaned out" from the LDS Church to assist the Utah team in drafting the state's own Ten-Year Plan. When he retired from the Church, the State of Utah hired him to continue the implementation of the Ten-Year Plan to End Homelessness as the Director of the Homelessness Task Force.

Pendleton's involvement was considered instrumental given his business expertise and previous experience assisting nonprofit organizations that needed restructuring. Raised on a ranch in the western deserts of Utah, Pendleton had dutifully completed his two years of service for the LDS Church, obtained an MBA degree, and worked for Ford Motor Company for 14 years before taking employment with the LDS Church for the next 26 years.

The meeting in Chicago was Pendleton's first introduction to Housing First and he was impressed by Philip Mangano's ability to speak the language of the business world—a vernacular steeped in problem solving and pragmatism. Two years later, Pendleton traveled to a similar national meeting in Las Vegas where he met Sam Tsemberis. Serendipitously sharing the airport shuttle with Sam, Pendleton asked him questions and got answers that intrigued him enough to advocate for HF at home.

When describing his experience implementing HF in Utah, Pendleton refers to his "epiphanies," or watershed moments. The first came as the Utah Task Force was planning the construction of a 100-unit building to house the homeless: Why not do a pilot test of the HF model while awaiting the completion of this large facility? Hearing of a luncheon sponsored by Salt Lake City's Housing Authority to thank local landlords for taking Section 8 vouchers, Pendleton made an appearance, described HF, and took the inevitable questions from the audience.

- *Who will pay for damage to the apartment*? Pendleton: the program will
- *Who will help out if the tenant creates problems?* Pendleton: a case manager from the program will be available 24/7
- *How can I be sure the rent is paid?* Pendleton: the local housing authority will be the leaseholder and ensure that the rent is paid
- *What if the tenant has to go to jail or the hospital*? Pendleton: If a short stay, no change. If longer than 90 days, another tenant will be moved in (and the original tenant offered another apartment upon release).

Pendleton's answers did the trick: 15 landlords volunteered on the spot and a budget of $150,000 was allocated for the pilot project. In deciding where to start, the Task Force identified 17 chronically homeless individuals to be given priority in housing. They were hard drinking and "housing resistant" ("the worse of the worst," according to Pendleton).

Epiphanic moment #2 came as resistance from the local Housing Authority and shelter providers was countered by explaining how HF had worked elsewhere and was worth a try. By the end of August 2005, all 17 men were given apartments and 22 months later 100% remained housed. Pendleton's epiphanic moment #3 came when he realized that taking a "whatever's necessary" approach—a roll-up-the-sleeves willingness to tackle every obstacle with the resources at hand—was his modus operandi. When the 100-unit facility finally opened in 2007, it became a HF building and a year later an 84-unit permanent supportive housing facility was completed. In 2009, a defunct Holiday Inn was bought and converted into 201 apartments with 52 reserved for chronically homeless families. As word spread of the success of HF in a conservative state like Utah, Pendleton became a sought-after spokesperson. An affable gentleman in conservative Western attire, Pendleton uses down-to-earth language mixed with occasional religious piety. His status as a former LDS employee has undoubtedly smoothed the way in Utah's rural towns where the Mormon presence is dominant.

When asked what made the difference in implementing HF, Pendleton did not hesitate: "You need a champion, otherwise you're dead in the water." Did the research conducted on HF make a difference? Pendleton replied, "That was done in New York City and that's an entirely different place to us here in the West."

In his travels around Utah, Pendleton preaches a "centrally led, locally developed" philosophy starting with vocal support from Utah's Lieutenant Governor. He reaches out to local political leaders, takes them to lunch, and uses gentle persuasion to point out the benefits of HF. He speaks of the need for the "effective invitation" to housing, one that makes sense to the homeless man or woman. "We have to make as big a change as they do," he says, to ensure that both parties meet halfway. Pendleton's last epiphanic moment (at least for the time being) is his understanding that middle-class values cannot be imposed on those who have had no access to middle-class comforts. Despite his homespun celebrity, Pendleton remains steadfast in his humility and piety, saying he might write a book in the future, but this decision will ultimately be up to the "Big Guy in the sky."

group of stakeholders interested in addressing chronic homelessness (see Box 7.4 for a description of Pendleton and his work on behalf of HF in Utah). The first program, a pilot demonstration project with an evaluation component, was intended for residents of the city's downtown shelter operated by the Road Home program.

The pilot soon demonstrated success in housing retention and cost savings and Pendleton and his colleagues quickly took the program to scale. By 2015, an estimated 2,000 formerly homeless individuals and families in the state were housed in single-site and scatter-site programs. A cost analysis showed that the average cost of serving an individual who remained chronically homeless was $19,208 per year compared with $11,000 for housing with support services. These results were remarkable for having been achieved in a conservative state.

What appeared at first to be a local success became a national sensation. Media attention grew after a *San Francisco Chronicle* article appeared in June 2014 with the headline, "What San Francisco can learn from Salt Lake City." The idea that a liberal secular city like San Francisco could take a few lessons from its religious and conservative counterpart was novel to say the least. Picked up by national media, Utah's success led to an interview with Lloyd Pendleton aired on National Public Radio and Comedy Central's The Daily Show with Jon Stewart. It was also the centerpiece of a story in *The New Yorker*. As the story's author noted, "Housing First isn't just cost-effective. It's more effective, period" (Surowiecki, 2014, p.42). The *New Yorker* writer goes on to note, "it may seem surprising that a solidly conservative state like Utah has adopted an apparently bleeding heart approach like giving homeless people homes. But in fact Housing First has become the rule in hundreds of cities around the country in states both red and blue" (p. 42).

Across the country, Charlotte, North Carolina celebrated its own HF success in March 2014. Moore Place, the 85-unit building where apartments were made available, opened in 2012 amidst the usual concerns about rewarding bad behavior with immediate access. Social work professor Lori Thomas from the University of North Carolina-Charlotte conducted a study of first-year outcomes and the results were striking: $1.8 million saved in the program's first year by drastically reducing the amount of time its tenants spent in emergency rooms (447 fewer visits) and were admitted to hospitals (372 fewer days). Arrests dropped by 74% and there were 84% fewer days spent in jail (Thomas, Shears, Pate, & Priester, 2014).

A local newspaper described a Charlotte HF recipient, Michael, a disabled 55-year-old man (Price, 2014). Michael had visited emergency departments 24 times in the year before he entered the program, accumulating $268,000 in medical bills. In his first year at Moore Place, he visited emergency departments five times and his medical costs dropped to $9,000. The interfaith program behind Moore Place, Urban Ministry Center, has plans to expand with $3.5 million in commitments from the City Council and other donations. Urban Ministry's Caroline Chambre stated, "You can't argue with the statistics. This approach was controversial at one time because of the stereotype of who the homeless are, and we had to change that stereotype" (Price, 2014).

In Pursuit of Fidelity and Evidence

Identifying what was and was not a "HF program" became increasingly difficult as time wore on. To address this definitional blurring and assist in the growing number of requests for help, the Pathways founder published a manual with Hazelden Press (Tsemberis, 2010). Written for practitioners and others interested in starting a HF program, the book addressed the many questions that had accumulated over the 18 years of Pathways existence. However, the manual did little to rein in variation as more and more programs called themselves "HF"—the examples provided in this chapter are just a few of many.

A key metric for evaluating HF as it spread was the extent to which adopting programs (or nonadopting programs for that matter) conducted outcome research and, if so, who did the study, how rigorous was the research, and what were the findings. The New York Housing Study's impact was largely due to its randomized experimental design and the involvement of a highly respected researcher (psychologist Dr. Mary Beth Shinn). Research findings from Seattle's DESC and Denver's CCH were based upon quasi-experimental designs (wait list controls or a pre–post longitudinal design, respectively). Seattle researchers and others conducting similar studies (Sadowski, Kee, VanderWeele, & Buchanan, 2009) have published their work in high-impact scientific journals. The HUD-VASH program has built-in research components ensuring that it is evaluated thoroughly. In San Diego, "full-service partnerships" using HF showed reduced service costs and higher quality of life for HF clients compared with homeless persons using outpatient services (Gilmer, Stefancic, Ettner, Manning, & Tsemberis, 2010). The Common Ground model, widely known and respected, is among the least documented by an evidentiary base. According to Parsell, Fitzpatrick, and Busch-Geertsema (2014), "notwithstanding claims to the contrary, there is in fact very little (research) evidence to support the efficacy of the Common Ground model, even in its original setting in the USA/New York City" (p. 70).

In 2003, a HUD-commissioned independent study of Housing First was begun by Carol Pearson of Walter R. McDonald Associates with the collaboration of Ann Montgomery (University of Alabama-Birmingham) and Gretchen Locke (Abt Associates). The study, which compared Pathways to Housing (PTH) in New York to "housing first" programs with different approaches, canvassed programs nationally and selected two: Seattle's DESC and San Diego's Project REACH (Reaching out and Engaging to Achieve Consumer Health). Eighty new or recently enrolled clients were recruited for the study, 26 from PTH, 25 from DESC, and 29 from REACH (Pearson et al., 2009). In addition to measures of outcomes, the research team made site visits to each setting and conducted focus groups with clients to ascertain satisfaction with services and compare this to the quantitative findings.

REACH bore a resemblance to both DESC and Pathways with one critical difference: Clients were recruited following low-threshold criteria, but the housing providers did not accede to this and imposed rules regarding sobriety, curfews, and supervision. Case managers attempted to bridge these conflicting practices but the authors acknowledge REACH "was not the best fit with the Housing First Model" (Pearson et al., 2009, p. 409). Following the lead of an earlier pioneering study by Burt and Aron (2000), the authors focused on housing stability as the relevant outcome. They found an overall rate of 84% for tenants remaining in their housing after 12 months, the rate for Pathways was 92%, and 80% for DESC and REACH. Reasons for leaving ranged from resistance to the program's expectations to relapse and death. Levels of impairment due to psychiatric problems or substance use did not change significantly over the 12 months.

The authors reported varied responses from the focus groups, along with overall client satisfaction. One resident of DESC resented living with others who had a mental illness; Pathways tenants tended to be grateful to be off the street, saying it was "too good to be true" (Pearson et al., 2009, p. 413). REACH participants spoke about the wait for independent housing and dissatisfaction with living in a single-room occupancy (SRO). Though relatively small, this first multisite study of Housing First produced results strikingly similar to other studies of the model.

Implementation Paradox: Case Management in Housing First and Treatment First Programs

Both the New York Services Studies (NYSS) and the New York Recovery Study (NYRS) described in earlier chapters involved in-depth interviews with case managers (CMs) whose clients had given consent. On the PHF side in the NYSS, case managers were part of ACT teams, sharing the responsibility for clients. In the non-PHF programs, case managers followed an intensive case management (ICM) approach in which each CM had his or her own caseload of clients. CMs were asked about their service philosophy, their experiences with the program, and their perspectives on the client (study participant). In keeping with each study's aims, CMs were also queried about what engaged clients or repelled them and about their views on mental health recovery and harm reduction.

In coding and thematic analysis of the CM transcripts, the search was for similarities and differences across programs as well as signs of "street level bureaucracy" (Lipsky, 1980) or the exercise of discretionary authority to bend or break program rules on behalf of clients. CMs talked about their work routines, their professional identities, and how much (or how little) they identified with the program's mission. True to form, CMs in the two approaches differed in how they "voiced" their clients, that is, how they described the client's needs and future prospects. (Henwood, Shinn, Tsemberis, & Padgett, 2013).

One of the more intriguing findings came from examining how CMs engage clients and work with them in the context of their program's mission. One of the most powerful messages given to incoming clients in non-HF programs is that permanent independent housing is within their grasp if they comply with program rules and prove themselves "housing ready"—anywhere from six months to two years is the typical window of time given to them upon program entry. We found in the interviews that CMs in the non-HF programs spent much of their time preparing their clients for the next step up the staircase, not, as expected, focusing on treatment for mental illness or substance dependence (Henwood, Stanhope, & Padgett, 2011).

Given the requirements associated with new placements, this was a time-consuming effort in which paperwork had to be pulled together from various sources (psychosocial evaluations, psychiatrist's evaluation, medical records, medication requirements, criminal justice history, etc.). A client living in a dormitory-style community residence, for example, might be deemed ready to apply to move up to a shared apartment program. He (or she) would be interviewed by staff at the apartment program and a decision made to accept or reject. To help their clients get accepted, CMs put their clients through role-playing exercises, coached them on what to say (and not to say) and urged the client to dress properly and act compliant.

When asked about the client's mental health status, one CM replied that she had little time to address that as long as the client was not a threat to himself or others (Henwood, Stanhope, & Padgett, 2011). Substance abuse, if suspected, meant going to addiction treatment and rehabilitation services and losing one's place in the line for independent housing. The paradox came from the fact that HF CMs were more likely to address their client's needs—treatment and otherwise—because they were already stably housed. PHF CMs also did not have a time limit on their services or a goal of "graduating" the client to go elsewhere.

This almost counterintuitive finding—HF staff were more treatment-oriented than their counterparts whose primary goal was supposed to be treatment—is one example of the surprising distortions or amplifications in a program's mission that can occur when enacted in unpredictable and changing conditions. And, as HF became the aspirational goal of more and more cities' homeless services, its implementation became subject to greater variability in interpreting its core tenets.

Applying the CFIR to the Diffusion of Housing First

Damschroder and colleagues' Consolidated Framework for Implementation Research (CFIR) (2009), discussed earlier in this chapter, included five domains that can be applied to the dissemination of HF. The first domain—the intervention—came with a value-driven philosophical premise of consumer choice, harm reduction, explicit service components, and immediate access to housing. It also came with a robust evidence base. The outer settings (political and economic host environments) of implementation ranged from liberal to conservative values, a surprisingly eclectic foundation for a rights-based program model. What these settings had in common was access to Federal, state, and local funds with a Federal endorsement of HF. Inner settings (local provider networks) ranged from enthusiastic agents of change to wary adopters to outright resisters. Individuals (another CFIR domain) played critical roles as local advocates, and providers became institutional entrepreneurs on behalf of HF or in pursuit of an alternative to HF.

Table 7.1 represents an application of the five domains to the programs described in this chapter. Although implementation of HF at these locations is a work in progress, the table shows variability in how, who, and what took place, in the scope of each effort (including the presence or absence of research) and the degree of fidelity to the HF model.

The final CFIR domain—the implementation process—took many forms. Program administrators had to secure housing units and make them ready for occupancy, while working with landlords and building owners to obtain leases and give assurances. They also had to hire, train, and supervise support staff—psychiatrists, social workers, case managers—to ensure multiple needs were met in accordance with the model's tenets. Previous training and experience were rarely a good fit for working in a HF program—hard-won expertise and guarantees of authority had to be subordinated to consumer choice and flexibility. Staff seemed more governed by these constraints than their clients.

And yet, after HF was put into place, gratification came early as clients expressed happy disbelief over the offer of an apartment with limited strings attached. Longer term, the model held fast and the vast majority of clients remained housed (although rehousing was not uncommon). We know of no occasion in which HF was adopted and failed to perform to this level when applied to

TABLE 7.1

APPLICATION OF CFIR* TO HOUSING FIRST PROGRAMS

Program	Intervention	Inner Setting	Outer Setting	Individuals Involved	Process	Research
PTH Westchester	PHF model (no modifications)	PTH's first venture into suburban context	Initial protests by local shelter providers	Run by and out of PTH NYC office	Strongly contested but no delay in start-up	Four-year follow-up by PTH research department
PTH Washington, DC	PHF model (no modifications)	Start-up; PTH's first expansion program	Key supporter among city officials enables HF	Director from PTH–NYC + local service providers.	Mixed beginning; inadequate financing; later endorsed by Mayor	Self-evaluation research; Doug Kent independent researcher
PTH Philadelphia	PHF model (no modifications)	Start-up; second PTH expansion; contacts with local providers	Support by city; wary local provider "already doing it"	Clinical Director from PTH–NYC + local leadership + providers	Strongly supported by city government; smooth adoption	Self-evaluation research; Scattergood Foundation
PTH Vermont	PHF model (modified for rural context)	Start-up; PTH third expansion and first in rural context	Supported by Federal grant and key state personnel	Director from PTH–NYC + local service providers.	Contested when Federal funds end in 2014, but Vermont Legislature approves	Follow-up study by PTH research department (Stefancic et al.)

Denver HF	HF model	Existing service providers adopt model	City and state support	John Parvensky	Little resistance	Self-evaluation research; cost savings
Seattle HF	HF model (major modification = single-site)	Focus on "chronic inebriates" and supervised living	Public disapproval of "bunks for drunks"	William Hobson and researchers from University of Washington	Housing facility located away from residential areas	Self-evaluation research by University of Washington; Cost-savings+ changed attitudes
Common Ground (CG)	Non-HF model; mixed tenants	CG staff committed to integrated housing	Strong civic–business partnership support	Roseanne Haggerty	Support services by Center for Urban Community Services (CUCS)	Limited research
100,000 Homes Campaign	Movement to end homelessness for 100,000 people	Small staff committed to "spreading the word" with public relations and advocacy	Increased pressure to address homelessness by cities adopting 10-year plans	Roseanne Haggerty & Becky Kanis	Campaign ended in June 2014 with success	No research; Urban Institute to evaluate results

(continued)

TABLE 7.1
CONTINUED

Program	Intervention	Inner Setting	Outer Setting	Individuals Involved	Process	Research
HUD-VASH	PHF model + Housing Choice vouchers	VA bureaucracy; services delivered at VA centers	National pressure and support to end veterans' homelessness	Vince Kane; PTH providing technical assistance	Ongoing work on fidelity; vouchers key to success	Self-evaluation by contract
Salt Lake City, Utah	HF model (single- and scatter-site models)	LDS Church and Ten-Year Plan	Little resistance	Lloyd Pendleton, Utah's Homeless Task Force	Close partnership with business community and landlords	Cost-benefit analysis
Charlotte, North Carolina	HF model (single-site)	Local pressure to alleviate homelessness	Some resistance from providers	Carolyn Chambre, Urban Ministry Center	Faith community plays key role	Cost-benefit analysis—University of North Carolina–Charlotte

*Consolidated Framework for Implementation Research

the target population (literally or recently homeless persons with serious mental illness and coexisting substance abuse problems) and when sufficiently funded to enact the model faithfully.[3] Moreover, recent findings show positive outcomes of HF calibrated to the degree of fidelity of the implementation (Davidson et al., 2014; Gilmer et al., 2014).

To be sure, there can be rough patches, especially when consumers are still using drugs, drinking heavily, or in a psychiatric crisis. Some have to be evicted and cannot be rehoused, some go to live with relatives, and a small number return to the streets. Tenants might have to be hospitalized for mental or physical problems, jailed for a criminal offense, or sent to treatment for substance abuse. Grappling with slender budgets, local landlords, and building regulations is only part of the challenge. Careful hiring and in-service training are needed to maintain fidelity to HF's values and job performance expectations. With so many moving parts, the model's implementation depends upon large amounts of dedication and willingness to ignore popular beliefs about homeless men and women.

A Candid Take on Implementing Housing First

Only a few individuals have been on the national frontlines of HF implementation and Becky Kanis is one of them. Kanis became a celebrity in the homeless services world after appearing on "60 Minutes," a popular television news show, on February 9, 2014. Speaking for the 100,000 Homes Campaign, Kanis described its approach to assertive outreach and housing. Accompanying the interview were video clips showing the 100K Campaign at work in Nashville, Tennessee, where it met success in housing the city's chronically homeless men and women.

In an interview for this book, Kanis relates how her career in homeless services developed after serving in the military. In 2003, she was hired to start the Street to Home program for Common Ground to address homelessness in the Times Square neighborhood of Manhattan. (This program was described in Chapter 3.) Not long afterward, Kanis heard Sam Tsemberis speak about Housing First at a conference. "It was as if I was hearing the most common sense thing I had ever heard in my entire life," she said.

Looking back, Kanis says that she "drank the Housing First Kool-Aid out of sheer pragmatics and common sense." HF, she said, "has informed my approach to ending street homelessness from the moment I learned about it, from a social justice standpoint, and largely from a practical standpoint. I had done just enough street outreach to realize that trying to sell something that someone isn't buying was a huge waste of time and effort."

Kanis views the 100K Campaign as a grassroots "Trojan horse" to get HF adopted across the country. "Because we framed the conversation in terms of people who are vulnerable to dying on the streets, we were able to leapfrog over the dreadful and boring community debates about housing readiness. Communities had epiphanies similar to the one I had ... they quickly discovered on their own that if they wanted to house the most vulnerable people, 'care as usual' wasn't going to get the job done."

Kanis notes that "the people who were attracted to the 100K Homes Campaign were predisposed to align with HF ... those were 'our people'." Yet these local enthusiasts had to convince skeptical stakeholders, including shelter providers and others accustomed to the status quo. Kanis refers to "laggards and a late majority" as those hindering adoption. Laggards, she says, "ain't never gonna change" and the late majority only responds to "regulation and punishment." "The Federal government," Kanis says, "has done a great job of incentivizing providers to embrace HF," but it should mandate HF up front, throwing in a stick with the carrot.

When asked what advice she would give to others seeking to adopt HF in their communities, Kanis ticked off a list immediately. First, "be willing to do whatever it takes to help someone maintain their housing. I heard Sam ask, 'Do you clean toilets?' I do think it takes a special breed of person to have as their job providing services to help people stay in housing. Find the best people you can, pay them well, and treat them right. Don't nickel and dime them or be stupid about it." Second, "use data to track your outcomes. Don't be satisfied with the 85% retention rate that the peer-reviewed literature suggests is possible with HF. Always be looking for ways to improve the outcomes in terms of housing retention and customer satisfaction. Measure it. Constant improvement. Be transparent."

Third, "Don't make your services model too complicated or too expensive. I'm not saying you should cheap out on it, but I've seen communities over-complicate it and make it too expensive, and as a result of that barely able to help anybody at all." Fourth, "Be pragmatic and open to new learning. Look around and see who is doing HF really well. Go learn from them, then improve so that you do something better than they did." Finally, "Share, be generous. Don't be all snotty about intellectual property. Just share, share, share. Let generosity be the basis of your business model."

Conclusion: Adoptions of and Variations in Housing First

Becky Kanis's experiences on the front lines and her sage (if salty) advice offers some levity to what is all too often a discourse of futility and frustration. The increasing support for HF carried with it seeds of hope that nonetheless required fertile ground to take root. In this chapter, we have seen some of the many variations of HF that emerged as programs across the United States adopted the new model. Many early adopters were advocates-turned-providers who found HF attractive even as they grappled with competing institutional logics and how to reconfigure services. As the pace of dissemination (or the "diffusion of innovation" in Rogers's terminology) increased, so did variability in interpreting the model's tenets. Some programs were attracted to the cost-savings of HF and others found Federal endorsements a sufficient incentive to try something new. The "pull" of innovation was more than matched by the "push" of decades-long failures to stem the tide of homelessness. Whatever their raison d'être, HF programs sprang up around the United States and challenged the institutional logic of the continuum model.

Adoptions of HF were driven by values-consonance, by robust research evidence, or by both. As federal and local governments became invested in HF, funding announcements promoted it more aggressively. HF programs that undertook well-designed research found consistent results in greater housing stability, decreasing use of drugs and alcohol, and cost savings.

Among the easiest to recognize were the direct spin-offs or affiliates of Pathways in New York, faithful to the original model, albeit with some changes necessitated by Vermont's rural setting. One of the most significant modifications in HF was introduced by Seattle's DESC. The program's wide-ranging impact led many to expand the definition of HF to include single- as well as scatter-site housing. The DESC was also the first to show positive results for a population deemed eligible by alcohol abuse rather than psychiatric disability.

More typical was the pragmatic experience of Denver, Boston, and other cities in offering single- and scatter-site HF options depending upon the funding stream being tapped, the type of housing stock available, and the population being served. A minimalist approach could entail grafting HF to an existing program's menu of options—in a sense, adding it as the top step of the staircase.

Aside from differences in housing type were variations in the services offered and associated contingencies. Harm reduction, for example, might be practiced via eased entry requirements and discretionary case management, but many programs steeped in abstinence-only practices (especially faith-based organizations) had difficulty accepting this new regimen. Similarly, Many psychiatrists and mental health workers view medication compliance to be a minimal requirement of program clients who are considered unstable and unable to care for themselves. Staff could be found and trained, but old habits die hard.

Perhaps the most independent of homeless organizations in this new era of HF was Common Ground. Its S2H initiative linked homeless adults to existing services (mostly variants of the continuum) but with an added layer of continuous support to help the individual move along the continuum. The successor to S2H—the 100K Homes Campaign—followed a similar pragmatic approach of using existing providers, this time to help homeless adults at risk of premature mortality.

The 100K Homes Campaign had a high diffusion rate and uptake around the United States and achieved its goals with impressive efficiency and coordination, although its promotion of HF was dependent on what local programs had to offer. For time-limited national campaigns such as 100K, long-term change depends upon sustained coordination repeated across hundreds of localities. In the meantime, few if any national efforts have been as successful in galvanizing homeless advocates and providers.

Passive resistance was and is an expected reaction in light of neo-institutional theory predictions. Casting a skeptical eye on research findings, viewing harm reduction as enabling addiction, believing that congregate living is superior to living alone, or simply standing firm with the status quo—one or all of these could be in play. As we will see in the next chapter, entirely new arenas of acceptance and resistance surfaced when HF spread internationally.

Notes

1. This was Philadelphia's second effort at implementing HF. The city was one of the 11 original USICH chronic homelessness initiative sites but because of problems in the coordination of clinical and housing functions that program did not perform to the satisfaction of the city's administration.

2. The original deadline for achieving the 100K goal was extended to July 2014 and was reached in June.

3. The authors were able to locate some news reports of HF "failures" in some cities but these were not failures of the model but rather of local funding and/or support for the HF program.

8 Housing First Internationally
CANADA, EUROPE, AND AUSTRALIA

WITH A GROWING track record of effectiveness, Housing First (HF) attracted attention in countries experiencing their own "epidemics" of homelessness, beginning with Canada and soon after extending to Western Europe and Australia. The visibility and persistence of poverty, especially among those with psychiatric disabilities, became a vexing public health and political issue, particularly in nations with generous social welfare policies and robust social service systems (Shinn, 2010). Although the occasional beggar on the streets was not unfamiliar in European countries, the sight of so many people sleeping rough in public spaces was a rude awakening. If a person could drop through the sturdy safety nets of Sweden or Denmark, a problem was at hand. As homelessness increased and existing systems failed to engage those with complex needs, more countries began to introduce HF programs into their array of homeless services.

It would be an understatement to point out that adoption of HF internationally was not a simple matter of political will combined with procuring funding and affordable housing. Invoking our framework of neo-institutional theory (DiMaggio & Powell, 1983), the institutional pillars (regulative, normative, cultural–cognitive) that supported varying international approaches to homelessness differed from those in the United States. Foremost in the host environments that greeted HF are sociopolitical philosophies that diverge from the private sector limited-government ethos of the United States (with the United States at one end of the spectrum, Northern Europe at the opposite end, and Canada, Australia, and other countries in Europe falling somewhere in the middle).

To complicate matters further, economic conditions could favor or inhibit adoption of HF in unpredictable ways. The degree of fit between HF tenets and local or national values and culture was always in play. These values pertained to the right to housing, government's responsibility for its citizens, prioritizing access to housing based upon vulnerability or other criteria, consumer choice in psychiatric treatment, and harm reduction approaches to substance use. Overall, the spread of HF to other nations involved its incorporation into more benefi-cent welfare systems whose openness to such a change—particularly one coming from America—was far from certain (Benjaminsen, Dyb, & O'Sullivan, 2009). In some places, local practices changed in order to accommodate HF's core prin-ciples, and in others HF itself was changed.

In this chapter, we address the ways that HF was introduced in the interna-tional arena, the reactions it prompted, and the status of the model internation-ally. Rather than simply noting broad international differences, we reintroduce the Consolidated Framework for Implementation Research (CFIR) from the pre-vious chapter in order to describe in greater detail the implementation of HF in Canada, Australia, and Western Europe. In the next section we describe some of the bridging actions that took place under Pathways to Housing's aegis, which assisted in international adoption.

The Housing First Partners Conferences and the Pathways National Office

Two events took place in 2012 that had direct implications for the adoption of HF beyond the United States. First, Pathways National was incorporated in New York City as a separate entity devoted to dissemination of HF through technical assis-tance, training, and partnering with local entities—communities, governments, and programs. Headed by Pathways's founder Sam Tsemberis, Pathways National (which might better be called "Pathways International") assisted in Canada's roll out of the Homeless Partnering Strategy in cities across the country, in the U.S. Veterans Administration HUD-VASH program for homeless veterans, and in sev-eral initiatives in Western Europe (to be described later in this chapter).

Second was the first-ever Housing First Partners Conference (HFPC) that took place in New Orleans in March 2012. The HFPC was a watershed event, attracting over 1,000 housing, health, and mental health providers—most from the United States but with a sizeable minority from other countries well on their way to adopting HF. Also in attendance were "federal, state and local government officials, researchers, advocates, trainers, peers, and thought leaders engaged in ending homelessness through Housing First" (http://www.hfpartnersconference.com/about). The conference's co-leaders—Seattle's Downtown Emergency Service Center (DESC) and Pathways to Housing (PHF)—viewed the meeting as a forum for attendees to share experiences and learn from one another.

At times resembling a family reunion, attendees applauded speakers at plenary sessions then broke up into smaller sessions where research findings were presented and providers and consumers shared experiences. The HPFC in New Orleans was remarkable in another respect: It featured two distinct versions of HF as co-equal partners, one the "traditional" PHF scatter-site approach and the other the single-site approach pioneered by DESC. Seeing Bill Hobson and Sam Tsemberis share the stage and the limelight was a visible reminder that HF had taken on new iterations.

The second HFPC (March 2014 in Chicago) was a larger more international gathering that continued the tradition of uniting researchers, policymakers, providers, and consumers under the HF umbrella. In addition to PTH and DESC, sponsors included the Bill & Melinda Gates Foundation, the Conrad N. Hilton Foundation, the Melville Charitable Trust and the U.S. Department of Housing and Urban Development (HUD). In addition to HF attendees from around the United States, presenters came from Australia, France, Portugal, Germany, the United Kingdom, and Canada among other countries. The friendly vibe was enhanced by the egalitarian nature of the event—psychiatrists, psychologists, social workers, and consumers rubbed elbows with high-level Federal government representatives and foundation directors (see http://www.hfpartnersconference.com/ for more information). Concurrent meetings of FEANTSA (European Federation of National Organizations Working with the Homeless) were being held in Western Europe, with a strong focus on HF implementation (more on this later in this chapter).

Income Disparities, Housing, and Social Services: International Contexts of Housing First Implementation

A nation's economic well-being affects many aspects of the lives of its citizens, including the homeless. Nations differ widely in their standards of living and there are significant differences in the costs of food, housing, and social services.

Thus, poverty is experienced differently from one country to another. One measure of a nation's standard of living is the Gini coefficient, a frequently used index of income inequality, specifically the disparity between the wealthiest and the poor. A World Bank ranking of Gini scores shows the Scandinavian countries have the smallest income disparities (around .25) with Canada, Australia, and the rest of Europe ranging between .30 and .33. In the United States, income disparity has been on the increase since the 1980s hovering around .49; putting it on a par with Mexico, Rwanda, and China, just under Brazil (.55) and below South Africa (.63), which has one of the highest Gini scores (http://data.worldbank.org/indicator/SI.POV.GINI)

Of interest here is the relationship between a nation's Gini score and its investment in social services (Toro, Tompsett, Lombardo ... & Harvey, 2007). In countries with higher income disparities, there are typically fewer social safety-net services and more people living in poverty and in need of those services. Another area where nations differ is the availability and accessibility of benefits and entitlements for those who are poor, or disabled, or both. For example, in Canada and Northern Europe disability benefits include a rent or "shelter" allowance, anticipating that beneficiaries will need additional support in order to secure housing. Such benefits are not available uniformly throughout Europe, especially in Southern European countries where developing or providing public housing is rare as is financial assistance for the poor.

In countries with substantial public housing stock, units are typically available pending long waiting times, thus essentially placing them beyond the reach of the homeless. One of the changes wrought by HF in some localities occurred when public housing authorities allowed access to the homeless, bypassing the wait list. These authorities came to realize that people who are homeless are at a disadvantage because they could not be reached when their turn arrived, even if on a waiting list.

Most HF programs abroad have budgets that include rent stipends or rent supplements so that program participants can add to their shelter allowance and compete for units on the private rental market. In France, Portugal, Ireland, and other countries, HF programs work with private landlords as well as public housing authorities to rent units on the open market. Using private market rentals has the advantage of bypassing public housing waiting lists and offering immediate access.

In Canada and Australia, as in the United States, the rental housing market is not tightly regulated and HF programs can compete on a first come, first served basis with other renters (albeit in lower-income neighborhoods). Not all rental housing is on the private for-profit market. Much of this housing in the

Netherlands and Scandinavia is owned and operated by not-for-profit corporations whose mission is to provide quality affordable housing. These corporations operate somewhat like public housing authorities, including the use of wait lists to ensure fair access to units as they become available.

This extended discussion of the types of affordable housing is necessary to understand the environment that greeted HF in Canada and Europe. In the United States, the only feasible housing options were on the private market, and a relatively volatile and broad-based rental market made the procurement of apartment leases difficult but not impossible. Outside the United States, HF programs had to learn to navigate the local public and private housing systems to provide immediate (or close to immediate) access for program participants. Although objections were raised that local occupancy rates were high and HF could not compete, this proved to be an objection overruled. In every city where HF programs were implemented, a sufficient number of units were made available; the number of eligible individuals in most cities rarely exceeded a few hundred (sometimes a few dozen). Of course, programs did need to be proactive in negotiating access and could not assume success.

In addition to the housing situation in other countries, differing mental health and healthcare systems influenced the implementation of HF. Social welfare services in Europe and Canada are typically set apart from health and mental health treatment. Case management is usually under contract from the government to nonprofit organizations while clinical services reflect a philosophy consonant with the more conservative, hierarchical tradition of biomedicine. Though poorly coordinated and underfunded, the conjoining of social welfare programs in U.S. homeless services (SSI, supported housing, Medicaid) eroded some of these distinctions between clinical services and case management and provided some flexibility.

While Assertive Community Treatment (ACT) teams and Intensive Case Management (ICM) have been an integral part of mental health services in the United States, this is not the case for a number of countries where such care—more affordable and accessible than in the United States—is nonetheless clinic-based. Adding to the operational challenges is the fact that the philosophical and practice orientations of HF teams call for consumer-driven and recovery-oriented services, whereas clinic services are typically based on the traditional medical model with clinician as expert. A high fidelity HF program implementation would require not only a change in practice involving leaving the office, but new ways of seeing consumers as capable and having decisional authority. Thus, what starts out as a "simple" adoption of HF can become an impetus for transformation in the wider housing and mental health systems.

Canada: Early Housing-First Initiatives

Canada's homelessness problem dates to the 1990s, due in part to the Canadian Federal government's policy that affordable housing should be a provincial responsibility. The provinces did not meet this challenge and it was not long before the number of Canadians who were homeless was on the rise. As with homeless populations in other nations, individuals with complex needs were represented in disproportionately high numbers and could be found among the repeat users in shelters, emergency rooms, jail cells, detox centers, and soup kitchens.

The lack of affordable housing became more problematic a few years later when the Canadian economy took a turn for the worse, especially in the Atlantic Provinces where the fishing industry was decimated. Many Canadians left home to find jobs in the oil sands fields of Alberta and this drove up the price of rental units locally. Those who could not find work frequently joined the local homeless population in cities like Calgary, Saskatoon, and Edmonton. Meanwhile, Canada's largest city of Toronto was experiencing growing immigration and its own homelessness epidemic—an increase of 400% in the numbers of homeless since 1980 (Falvo, 2009).

Toronto's Streets to Homes Project

A notable exception to the continuum or mainstream model in Canada was a program in Toronto called "Streets to Homes" (S2H). By 2003, concerns about homelessness on Toronto's city council had reached a peak with widespread media coverage and public outcry over police sweeps and evictions of encampments. Among other places attracting rough sleepers, the Bathurst Street Bridge had several dozen sleeping underneath it and 100 persons were camping on the square in front of City Hall.

Beginning in 2005, the S2H mission was to assist *all* homeless people in finding a place to live, people with complex needs among them. The program's name, the same as the title of the first publication of the Pathways program (Tsemberis, 1999)[1], indicated its commitment to immediate access to housing without first requiring treatment or abstinence. However, S2H in some ways more closely resembled the U.K.'s Rough Sleepers Initiative and New York's "Street to Home" program in its emphasis on helping people get off the streets without diagnostic or other criteria for service eligibility. Outreach workers had long since learned that to promise access to an apartment was a useful tactic for engaging homeless persons—but S2H backed up this promise. An estimated 600 persons per year were housed in the first three years of operation (Falvo, 2009).

A one-year postoccupancy survey of S2H clients found that 90% of those contacted were still housed, a remarkable outcome (Falvo, 2009). However, there were a few problems in the implementation. First, there was high turnover and rehousing of tenants due to instability in the rental agreements and living conditions. Related to this, only 61% of S2H tenants lived in their own apartment, the remaining 39% had to share accommodations. According to a city report:

> Those in shared accommodation are less likely to feel secure about their housing, are far more likely to move and need more help from their follow-up workers to relocate. People in shared accommodation frequently reported issues with roommates/housemates that made it difficult to keep their housing. Most quality of life indicators also showed less improvement for people in shared accommodation. (City of Toronto, 2007, p. 2)

Other shortcomings included S2H's inability to enforce a strict affordability requirement (clients paying no more than 30% of income toward the rent) and to integrate services (clients were frequently referred to existing mental health services ill-equipped to make the house calls needed to support them in their housing) (Falvo, 2009). Nevertheless, S2H was first to introduce the idea in Canada that people who are on the streets do not have to comply with continuum requirements in order to succeed in housing.

Pathways Housing First in Canada: Calgary's The Alex Health Center

The first high-fidelity HF program in Canada was introduced in 2007 by the Calgary Homeless Foundation led by Tim Richter. The Homeless Foundation, which was formed a year earlier as the philanthropic arm of Alberta's wealthy oil industry, organized the city's homeless service providers, who identified 54 individuals who were "frequent fliers" at the city's emergency rooms during the previous year. With technical assistance from Pathways New York staff, the Foundation provided the funding for an ACT team and rent supplements. The Alex Health Center, a community health clinic with a long history of services for people who are homeless, was selected as the program provider that would outreach, engage, house, and support them. The ACT team, which included a family practice physician, was trained by Pathways staff.

The Alex website reports that the program resulted in a 66% decline in hospital days, a 38% decline in times seen in emergency rooms, a 41% decline in emergency calls or visits, and a 79% decline in jail days (http://www.thealex.ca/). As of

2013, the program had expanded to include a case management component and was serving 150 individuals in scatter-site apartments (http://www.thealex.ca/programs-services/housing/pathways-to-housing/).

These results provided the impetus to create a province-wide coalition of organizations called "Alberta's 7 Cities on Housing and Homelessness" responsible for the implementation of local Plans to End Homelessness (Cameron & Makhoul, 2009). Calgary's experience exemplifies the power of philanthropic leadership arising from local wealth (Pearson, 2014). It also demonstrates the usefulness of starting with a local demonstration project, evaluating the results, and using that to push for system-wide adoption of the model.

Canada's National Implementation of Housing First: The At Home/Chez Soi (AH/CS) Project

Canada's national commitment to implementing HF—unprecedented in its cost, scope, and ambition—had its beginnings in the 2008 Winter Olympics held in Vancouver. Senator Michael Kirby succeeded in persuading the federal government to take this opportunity to address visible homelessness in Vancouver and throughout the country. The Canadian Parliament responded by allocating $110 million for a national research demonstration project in five cities: Vancouver, Winnipeg, Toronto, Montreal, and Moncton. The rationale for HF in Canada was fairly simple: It focused on the right population, it was evidence-based, and it was cost-effective. With an estimated $7 billion per year in health, justice system, and social services costs, homelessness took a financial toll on the Canadian budget, with no end in sight. Mounting a national trial, though expensive, was deemed a worthwhile next step given that previous models had demonstratively failed in stemming the tide of homelessness in Canada's cities.

Previous work by Canadian researchers already had begun to contribute to a growing awareness of the benefits of HF. Nelson and colleagues examined choice and control in supported housing as compared with group living in an Ontario housing initiative and found more positive outcomes for the HF group, including quality of life and community integration (Nelson, Sylvestre, Aubry, George, & Trainor, 2006). Qualitative narrative findings reported gains beyond numbers of hospital days or days spent homeless (Nelson, Clarke, Febbraro, & Hatzipantelis, 2005).

The funding for "At Home/Chez Soi" (AH/CS) was awarded to the Mental Health Commission of Canada (MHCC). MHCC's Jayne Barker coordinated the project and Paula Goering, a University of Toronto senior researcher, was selected to oversee the implementation and the research needed to evaluate this complex nationwide effort. Goering and Barker approached the Pathways HF program in New York City and worked with Tsemberis and Pathways staff to provide training and ensure fidelity to PHF across all five cities.

When AH/CS began in 2008, HF was still a rarity in Canada, with the majority of homeless programs relying on outreach, shelters, emergency housing, and transitional housing. The MHCC contended that HF was an evidence-based intervention targeted to this population, adding that it was worth testing HF in Canada given the differences in social policies, healthcare delivery, and target populations compared with the United States (Keller et al., 2013).

The implementation of the HF programs in the AH/CS project was both high fidelity and adapted to the local context. Data collection, which began in 2009 and ended in 2013, involved 2,148 clients across the five sites (1,158 in the PHF group), all recruited from shelters or the streets. Structured interviews were administered every three months for two years of follow-up to assess housing stability, service use and costs, quality of life, and social functioning. Predominantly male (68%), the study participants included aboriginal people (22%, most in Winnipeg) and members of non-White ethnic groups (25%, most in Toronto) (Goering et al., 2011).

Site-specific enhancements included a congregate version of HF in Vancouver, a revamped hotel where residents shared meals and on-site services (see Box 8.1).[2] In Winnipeg, a Medicine Wheel approach to service delivery and use of tribal elders in support services fit the First Nations composition of the study sample. Montreal included an Independent Placement and Support (IPS) employment program, Toronto's multiethnic study population prompted the development of Anti-racism/Anti-oppression principles, and the Moncton site included a rural service delivery option.

Randomization assigned participants to one of three arms of the intervention across the five cities. Two were HF, differentiated by whether participants received Assertive Community Treatment (ACT) or Intensive Case Management (ICM). The third arm, Treatment as Usual (TAU), consisted of local service system offerings. Findings at 12 months of follow-up showed that HF participants spent 73% of their time in stable housing compared with 30% of the TAU group (Goering et al., 2014).

Central to the study's mixed method design was the incorporation of in-depth narrative interviews (Macnaughton, Goering, & Nelson, 2012). Narrative interviews were conducted with an approximate 10% subsample of 225 participants from December 2009 to July 2011 (Piat et al., 2012). The study also conducted assessments of program fidelity to document the quality of each program. An

BOX 8.1

VANCOUVER'S DOWNTOWN EAST SIDE: CONGREGATE
HOUSING FIRST AND HARM REDUCTION

Vancouver's Downtown East Side (DES) neighborhood achieved notoriety for its public drug use, drinking, and prostitution, along with its communalist values. The city's unique contribution to At Home/Chez Soi (AH/CS) was a congregate-site version of Housing First (HF) located at the Bosman Hotel in the DES. Along with a focus on substance users, the Bosman HF site fostered community-building through an art gallery and studio, rooftop gardening, and street soccer games. Well before the AH/CS project, local authorities had implemented harm reduction programs of needle exchange and injection sites for IV drug users. The AH/CS project included access to methadone and nasal Naloxone (to prevent death from overdose) as well as managed alcohol use (voluntary self-monitoring) and medical services.

The Vancouver site also had a scatter-site version of HF along with the Treatment as Usual (TAU) arm. Two results stand out from the AH/CS experience there. First, 67% of the study sample reported involvement with the justice system prior to recruitment (the most frequently reported crimes were property offenses). At the 12-month follow up, the scatter-site HF group had a significantly lower number of arrests compared with the other two comparison groups. Second, study participants in the scatter-site HF group chose, perhaps not surprisingly, to live away from the DES, yet this did not create a problem. Previous efforts to move DES residents elsewhere had met with stiff NIMBY ("not in my backyard") opposition from Vancouver neighborhoods like Yaletown and Abbotsford, the latter organized by local business owners who feared a congregate-living building would scare away customers. According to Dr. Julian Somers of Simon Fraser University, acceptance by other tenants and landlords in these new locations was a "hugely powerful part" of the success shown by this group (Culbert, 2014).

unusually well-funded project by any standard, AH/CS was designed to help identify what works, at what cost, for whom, and in which environments.

Housing First as Canada's National Policy: Cost and Other Considerations

The results of the AH/CS study provided a rare example of a national government using research to directly influence its decisions. In 2013, Canada's Federal government announced that HF was the national policy for ending chronic homelessness. The government also put its money where its policy is, requiring that the bulk of the $600 million in federal funding go to HF programs over the next five years. Its *Homelessness Partnering Strategy* (HPS) was (and is) to be used to implement HF programs in all 62 jurisdictions throughout the nation that receive such funding. These include Canada's 10 largest cities and other localities ranging from suburbs to rural towns to remote villages.

Because there are no additional funds allocated by the HPS, communities will have to make important choices about what services will be eliminated or transformed into HF programs. Cost savings calculations from AH/CH will likely influence such decision-making, just as they did in the United States. Yet such calculations are more complicated than is usually acknowledged in political and advocacy discussions. For example, when looking at the subset of individuals in the AH/CS who were high service users, every $10 invested in HF resulted in an average savings of over $21 from other health, social, and criminal justice service use (excluding medications). But because AH/CH also targeted individuals who were not service users, the cost offset overall was $10 invested in HF resulting in just under $7 in savings.

Here is where the broader context comes in. Robust cost savings in the United States are in part a reflection of the high costs of health care and the lack of primary care (creating a reliance on the most expensive of all forms of health care—emergency departments in hospitals and hospital stays). Then there is the cost of jail stays in the United States. By way of example, Merrimack County in New Hampshire had a budget of $81.6 million in 2014, $14.5 million of which was devoted to its corrections department. In an editorial, the *Concord Monitor* suggested taking a small amount of the corrections budget ($100,000, or .007%) to pay for HF and save costs. (http://www.concordmonitor.com/home/15032332-95/editorial-county-must-step-to-help-the-homeless)

Canada's incarceration rates are much lower and the country has a very different public healthcare system. Intrigued by their findings regarding costs, researchers in the AH/CS project took advantage of the large sample size and bifurcated the HF sample into high and low users of services. Looking at the high user group, they found the same cost-saving differences as found in the U.S. studies. The portion of the sample that was using few services before entering the program—but still meeting study criteria and thus having needs—showed a slight increase in healthcare costs.

A narrow focus on cost savings neglects the larger concern of human costs beyond dollars and cents. In countries with more generous health and social care systems, cost savings are likely to be less because the level of unmet need is lower (and access to care more affordable). Healthcare costs in the United States tend to be so high (consider Gladwell's Million Dollar Murray from Chapter 4) that any targeted intervention is likely to help bring them down. That HF reduces healthcare costs for high utilizers is a bonus, but it is not the raison d'être of HF.

The decision to implement HF strictly from a cost savings standpoint would likely mean focusing on those with the highest needs and service use. For communities seeking to help the homeless overall, the effectiveness of the approach in other outcomes (e.g., more people stably housed or in better health) could be seen as justifying any additional costs. These are ethical as well as financial decisions.

Meanwhile, there will be much to learn from Canada's AH/CS experience as the nation strives to move from "serving the homeless" to "ending homelessness." Almost from the beginning of AH/CS, Canada's experience with HF was getting well-deserved national and international attention, with European nations watching to see whether HF could work outside the United States.

Defining Homelessness in the European Context

The formation of the European Union (EU) in 1993 opened up enormous possibilities for individual mobility and economic growth among member nations. One consequence of this was greater cross-national migration, with immigrants from poorer member nations seeking employment in the more affluent ones. Simultaneously, many European nations were welcoming asylum seekers and refugees from politically turbulent and war-torn nations in the Middle East and Africa. The traditional model of social housing was stretched beyond its limits as unemployed and distressed immigrants joined the ranks of the local homeless population (Benjaminsen, Dyb, & O'Sullivan, 2009).

The ways in which the EU defined homelessness provide a window into the strength of the social safety net where it was available. The 2005 definition—the European Typology of Homelessness and Housing Exclusion (ETHOS)—was promulgated as a means of standardizing prevalence counts as well as policies related to service provision. Here are its definitional components:

- People without a roof over their heads who sleep rough or in overnight shelters;
- People without a home who, while they have a roof over their heads, are excluded from the legal rights of occupancy and do not have a place to pursue normal social relations (such as those living in hostels or temporary accommodation for the homeless, women living in refuge accommodation, migrants living in specific accommodation, and people living in institutions);
- People living in insecure housing, who do not have a secure tenancy and/ or are threatened with eviction or are a victim of domestic violence;

- People living in inadequate housing conditions (such as with friends or relatives, in squats, in caravans or illegal campsites, in conditions of extreme overcrowding, and in other generally unsuitable places).

The last three of the above are the criteria of a much more tolerant and accommodating approach to homelessness. Perhaps not surprisingly, EU member states did not agree on ETHOS and reliable counts within and across nations were hard to come by (Fondeville & Ward, 2011). In Scandinavian countries, not having a lease or living in transitional housing was considered a form of homelessness. In most other European countries, this was not acceptable as a definition. Despite such differences, there was a unity of purpose within the EU that something needed to be done.

Housing First in Europe

AMSTERDAM, NETHERLANDS. In 2003, a nurse from Amsterdam named Rokus Loopik contacted Pathways to Housing in New York City and requested assistance in obtaining a work visa to volunteer on one of Pathways's teams. In one of many instances of "seeing is believing," Loopik joined the Pathways Brooklyn ACT team for six months and returned to Amsterdam to advocate for the HF model. It took a few years to implement a HF program and the cooperation of a director of a large social housing program was needed.

What was probably the first HF program in Europe began operation in 2006 as Discus Housing First. Discus was operated by a nongovernmental organization (NGO) that cooperates closely with municipal health services and local housing associations. Funding was provided by national health insurance. The aim of the program was to house homeless people with complex and multiple problems including mental illness and addictions.

Here is how the program works: The target group, people living on the streets, are referred to Discus by professionals under supervision of the municipal health service of Amsterdam. They are provided with housing on condition that they cooperate with money management (i.e., to avoid rent arrears and to settle existing debts). Program participants pay a contribution to the program (about 30% of their benefits) and are responsible for rent payments for which they may receive rental allowances from the state.

From a treatment philosophy perspective, Amsterdam's HF program is highly compatible with the Netherlands' strengths-based case management and harm-reduction approaches, which are delivered through community-based services. Support is available on a 24/7 basis and housing is provided by a social housing provider that prioritizes Discus clients and offers individual apartments scattered throughout the social housing program. The apartments are rented by the agency and sublet on the basis of a combined "rent-and-care contract" to the service user. After a period, the tenant may have the opportunity to acquire a direct contract with the housing association.

The program has seen a slow and steady expansion in the Netherlands through working with housing associations (Wewerinke, Wolf, Maas, & Al Shamma, 2012). At the beginning of 2014, there were 18 HF programs in the Netherlands. This is a rather steep and accelerated growth curve given that the second program only started in 2009 (Wewerinke & Wolf, 2014).

LISBON, PORTUGAL. The HF project in Lisbon (*Casas Primeiro*) is a high-fidelity HF program developed in 2009 by Jose Ornelas, Director of the nonprofit organization known as AEIPS (Associação para o Estudo e Integração Psicossocial) and his associate Theresa Duarte. Staff from Pathways in New York provided technical assistance.

Ornelas, a tireless advocate for people with disabilities in Lisbon, secured a grant from the Portuguese government for housing and case management support. *Casas Primeiro* replicated much of the original Pathways approach, that is, it rented apartments from the private sector, took 30% of client income to help pay the rent, and offered an array of support services. Linked to the larger EU project targeting homelessness (described later in this chapter), *Casas Primierio* housed 50 persons and began evaluating outcomes right away using quantitative surveys and qualitative interviews. The results of the evaluation were quite favorable: 80% remained housed with an 87% decrease in emergency room visits and 90% decrease in psychiatric admissions. Other outcomes—perceived choice, life satisfaction, improved social relationships—were also positive. Costs per day were less than a shelter bed, a hostel night, or a hospital stay (Ornelas, 2013).

For the first two years, *Casas Primeiro* was funded by Portugal's Social Security Institute (see Box 8.2). In 2012, this support was dramatically reduced (by about 45% compared to the previous year) but new sources of funding were found, including the City of Lisbon and local foundations. Following these cuts, and in order to secure the sustainability of the project, rent subsidies from the project budget were reduced (with lower rents negotiated with landlords and higher subsidies procured from elsewhere). The number of service users had to be decreased (from 60 to 50) and staff numbers had to be reduced from six to four. Referrals

BOX 8.2

CASAS PRIMIERIO: PARTICIPATORY ACTION AND RESEARCH IN LISBON

Jose Ornelas, a community psychologist, can be credited with bringing Housing First (HF) to Portugal with his own quasi-religious fervor. As related in an interview for this book, Ornelas learned about HF from his psychologist colleague Mary Beth Shinn while both were attending the annual meeting of the American Psychological Association. Intrigued, he invited Shinn to give a seminar in Lisbon and share early findings from the New York Housing Study (NYHS), where she had served as a co-investigator.

Portugal had gone through its own struggles with community-based care after deinstitutionalization of psychiatric hospitals, and Ornelas dedicated himself to working with the growing numbers of homeless mentally ill adults on the streets of Lisbon. A major opportunity arose when the national government began searching for alternatives to shelters. Ornelas engineered a visit by Shinn and Tsemberis to Lisbon and also visited New York in January 2009 to see Pathways to Housing for himself.

Ornelas is especially proud of the participatory action research approach at *Casas Primiero*. Stepping away from traditional support services such as ACT or ICM, Ornelas helped forge what he calls the "ecological/collaborative" modality to involve clients and staff in joint decision-making. As HF spread to other parts of Portugal after 2012, Ornelas helped form a network of HF professionals in several cities with the ambitious goal of housing 1,000 of the estimated 3,000 homeless persons in the country.

In his interactions with Portuguese and EU colleagues discussing their own implementations of HF, Ornelas has been steadfast in promoting the scatter-site aspect of HF (at a FEANTSA meeting he was accused of being a scatter-site "fundamentalist"—a loaded term in European political circles). Advocating for scatter-site living is not necessarily a winning argument, because some European HF proponents express great affinity for congregate living as being consonant with European values. (The European Union announced 2010 as the "Year of Combating Poverty and Social Exclusion.")

At times, Ornelas sounds more like an evangelist than a scientist. "Follow the principles," he advises. Research evidence is important but one must also "be converted" to believe in HF. (Ornelas is optimistic that Pope Francis's generosity of spirit will eventually extend to housing the homeless using HF.) Ornelas's missionary zeal has led him to cities in Norway and Italy, where he advises HF programs just starting up. Though having little opposition at home, his experiences with FEANTSA have prepared him for the usual objections, such as, "We don't have enough apartments available." Before arriving at his host European city, Ornelas checks local newspapers online for apartment vacancies and calls local rental agencies. Armed with this ammunition, he counters questions almost before they can be asked.

to the project came from the city's outreach teams and other organizations or through recommendations from program participants (Ornelas, 2013).

There was a silver lining to this cloud of reduced funding, a twist of fate that favored scatter-site housing. Ornelas's insistence on this tenet of PHF was bolstered by the economic crises that plagued countries in Southern Europe after the 2008 worldwide economic recession. As rents dropped, private apartments become more available. Having fewer social housing units to begin with, HF programs in Portugal had few difficulties renting in the private sector.

GLASGOW, SCOTLAND. By 2008, Glasgow—a gritty but friendly city with its share of poverty—had witnessed several drug overdose deaths on the streets, which raised public alarm. In response, the Scottish Government set up a Working Group to examine the relationship between substance abuse and homelessness (see Box 8.3). The group asked Nicholas Pleace, a professor at York University, to provide a report. His subsequent analysis gave positive mention to Housing First as initiated by Pathways to Housing.[3]

BOX 8.3
TURNING POINT'S IAN IRVINE IN GLASGOW, SCOTLAND

Much of the credit for adoption of Housing First (HF) in Glasgow, Scotland goes to Ian Irvine, the Director of Turning Point Scotland, who provided information for this book in an interview. During a holiday trip to New York in 2008, Irvine took the opportunity to visit Pathways and became convinced of the soundness of the HF approach, as well as of the importance of peer support workers. Upon his return, Irvine helped set up an interagency focus group to explore a HF program in Glasgow. With funding primarily from Turning Point Scotland reserves, Irvine and his colleagues began a HF pilot project with 10 units provided by two social housing associations. They also employed a part-time occupational health worker. The project was evaluated by professor Sarah Johnsen from Heriot Watt University in Edinburgh—the final report can be found at: https://pureapps2. hw.ac.uk/portal/files/5945730/TPS_Housing_First_Final_Report.pdf

HF Glasgow subsequently won positive recognition from the Glasgow City Council, whose staff assessments mirrored the positive findings from the Heriot Watt University evaluation report. Initial skepticism gave way to growing awareness of how many others had been written off as failures, consigned to programs where they failed yet again. As word spread of Glasgow's HF experience, Turning Point attracted visitors from Belfast, Ireland and other cities in the United Kingdom. In June 2014, Glasgow Housing First was awarded the Scotland Social Services Council Care Accolade for Adults and Older People.

As a result, consensus was growing among Scottish social welfare officials that:

- Homeless people with complex needs are unable to meet the demands of a "linear" approach, resulting in a high attrition rate and a repeating cycle of homelessness;
- Temporary accommodation can have a damaging influence on vulnerable people and can itself increase substance abuse—this was evident in individual accounts as well as academic research;
- Academic reports and individual experiences endorse the positive role of peer support workers.

Key features of HF in Glasgow followed the tenets originally promulgated by Pathways to Housing with alterations to fit local needs (serving primarily homeless drug users). According to Ian Irvine, the Director of Turning Point Glasgow where HF was first tested, these tenets are:

- Housing comes first. Registered social landlords are sought out to place clients in safe and secure permanent tenancies from the outset.
- An holistic package of support is built around each individual to develop his/her tenancy management skills.
- A harm reduction approach encourages recovery from substance abuse and mental ill-health.
- The staff includes peer support workers, each having experience of homelessness and/or substance misuse.
- HF Glasgow contributes to the international evidence base alongside other European nations developing their own HF services.

Implementers of HF at Turning Point first had to confront a fear of failure and a very real legal concern. Glasgow's HF tenants—young predominantly male drug users—were among the most difficult to place in previous outreach efforts. Could HF make a difference? There was also genuine concern about harm reduction under current law. Great Britain has a national Misuse of Drugs Act dating to 1971 and Section 8 of the Act states that landlords and housing agency staff are committing a criminal offense if they knowingly allow individuals to use drugs in their tenancy. At least one agency in England had previously been charged with breaking this law and alarm bells immediately rang when HF was first put forward in Glasgow.

Creative but thoughtful planning helped to ameliorate the situation. Turning Point staff reached out to a senior police officer working with the Scottish government and another senior officer from the Glasgow police force. Through negotiations, Turning Point was able to develop a protocol such that the police excluded HF services from enforcement. Soon thereafter the police became openly supportive of HF, and the protocol allowed a number of Glasgow's Housing Associations to offer accommodation. As noted by Irvine,

"We felt the best way of responding was to quietly develop the pilot and provide that the level and nature of responses agreed with the individual service users. We also accommodated a wide range of visits to Glasgow Housing First from other cities in the U.K. and other European countries. We often include a visit and engagement with a tenant as a key part of learning about Housing First. We believe that the message and feelings they get from their visit were positive and encouraged them to pilot HF services."

FRANCE AND *UN CHEZ-SOI D'ABORD.* France pursued its own HF adoption in the form of a two-year randomized trial beginning in 2011—the only large-scale randomized clinical trial (RCT) among the many European evaluations of HF. HF–France began in four cities: Toulouse, Marseille, Lille, and Paris. Known as *Un chez-soi d'abord* ("A Home First"), the trial used both quantitative and qualitative methods to evaluate outcomes including cost savings and service use (Tinland et al., 2013). The research team and clinical directors of the project worked closely with the Canadian At Home/Chez Soi project, sharing research protocols, technical advice, and other supports. Staff from Pathways also provided training and technical assistance.

Under the leadership of Vincent Girard, Pascale Estecahandy, and Christian Laval, *Un Chez-Soi d'abord* began in June 2011 and housed its first client two months later, growing to 700 enrolled in the trial by 2014. Closely following the PHF model, the project used scatter-site independent apartments and ACT teams for support. Funding for rent was provided by the national housing ministry with services paid for by the social welfare ministry.

In presentations given at the 2014 Housing First Partners Conference in Chicago, Girard and colleagues cited the familiar litany of local concerns they encountered—fears of being evaluated, ethical concerns with randomization, suspicion of the government, and the "we're already doing it" rebuttal (Rhenter & Girard, 2014). They also found programs eager to be part of the experiment, not to mention eager for the additional funds coming their way as participants.

Interestingly, they took a distinctly subversive view of HF's potential, a sort of Trojan Horse that would shake up the establishment by introducing consumer choice. Decrying the "psychiatrization" of homelessness in a talk titled "Marx and not Freud," Pauline Rhenter and Vincent Girard cast HF as a driver of change, consonant with the values of social activism (2014). On balance, in France as in other countries, the continuum approach is far from obsolete despite government pronouncements favoring a "clean break" with the past (Houard, 2011, p. 83).

Early adoption in Amsterdam and Lisbon, along with the growing evidence base in the United States and Canada, helped representatives from EU member countries advocate for and implement HF programs. In August 2011, the European Commission-funded Housing First Europe (HFE) began. A 24-month demonstration project, HFE was contracted to the Danish National Board of Social Services with research and evaluation directed by Volker Busch-Geertsema, a senior research fellow in Bremen, Germany. Busch-Geertsema was also the coordinator of the European Observatory on Homelessness, a research organization under FEANTSA (European Federation of National Organizations Working with the Homeless). FEANTSA is an NGO established in 1989 to "prevent and alleviate the poverty and social exclusion of people threatened by or living in homelessness" (http://www.feantsa.org/).

In the belief that "swimming can be learned better in the water than anywhere else" (Busch-Geertsema, 2013, p. 9), HFE had five test sites (Amsterdam, Budapest, Copenhagen, Glasgow, and Lisbon) and five peer sites (Dublin, Ghent, Gothenburg, Helsinki, and Vienna). Test sites followed a strict definition of HF as developed by Pathways in consultation with Pathways founder Tsemberis. Essential elements meant that the test sites:

- Offered self-contained living units (e.g., not hostel accommodation);
- Ensured that tenants would have some form of secure tenure;
- Targeted persons with mental illness/drug/alcohol problems or other complex support needs (i.e., who could not access housing without support);
- Provided proactive support, with housing not conditional on acceptance of this support;
- Did not require previous stays in transitional accommodation or any other type of preparation for independent living (source: www.housing-firsteurope.eu).

One of the test sites (Copenhagen) added a single-site congregate version of HF. The peer sites implemented some but not all of the elements of HF. All of the sites were considered part of a mutual learning network of participants—providers, NGOs, government officials, and academic researchers. In addition to Busch-Geertsema, the latter included European experts in homelessness, such as Suzanne Fitzpatrick and Sarah Johnsen (Edinburgh and Glasgow), Judith Wolf and Lars Benjaminsen (Copenhagen), Elizabeth Gosme (Brussels), Paula Mayock and Eoin O'Sullivan (Dublin), Anna Balogi and Boroka Feher (Budapest), and Jose Ornelas (Lisbon).

HFE did not measure fidelity or have treatment-as-usual comparison groups as was the case in New York and Canada. Staff–client ratios at the sites were robust (from 1:3 to 1:11), client visits were at a minimum weekly in frequency, and support was available by mobile phone 24/7. The demographic profile of clients had common and familiar aspects—mostly men in their thirties and older—as well as cross-site variation (e.g., Lisbon having the lowest vs. Glasgow the highest prevalence of substance abuse). Sample sizes in the test sites ranged from a low of 16 in Glasgow to a high of 165 in Amsterdam (Busch-Geertsema, 2013).

HFE collaborators met in Brussels in November 2013 to review results. At the end of two years, the vast majority of clients were still housed with support from their HF programs: 86% in Amsterdam, 89% in Copenhagen, 93% in Glasgow, and 66% in Lisbon. The number of clients who had negative outcomes, such as dropping out to return to homelessness, imprisonment, and eviction, was minimal: 4 out of 165 in Amsterdam, 4 out of 80 in Copenhagen, 1 out of 16 in Glasgow, and 14 out of 74 in Lisbon (Busch-Geertsema, 2013).

Similar to the positive findings in the United States and Canada, HFE yielded further evidence that HF can be used to good effect for clients with addictions (Greenwood, Stefancic, Tsemberis, & Busch-Geertsema, 2013). The findings also countered one of the stronger arguments against HF in Europe—that it is unsuitable to European preferences for congregate living. Indeed, HFE clients strongly preferred scatter-site living. As the report stated, the research found "strong indications that gathering many people with complex problems in the same buildings may create problematic environments, conflicts and unintended negative consequences" (Busch-Geertsema, 2013, p. 12).

Other lessons learned from the HFE implementation ranged from the expected challenges (finding scatter-site apartments) to the less expected (e.g., a fixed address makes a person "findable" to debt collectors and local law enforcement seeking unpaid fines or serving outstanding arrest warrants). The importance of individualized and intensive (but flexible) support services underscored the point that HF was much more than housing-only (some in HFE preferred the term "housing-led" to "housing first"). Smaller-scale studies were conducted at many sites, and FEANTSA's journal (*European Journal on Homelessness*) was a key forum for ongoing discussions of HF, especially among academicians and researchers. In addition to research reports, the journal features articles about the experiences of individual countries as well as thought pieces on suitability for the model in Europe.

Challenges to Housing First Implementation in Europe

Although HF is being implemented in many cities and countries in Europe, it is unevenly distributed, ranging from "a national strategy" to "not at all." The EU is made up of 28 member states and only a few countries such as Finland, Sweden, Denmark, and Netherlands have established national policies encouraging HF programs.

There have been a few challenges in introducing HF into Europe. First, the EU has its own tradition of the staircase model, albeit in highly variant forms, with shelters, social housing, and disability assistance in the mix. As in the United States, the success of HF programs flies in the face of long-held assumptions regarding the need for psychiatric treatment, abstinence-based drug/alcohol programs, and housing supports.

Another challenge concerns access to affordable or public housing. In the wealthier European nations, social housing is operated on the principle of fairness in access and governed by waiting lists. The adoption of HF in some cities created controversy concerning the fairness of a waiting list for those who were chronically homeless and could not compete for placements. Concerns also were raised about the rights of citizens versus noncitizens because citizenship status affected eligibility for social welfare benefits and other services. Last but not least, the social welfare state is based on the assumption that all citizens are equal and must follow the same rules. Thus, HF programs present a dilemma: How can an individualized, person-centered approach be implemented in a culture based on uniform expectations and a guarantee of fairness?

There are also geographic differences, especially between Southern European countries and their neighbors to the north. Portugal, Spain, and Greece were experiencing economic crises related to their membership in the EU. The economic consequences of adopting the euro as currency and the debt and social unrest wrought by that financial policy change have been extensive. While poverty and disparities have increased, Southern European countries do not have the social welfare benefits or public housing stock to meet rising needs. Nor are there sufficient social and treatment services available for people who are homeless—many services are emergency treatment and shelters only. Recent influxes of refugees from Northern Africa, Eastern Europe, and the Middle East have contributed to crowding in shelters formerly reserved for homeless residents.

Ironically, implementing HF programs has been easier in some Southern European countries as long as funding for the program can be secured. After all, where there are few services, any additional help is welcome, and there are few existing structures typical of the continuum of care to stand in the way. An additional facilitating factor emerging from these struggling economies is a more favorable rental market. Rental housing is generally privately owned rather than owned and run by local governments and nonprofit corporations. With less regulation, rents are lower because of the economic crisis. Hiring staff is also easier given a shortage of jobs.

Finland, probably the first European country to adopt a national HF policy of its own, used profits from its national lottery to transform existing shelters into individual housing units. Similar to Seattle's DESC model, this single-site congregate housing uses a harm reduction approach and is neither abstinence-based nor treatment-first in philosophy. Most residents have substance abuse problems rather than mental illness—a commonality for Northern Europe. Evaluations of the HF programs aimed at ending long-term homelessness in Finland are underway at this writing.

In Denmark, HF has been the guiding principle of the national homelessness strategy since 2009. Besides Copenhagen, HF projects have been established in 17 municipalities testing two other support methods—Intensive Case Management (ICM) and Critical Time Intervention (CTI).[4] In Sweden, a number of small HF projects have been launched in Gothenburg, Helsingborg, Stockholm, Malmö, Karlstad, Örebro, Sollentuna, and Uppsala. In Norway, the development of HF projects started during Housing First Europe (HFE) with Bergen as one of the first cities to implement the approach. In the Netherlands, about 13 projects—apart from the HFE test site in Amsterdam—operate HF programs, most of them launched between 2011 and early 2013. They are located in The Hague, Utrecht, Dordrecht, Eindhoven, Haarlem, and other cities.

Other European countries where HF programs are being implemented include Austria, Belgium, Germany, Italy, and Great Britain (see Box 8.4). Programs vary in size (most are small) and in fidelity to the PHF model. Some countries, like Germany, have programs that use scatter-site housing and flexible supports but do not refer to this as HF.

Summing up, HFE is gaining ground as a program and as a policy, although adoption has been uneven and research on outcomes remains in its early stages. It is reasonable to assume there will be obstacles given the wide array of social, political, and economic differences. Among the EU's member

BOX 8.4

GREAT BRITAIN'S ROUGH SLEEPER INITIATIVE

Great Britain has been somewhat less favorable territory for Housing First (HF), in part because the country has its own tradition of homeless services. Britain's Rough Sleepers Initiative (RSI) began in 1990 at about the same time as the McKinney-Vento Act was funded by the U.S. Congress. Alarmed by over 1,000 homeless adults sleeping on the streets of central London, the British government allotted 96 million pounds to pay for increased outreach, new emergency hostels, and a range of temporary and permanent housing units located in properties leased from private landlords and permanent lettings provided by housing associations.

Surveys of the homeless in London revealed a demographic profile similar to the United States, namely, mostly men over age 25 but with a significant minority of women. Over half had a substance abuse problem, with drugs more common among younger and alcohol among older street homeless. The discourse on homelessness in government and media reports similarly focused on individual crises and proximal causes—family arguments, domestic violence, and physical and sexual abuse. Mental and emotional problems received mention but were not the subject of epidemiological assessments as in the United States.

The RSI model brought multiple providers together to offer an array of accommodations, including hostels, apartments in the private sector, and a winter shelter program. The RSI met its goal by reducing central London's homeless population by more than half to around 420 by November 1992 and down to 270 by May 1995 (http://www.unesco.org/most/westeu18.htm). Subsequently, government funding was expanded to enable the RSI to be implemented in cities outside London.

The fundamental elements of RSI—assertive outreach to street homeless without psychiatric or other vulnerability criteria—inspired similar efforts in the United States, Canada, and Europe. In its philosophy, RSI was focused on the frontlines, on engaging homeless persons and referring them into existing services. It was not a model designed to create new forms of housing integrated with services, but it was pioneering in its approach.

nations, there is considerable diversity in homeless populations and services available.

In the European cities where data are available, HF programs are selecting the chronically homeless who have presented difficult challenges to traditional providers. The majority of program participants are men, between the ages of 45 and 55 and with complex health, mental health, family, addiction, and other problems. The vast majority are local residents but with a proportion of ethnic minority groups represented. Services are provided using a range of off-site support teams from ACT to case management models and peer support. In spite of national differences, housing retention rates across all of the settings have generally been between 80% and 90%; evidence also suggests that better program outcomes are associated with high-fidelity HF programs (Busch-Geertsema, 2013).

Wide national and local diversity is in full evidence at the FEANTSA-led annual European Conference on Homelessness (whose theme in 2013 was "Housing First, What's Second?" and in 2014 was "Homelessness in Times of Crisis"). Here, researchers, policymakers, and providers from across the EU come together to discuss homelessness among youth, immigrants, and ethnic minority groups, as well as in the countries hardest hit by economic crisis. Researchers from Canada's AH/CS project share their findings in a continuing cross-Atlantic relationship with European researchers. Indeed, the success of AH/CS provided an opportunity for "seeing is believing" in a country more akin to Europe in values and social welfare spending.

Australia's Adoption of Common Ground

Australia has the lowest number of homeless persons per capita of the countries covered in this chapter, but its major cities have nevertheless been active in combating homelessness. Similar to European countries, Australia's housing and health sectors lack integration and thus place persons with psychiatric disabilities at greater risk of homelessness and poor service follow-up (Battams & Baum, 2010; Johnson, Gronda, & Coots, 2008).

In contrast to Canada and Europe, however, Australia has favored Common Ground (CG), the New York-based housing and business model approach described earlier in Chapter 3. Visits to Australia by CG's founder Roseanne Haggerty (including a stay as an Adelaide Thinker in Residence in 2005–2006) were successful in galvanizing government and private businesses (including a major construction company) to cooperate in new construction (Haggerty, 2006). According to Parsell et al., eight CG buildings were constructed in five of Australia's six states and more are being planned. CG in Australia brought about unprecedented levels of philanthropy as part of public-private partnerships (Parsell, Fitzpatrick, & Busch-Geertsema, 2014).

That CG's footprint in Australia was made so quickly and in so many cities is remarkable, but there are other reasons to take notice. First is the marked contrast to Canada and Europe—where HF was the leading import. Although interest in CG (and its spinoff 100K Homes Campaign) has been shown internationally, it has not achieved the traction of HF.

Second, CG does not have a track record of research showing its effectiveness (Johnsen & Teixeira, 2010). Australia's government openly espoused the importation of evidence-based practices, but CG's success attests to a willingness to suspend judgment on this count (Parsell et al., 2014). Perhaps this is because CG in Australia made an appealing proffer. CG was innovative and had architecturally attractive buildings in New York City to show for its efforts. CG in Australia produced majestic new buildings with socially mixed tenancies and this found favor with many local advocates. Largely a top-down initiative, with government ministers spreading the word (and sometimes competing for CG buildings in their districts), CG captured the imagination of many, including the Prime Minister's wife, who was CG's Patron when it began in 2008 (Parsell et al., 2014).

Not surprisingly, perhaps, CG encountered some of the same objections as HF, for example, resistance based on "we're already doing it" or distaste for a program from the United States (Johnsen & Teixeira, 2012). As one homeless advocate stated, "There's a real element of anti-American thinking and I am the first to agree with that. I would not look to America for insights on how to run a civil society or how to assist the most vulnerable people" (Parsell et al., 2014, p. 80).

And yet, what Parsell et al. refer to as "evidence-free policy transfer" took place because of the attractiveness of CG and its polished portfolio. Anecdotal accounts of visits to CG buildings by government officials, advocates, and business executives revealed that they were impressed by what they saw, including clean habitable units with rooftop gardens. Begging the questions of "What is evidence?" and "Does evidence have to come from well-designed systematic research?" CG embodies values with popular appeal—social inclusion, affordable housing, community-building, and private investment for public good. Ribbon-cutting ceremonies in front of gleaming new buildings are feel-good events for local politicians, organizational leaders, and benefactors. The enthusiasm of the business community and the invigoration of philanthropic giving was a repetition of what had occurred with CG's success in New York City.

Australia's Housing First Experience

The rise of CG in Australia did not result in a national policy change (Parsell et al., 2014) and HF also found its place there. In Sydney, a city of approximately 4.5 million, a coalition of city officials, service providers, landlords, foundations and businesses advocated for a PHF program and sought consultation from Pathways in New York. Sydney began with the Way2Home program to engage and house rough sleepers in the Wolloomooloo neighborhood and its environs. A 12-month evaluation of the project reported that 90% of program participants sustained housing over that period and 81% of program participants reported positive life changes (Parsell, Tomaszewski, & Jones, 2013).

In Melbourne, the Mental Illness Fellowship, a mental health agency led by Elizabeth Crowther and psychiatrist Julian Freidin, led the way to introducing HF. They targeted patients in psychiatric hospitals, "frequent flyers" in emergency rooms, and residents of congregate and restrictive group homes. The Melbourne "Opening Doors" and "Doorway" projects used HF principles of self-determination to assist individuals with severe psychiatric disabilities move into more independent settings in the community (Mental Illness Fellowship, 2014). The rationale is similar to opposition to institutional settings in the United States, where the Department of Justice is bringing lawsuits against congregate-care providers and courts are mandating "least restrictive" settings integrated into the community (more on this topic in Chapter 9).

HF in Australia has strong proponents but less visibility (or funding) compared with CG. The difference in costs can be profound. The $34 million CG project that was opening at the same time as Way2Home in Sydney took four years to build in order to house 50 low-income families and 50 homeless individuals. In contrast, the $1.5 million budget for Way2Home provided scattered-site apartments and off-site supports, had a 3-month start-up and after 12 months showed a 90% housing retention rate for its 100 clients. This difference in cost does not take into consideration the fact that the CG model adds to existing housing stock (a plus for some housing advocates).

We conclude these descriptions of international adoptions of HF by acknowledging the complex nature of implementation when carried out in different countries with their own organizational cultures and welfare policies. Returning to Damschroder et al.'s CFIR (2009) as a schema, Table 8.1 offers a summarization

TABLE 8.1

APPLICATION OF CFIR FRAMEWORK FOR HOUSING FIRST PROGRAMS INTERNATIONALLY

Program (year of beginning)	Intervention	Inner Setting	Outer Setting	Individuals Involved	Process	Research
Canada Calgary Alex Health Center (2007)	High-fidelity PHF program + integrated health care	Alex Center experience in serving homeless population	Calgary Homeless Foundation (CHF)	Tim Richter, CHF leading plan; leadership at the Alex	Community planning to identify the 54 highest users	12-month follow-up by CHF
Canada At Home/ Chez Soi Project (2008)	High-fidelity PHF RCT in five cities	MHCC oversees project	Each city designs local HF intervention to meet needs	Michael Kirby; Jayne Barker; Paula Goering et al.	Top-down, Federal funds; becomes national policy (HPS)	National Research Team; local plus national site collaboration
EUROPE Netherlands Amsterdam Rotterdam Utrecht The Hague (2006)	PHF model, modified ACT team and social housing	Discus Agency + Alliantie Amsterdam Housing Association	Funding by national health insurance; four-city alliance	Rokus Loopik, Wessel de Vries	Strong support + smooth adoption; national policy	Radboud University, Dorieke Wewerinke & Judith Wolf
Lisbon Casa de Primiero (2009)	PHF program using ICM; scatter-site	Psychiatric rehabilitation compatible with HF philosophy	Pressure re: growing number of homeless	Jose Ornelas, Theresa Duarte	Advocacy successful in securing funding	Self-evaluation

(continued)

TABLE 8.1
CONTINUED

Program (year of beginning)	Intervention	Inner Setting	Outer Setting	Individuals Involved	Process	Research
Glasgow Turning Point (2009)	Single-site HF for persons with drug problems	Concern about harm reduction under current law	Government work group to address homeless deaths	Ian Irvine, Director of Turning Point	Worked with senior police officers and Scottish government	Heriot-Watt researchers Sarah Johnsen & Suzanne Fitzpatrick
France Marseilles Toulouse Lille Paris (2011)	PHF model, ACT teams + scatter-site	System change for mental health and housing	National funding but limited time	Vincent Girard, Pascale Estecahandy et al.	Top-down funding; staff training to learn new model	Evaluation using Canada's Chez-Soi protocols
Copenhagen (2007)	PHF ACT team with scatter-site social housing	Focus on chronic homelessness	Strong local and national support	Pilot to determine effectiveness for national in 2009	Policy and research staff from city and national ministries	Danish National Center for Social Research
Australia–Common Ground (2011)	Common Ground model; large new buildings	Multiple business and service providers	Top-down initiative; Some opposition to any U.S. innovation	Roseanne Haggerty et al.	Mobilize government and private businesses for new construction	N/A
Australia Sydney (2010) Melbourne (2012)	PHF Way2Home; PHF Doorway Project	City + coalitions Mental Illness Fellowship	Local support including mental health community & private support	Liz Giles, Elizabeth Crowther, & William Frieden	Local advocates and foundations	12-month evaluation Parsell et al. Self-evaluation

and comparison of the examples in this chapter. We caution that this represents just some of the sites of international HF implementation. Given current rates of adoption, there are undoubtedly more to follow.

Reactions to Housing First Internationally: Differing Constituencies, Values, and Priorities

If Canada's embrace of HF can be described as wholehearted (albeit with some resistance from the left and the right), HF's implementation in Europe and Australia has been more complicated. The growing body of research evidence from the United States and Canada played a positive role in adoption as did economic incentives such as cost-savings, but sociocultural consonance (or dissonance) was also important. European values promote social welfare, inclusionary policies, and harm reduction. Australia's two-part approach favored "big buildings" erected through business community partnerships but also encouraged HF adoption in Sydney, Melbourne, and other cities.

Some advocates objected that HF does not fit prosocial values. They cited its emphasis on individual choice and the unintended but presumed consequence of social isolation, thereby inhibiting collective action (Klodawsky, 2009). Other objections include: (1) HF channels public funds to private landlords; (2) HF is unnecessary (local providers are doing just fine); and (3) funding for HF deprives existing service systems. Such concerns were not new. As cautioned by U.S. investigators early on, "Preventing homelessness is not identical to ending poverty, curing mental illness, promoting economic self-sufficiency, or making needy people healthy, wealthy and wise" (Shinn & Baumohl, 1999, p. 11). Certainly, the European Union had far more consensus that helping the needy become "healthy, wealthy and wise" was a worthwhile goal.

There were a few salient on-the-ground differences in the implementation of HF in Europe compared with the American experience. First, mental illness was less prominent in its rationale even if individuals with mental illness were often the desired user group. This signified a trans-European sentiment that poverty and homelessness were sufficient to warrant action. Secondly, a tension inhered where social housing was considered the ideal outcome with private housing a distant second. Long wait lists for the former made the latter a necessary option even though tenure was much less secure, given that private landlords could evict more easily than local authorities (Fitzpatrick, Quilgars, & Pleace, 2009).

With respect to service modifications, ACT was not (and is not) a common part of the European experience. (Some version of ICM is far more common.) In addition, there is a lack of integration of services for individuals with a dual diagnosis, which often results in the rejection of substance-using psychiatric patients by mental health clinics and mentally ill substance abusers by "drying out" rehabilitation programs (Atherton & McNaughton-Nicholls, 2008). The lack of systems integration took on additional meaning in Europe, where social housing did not traditionally accommodate clinical care. This rendered service providers unaccustomed to working closely with housing authorities and left housing authorities unfamiliar with support staff entering their properties to assist clients in their homes.

As mentioned earlier, social services in Europe were rooted in rights-based advocacy while medical and mental health care remained under the more conservative purview of biomedicine. This disconnect surfaced in various ways in the discourses on homelessness in Europe. For example, the primary challenge to maintaining a tenancy was labeled "antisocial behavior" rather than mental illness or addiction (Fitzpatrick et al., 2009). This demonstration of a preference for labeling behaviors rather than people recalls the lamenting of "psychiatrization" by Rhenter and Girard in their description of HF in France (2014).

If the disability ethos was not essential in Europe's adoption of HF, early implementers in France and Portugal were mental health providers nonetheless. For them, HF brought a welcome side benefit through breaking down traditional walls separating social and health services and infusing mental health services with a consumer rights-based ethos.

Housing First's Implementation Internationally: Neo-institutional Theory Revisited

HF's adoption internationally was assisted by local institutional entrepreneurs as well as by government entities—many such individuals had the vision and wherewithal to make HF a reality. Acting as a midwife at the birth (or adoption), Tsemberis travelled to all of the cities and countries mentioned in this chapter to consult and cajole. Interviews conducted with "early implementers" for this book invariably included a vivid memory of one or more of his visits.

In Canada and Europe, we see a pattern of government initiative in funding that is less common in the United States, namely, initiatives not as dependent on disability income or on private business and philanthropy. Values consonance with HF outside the United States was enhanced by its "housing is a right" tenet and, in most places, by harm-reduction practices.

As in the United States, the fit was somewhat less true for HF's emphasis on community-based support services coordinated with housing needs, and for reduced power of the medical and psychiatric establishment (although many individual providers welcomed this change). Contrary to expectations, the fit with scatter-site housing proved to be a good one—HF clients in Canada and Europe preferred the same independent living arrangements as their counterparts in the United States (Busch-Geertsema, 2013).

Some academic critics charged that HF served neoliberal policies and diverted attention from larger causes such as poverty reduction (Klodawski, 2009; Lofstrand & Juhila, 2012). As we will see in the next and final chapter, larger causes and structural determinants are necessary to understanding the constraints placed on HF and the entire homeless services industry. The stakeholders involved in HF's implementation are diverse, sometimes united and sometimes at odds, and not always predictable in where they will stand on the issues. United by a commitment to help the homeless in their midst, they risk being pulled apart by the centrifugal forces of professional pride, activist impatience, and job-loss fears of those working in the "industry."

Conservative governments want to cut costs and remove the homeless from public areas such as shopping districts. This does not preclude empathy or charitable giving, but it fails to address the deep structural fault lines that produce economic inequality. Staunch advocates are needed to galvanize action to address those fault lines, but they can be uncompromising and delay or divert action. Then there is the vast middle ground of bureaucratic inertia. The stalwartness of the status quo, as well as Weber's "iron cage" of bureaucracy, ensure that proponents have to push and push hard for any change to take place. Adoption of a new program on a trial basis is one thing, rigorous evaluation and wider implementation are another.

In this regard, the experiences of HFE are not all that different from those of HF in the United States and Canada. The usual debates took place abroad—scatter-site versus single-site housing and disability as eligibility for some versus homelessness as eligibility for all—and they were enlivened by doubts about an innovation coming from the United States. Yet, cost savings and research findings that had traction in the United States were less influential in European countries with more generous social policies and less emphasis on monetization and evidence-based practices.

Conclusion: Philosophical Stances of Housing First Implementation

At the risk of over-simplification, two philosophical stances were instrumental in the dissemination of HF both in the United States and internationally. One of these, which we refer to as "the mental health priority group," was the major force in the early days of HF and its subsequent spread to Canada. Aided by funding streams supporting a disability ethos, homeless service providers and advocates prioritized helping persons with serious mental illness recover their lives while residing in the community. Bolstered by the mental health recovery movement, this contingent was led by forward-thinking mental health providers and family and consumer advocates.

Because mental illness was so often combined with addiction and health problems, the mental health contingent pragmatically expanded its purview to include homeless persons with complex needs (but still not *all* homeless persons). These individuals, more likely to be called the "chronically homeless" in the United States, had greater vulnerability and incurred much higher costs to the system. They thus were accorded higher priority for receiving housing and services.

The other philosophical stance behind the spread of HF was less concerned about clinical diagnoses or duration of homelessness. The "social advocacy priority group" had a more ambitious value-laden agenda: to end homelessness for everyone. Similar to their counterparts in the United States, social advocacy groups in Canada, Europe, and Australia espoused a rights-based argument that homeless assistance programs needed to help all rough sleepers whatever their problems. Their assertive outreach and housing efforts were egalitarian in practice and rooted in the principle of housing as a right for all in need.

The tradeoffs associated with each of these are probably obvious by now. Mental health priorities exclude homeless persons without mental illness, families, and youths, but yield the tangible benefit of ending homelessness for those deemed eligible. Social advocacy priorities are targeted to the structural problems that undergird homelessness—laudable and necessary but not easily translated into programs on the ground when resources are scarce and the powers-that-be are uncooperative.

One can see echoes of the "three lineages" described in Chapter 3. Charities and faith communities are major sources of help for the homeless in Europe. The Simon Communities in Ireland and the United Kingdom, for example, have been leaders in programming assistance (including a HF program in Dublin). The second lineage—advocacy and action—aligns closely to the second philosophy described here—an orientation that has retained a vigorous presence in Canada and Europe where the values of social responsibility are alive and well. Finally, there is the business-model lineage. This approach has found fewer adherents outside of the United States (with the possible exception of Australia's adoption of Common Ground). Erecting or renovating multistory buildings to house the homeless—and monetizing programs that help the homeless—are not very common practices in Europe. Nor is the American-style use of tax credits and capital investment incentives typically used to finance such public works. A central tenet of European welfare policies—that governments assume responsibility of fundamentals such as housing—makes this type of approach unlikely.

Returning to the two philosophies (mental health and social advocacy priorities), the second of these has had much more traction outside of the United States, but the first could be considered a "hidden asset" in many a program's claim to legitimacy and public support. Of course, as we have seen, these are not mutually exclusive when put into practice. Psychiatrists with strong social activist allegiances lead HF in France, where they view it as a means of shaking up the establishment. The 100K Campaign was a blend of both with its "housing for all homeless" slogan paired with a triage-type eligibility requirement. Britain's Rough Sleeper Initiative and CG's Street to Home program were similar to 100K in focusing on homelessness in given geographic areas and in drawing on linkages to existing homeless programs with additional supports. (HF may or may not be a part of these offerings.)

The integrated approach pioneered by Ellen Baxter and Common Ground—large architecturally attractive buildings built or renovated to accommodate disabled as well as nondisabled low-income tenants—skillfully draws on both philosophies even as it remains distinctly American in its origins and financing. It creates new housing and the potential for community empowerment—both attractive to advocacy coalitions. And yet this "big building" approach requires large capital outlays and lengthy waits for construction to be completed. Like all single-site housing programs, expenses are incurred in building security, building maintenance, and staff supervision (a challenge when a substantial number of residents are working on their recovery at the same time). Though designed to be "normal community living," a single-site approach risks becoming "institutional care" if the balance tilts toward supervision rather than normality.

We end this chapter with the recognition that HF implementation continues to be a work in progress even as it proceeds apace. Existing side-by-side (or integrated) with programs driven by charitable, advocacy, and/or business models, HF has taken on varied forms with varied fidelity to the original model. In some instances, the mental health priority philosophy has smoothed the way and in others social advocacy has been the route to adoption.

Notes

1. The acronym S2H was also used to describe Common Ground's "Street to Home" program in New York City.
2. In its emphasis on congregate living and substance use as the primary reason for program enrollment, the Vancouver site resembles a program not far away in the United

States—Seattle's DESC. Notably, this trend seems to be a West Coast phenomenon, given that U.S. cities such as Portland, San Francisco, and Los Angeles also have focused on single-site programs for chronically homeless people who are substance abusers.

3. This description came from an interview and subsequent e-mail communications with Ian Irvine of Glasgow's Turning Point organization.

4. Critical Time Intervention (CTI) is an evidence-based intervention designed to prevent homelessness through time-limited case management for clients facing discharge from institutional care (Herman et al., 2011).

9 New Beginnings

TRANSFORMING SYSTEMS AS WELL AS LIVES

IN JUNE 2014, the U. S. Interagency Council on Homelessness (USICH) website featured a policy blog entry that reflects how far Housing First (HF) has come. Criticisms that HF "is just one program among many" or "isn't for everyone" are countered with a reframing: HF is a whole-system response. HF portends changes that are systemic, not just programmatic. Questions are no longer about which program does the best job but about how existing programs can join in the transformation. Regardless of one's problems, having a home is the route to a better life (Cho, 2014).

The profound impact of HF is in evidence each day on Google Alerts where media and other reports offer glimpses into its reach. In Bristol, Tennessee, deep in the heart of Appalachia, the director of a homeless program for veterans states, "We follow the 'housing first' model. We house them first and then you look at all the other services they need to keep them in housing." (Brooks, 2015). The localities endorsing HF, no longer just big cities, run the gamut from First Nations communities in Canada to small towns in Sweden.

Herein lies a dilemma of popularity and widespread dissemination: Does HF risk becoming co-opted and conflated with other approaches? What if providers say they are doing HF and then go about business as usual with an occasional nod to harm reduction or to scatter-site placements? Is it "systems change" if HF is simply added to the top of the still-standing staircase? Surely the latter is better than no top step at all (or better than a promised but largely nonexistent top step). But such a desirable outcome must still be achieved through good behavior, thus violating a central premise of HF.

Definitional blurring has led to conflating permanent supportive housing with HF—a sign of progress, of course, but not if HF is positioned as one program among many (Cho, 2014). We know that the majority of homeless persons exit their unfortunate status within days or months; only a small minority remain chronically homeless. If emergency shelters are retained for the "quick exiting" majority, the shift to rapid rehousing efforts and HF would virtually eliminate the need for (and expense of) outreach efforts and transitional housing programs. Moreover, such a shift would considerably reduce costs related to emergency room visits, jail stays, and hospitalizations. Such a massive reconfiguration of services has yet to occur, although dismantling of the staircase is starting to happen in conjunction with adoption of HF. Canada is proceeding forthrightly in this direction.

We begin this final chapter by noting that the story of HF is far from over. Yet, whatever the future holds, this story has few parallels in the annals of systems change in social and health services (Greenwood, Stefancic, & Tsemberis, 2013). Permanent supportive housing using a HF approach has been credited with reducing the number of chronically homeless adults by 25% from 2006 to 2013 (U. S. Department of Housing and Urban Development, 2014)—and by 73% in the state of Utah alone. The Veterans Administration's adoption of Housing First in 2010 has brought a 33% reduction in homelessness among veterans and is the basis for a drive to end veterans' homelessness in 2015 (Kane, 2014).

Recalling the questions posed in the Preface, how often does a program start small in a large city in the United States and in less than 20 years become the stated policy of an entire nation (Canada), of the U.S. Federal government, of many U. S. cities, and of several member nations of the European Union? Emerging from an entrenched "industry" of homeless organizations, HF's success attests to the rarity of breakout innovations as well as to the near-inevitability of pushback rooted in self-preservation and philosophical differences. This success has, in turn, profoundly changed the conversation around homelessness and the benefits of having a home of one's own, however humble.

Thomas Kuhn's paradigm shifts and Max Weber's "iron cage" of bureaucracy help in understanding the resistance that HF encountered. In returning to DiMaggio and Powell's neo-institutional theory (1983) from Chapter 1, the three pillars that maintain institutions—*regulative, normative,* and *cultural–cognitive*—are instructive in their applicability to the story of HF. Regulatory dimensions enhancing

HF's challenge to the institutional status quo included the Federal government's policies via the Department of Housing and Urban Development (HUD) and USICH, as well as the Olmstead court decision (more about this landmark decision later in this chapter).

Normative dimensions—assumption or ideals governing behavior—have shifted dramatically. Thus, homeless service providers in much of the United States, all of Canada, and many parts of Europe and Australia start from the premise of HF as optimal and then strive to enact its tenets. Fundamental changes in the cultural–cognitive pillar—schemas or taken-for-granted scripts underlying behavior—have emerged as homeless persons are increasingly aware of (and acting on) their desire for a home, service providers are operating under HF assumptions (even if not enacting all of the tenets), and policymakers share in the vocabulary of HF.

DiMaggio and Powell noted that institutional change could be *coercive* (top-down enforcement), *normative* (altering perceptions of what is expected and desirable), or *mimetic* (copying best practice models) (1983). In this book, we have seen examples of all three. Top-down enforcement of HF as a policy has occurred in Canada. Elsewhere it has been more hortatory (although some providers might feel otherwise). Normative institutional change has been pervasive such that HF has become an expected and desirable outcome in many localities. Finally, mimetic change can be found in the many reports of HF implementation where localities have sought to replicate (or approximate) the model. The hallmark of institutional change, a new *institutional logic*, is exemplified in the first paragraph of this chapter, which points to a "whole-system response" wrought by HF.

With the possible exception of Rogers's work on innovation, there are few frameworks for understanding how HF achieved such institutional prominence in less than 20 years. In many places, an energetic institutional entrepreneur seized on HF's message and led the way in its implementation. Alternative models and approaches also emerged and were adopted, but they did not have the same impact or track record of rigorous evaluation.

What propelled HF to center stage was most likely a combination of research evidence, social and cultural consonance in new settings, and widespread (if sometimes begrudging) agreement that existing programs were having too little effect, especially for the costs being incurred. To be sure, there were and are persons who do not fare well in HF—about 15%–20% on average across the quantitative studies but a considerably lower proportion in qualitative studies (as shown in Chapter 6). The most likely to encounter problems are those in the worst throes of addiction, mental illness, poor health, or some combination of these (Goering et al., 2014). With rehousing, some will eventually stabilize, leaving a small number who cannot sustain an independent tenancy in an apartment even with support services.

The kicker here is that it is almost impossible to predict in advance who will succeed and who will fail. If addiction and severe psychosis are at the forefront of reasons for failure in HF, these same problems—at a similar or worse level of severity—more often have been part of success stories, as individuals overcome them once housed. The benefit of the doubt would seem better placed in assuming success rather than failure.

The above observations are a sure sign of the change in conversation. Not long ago, providers of housing for the homeless were lamenting the "housing resistant," those who seemed to prefer the freedom of life on the streets. Nowadays, it is hard to justify such a belief when there is ample evidence that a homeless man or woman—if given the choice of a home—will gladly come indoors. Another entrenched belief—that only a small minority of the chronically homeless could move immediately into and then live stably in their own apartment—has been turned inside out by the evidence.

Consider Figure 9.1 as part of a reconfigured services system based upon lessons learned from HF. Beginning from the premise of consumer choice, homeless adults would be given the opportunity to move immediately into independent supportive housing. If they preferred more structure, they could move down a step or two as needed. If an individual at the top step is not able to maintain independent housing, he or she could approach the program case manager and say,

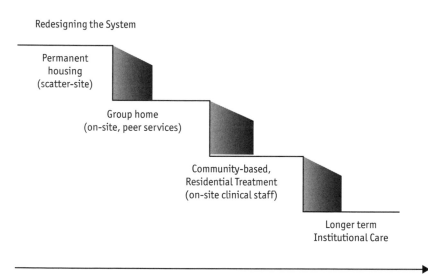

Redesigning the System

Permanent housing (scatter-site)

Group home (on-site, peer services)

Community-based, Residential Treatment (on-site clinical staff)

Longer term Institutional Care

Least restrictive to more restrictive setting

FIGURE 9.1 The Staircase or Continuum Reversed.

"I think I need more on-site support" or "I prefer living with people and services around me." The direction of movement is downward toward more structure and does not involve a long upward climb where it is easy to fall off.

There are still subpopulations whose suitability for HF is relatively unknown and understudied, most notably young people (Atherton & McNaughton-Nicholls, 2008; Gaetz, 2014). This book's focus on single adults omits other categories of homeless persons—families and adolescents especially—and thus is far from comprehensive. As we will see later in this chapter, Housing First for families and young adults is new territory now being explored.[1]

The emphasis on the chronically homeless in the prioritizing of public funds, a policy change that positioned HF as the "answer," raises an obvious question: Who are the nonchronic, or "situational," homeless? These individuals use shelters for shorter finite periods (usually less than six months) and are likely to be newly released prisoners, women fleeing partner violence,[2] or down-on-their-luck men and women subsequently "rescued" from homelessness by family members. Far less is known about this group in large part because public data systems are focused more on chronic service users.[3]

However, enough was known to initiate "rapid rehousing" programs to prevent individuals and families from crossing the threshold into chronicity. In 2008, HUD began financing rapid rehousing demonstration projects, and a year later the U.S. Congress appropriated $1.5 billion for the Homelessness Prevention and Rapid Re-Housing Program (HPRP). Also in 2009, the McKinney–Vento reauthorization was expanded by Congress to include the Homeless Emergency Assistance and Rapid Transition to Housing (HEARTH) program. Offering mostly emergency financial assistance with some tailored services, HPRP and HEARTH have been credited with significantly reducing rates of homelessness in many cities. Up-to-date information on these programs can be found at: http://www.endhomelessness.org/.

The adoption of homelessness prevention programs such as Critical Time Intervention (CTI) (Herman, Conover, Gorroochurn, Hinterland, Hoepner, & Susser, 2011) has become integral to many rapid re-housing initiatives. An evidence-based intervention, CTI has been tailored for a number of populations at risk of homelessness, including those exiting prison and substance abuse treatment as well as those leaving psychiatric hospitalization. (More information can be found at: www.criticaltime.org/)

Giving more attention to nonchronic as well as chronic homelessness opens the door to consideration of broader demographic trends and what this might portend for homeless services. Based upon New York City homeless data from 1990 to 2010, there was a marked bimodal increase in two age groups: young people (ages 18–30) and older adults (in their fifties). Moreover, 35% of the adult homeless over 50 years of age were experiencing homelessness for the first time in their lives (Culhane, 2014).

Young adults aging out of foster care are likely responsible for some of this increase, although why it appears at this time versus any other is not clear. The presence of a significant number of older "new homeless" individuals, however, is striking (see Box 9.1 for one example). Anecdotal reports point to a few likely scenarios: disabled individuals who lost their aging caretaker parents, men and women with manual

---

BOX 9.1

BECOMING HOMELESS AFTER AGE 50: THE BILLS KEEP PILING UP

The recent uptick in the numbers of "new homeless" over age 50 is puzzling on the face of it. Perhaps a result of Baby Boomers growing older, this phenomenon is nonetheless counterintuitive given the Social Security and Medicare safety net protections possessed by older Americans (at least compared with younger Americans). The story of one such individual appeared in a Springfield, Massachusetts news story dated December 30, 2014. Sherri, a 50-year-old woman, became homeless late in 2014 after a lifetime of minimum wage jobs that barely sustained her. A high school graduate, Sherri worked in a potato chip factory and other low-threshold jobs, got married and divorced, and gradually lost her home and car as the bills piled up. When her last job ended—repairing vending machines for $9 an hour—Sherri had to move into a homeless shelter where she works in the kitchen for $40 a week. Like so many in her situation, Sherri took out a loan to get a vocational-school training certificate, but the school closed, leaving her further in debt.

Having no children or family to assist her and with relatively good health, Sherri has few options. The shelter director where she lives noted, "For those people [like Sherri] it's going to be the old-fashioned solutions—you hustle; try to find work; you house share, that kind of thing." He added that he believes subsidies can be a disincentive to work in comparison with struggling to survive on salaries that barely exceed minimum wage. Sherri does not necessarily agree: "I feel an individual should be able to work a full-time job and be able to support themselves—buy a car; maintain a car; put gas in that car; pay their rent and buy groceries without being fearful it will all fall apart at any moment," she said. "I worked hard and lived like that for years."

Noting that the Commonwealth of Massachusetts strongly supports Housing First, the shelter director concurred, "Study after study shows that 80% to 90% of Housing First participants are successfully maintaining their housing. There is probably more attention being paid to homelessness now in these last six or eight years than in any other time that I can remember from a government level" (Barry, 2014).

labor jobs who aged out of their ability to work and support themselves, individuals discharged from long sentences in prison and unable to find a place to live.

Implications for services point to more job training and education for the younger cohorts, and a number of services for youth have been configured in this direction. But the needs of older homeless persons, whether living in a shelter, transitional housing, or a Housing First apartment, are given much less consideration in service planning (Henwood, Cabassa, Craig, & Padgett, 2013). Chronic disease management, mobility problems, injurious falls, and cognitive impairments are some of the age-related problems needing more attention (O'Dwyer & Alexander, 2014).

Here is a question that illustrates how much HF has changed the conversation: Are there *any* populations for whom congregate housing with on-site services is a good fit? Answers to this question depend on who is being asked. There are undoubtedly some consumers and homeless persons who would prefer to live this way even if the overwhelming majority does not. If providers and clinicians are asked, they are more likely to answer "yes," based on classes or groups such as people with addictions, young people, or ex-prisoners on parole. As we will see later in this chapter, the provider's answer can no longer include "persons with psychiatric disabilities" without introducing legal implications.

Housing's First, What's Second?

Small victories accrue to those who obtain a home after being homeless. These include dreaming about the future rather than worrying about daily survival, reuniting with children and grandchildren, calling relatives and being able to leave a number for a return call, taking an exercise class, finding a place of worship, taking up a new interest or resuming one abandoned long ago. All of these things have happened to individuals we have interviewed in our studies and to beneficial effect.

The proximal answer to the "What's second?" question is, quite simply, services. Support for clients to stay housed, to recover from and in mental illness, to recover from and in addiction, to get healthier, and to pursue the life that they want to lead. Support services also may be needed to get a job, go back to school, obtain entitlements, learn how to cook and eat nutritionally, exercise more, find friends, reconnect with family, straighten out legal problems, and pursue creative activities. HF is about the whole person, even if not every service can be provided.

The distal answer to this question is a matter of linking the individual's capabilities and experiences to the bigger picture, that is, overcoming structural barriers to fulfilling several of these "secondary" needs. For the individual, the time after being housed is one of reflection and reorientation. The past has not been erased and the burdens of trauma, loss, and lingering health problems cannot be either. Researchers have found significant associations between childhood adversity and adult homelessness even when controlling for adult problems such as mental disorders (Roos, Mota, Afifi, Katz, Distasio, & Sareen, 2013).

No amount of a program's success or its paradigm-shifting proclivities can reverse the effects of structural inequalities, social exclusion, and poverty (Hopper, 2012). For activists seeking a major transformation of society, HF might appear to be little more than a stopgap solution that makes the system look better than it deserves to look. The honoring of consumer choice can make a tremendous difference in an individual's life, however, and it is difficult to imagine a more fundamental change than getting a home of one's own after months or years of surviving without one. But those troubling What's next?" questions (Padgett, 2007) reflect what is left unaddressed and inaccessible.

Notwithstanding the occasional person who descends into homelessness from a comfortable perch in the middle class, most homeless persons have grown up in poverty. For them, becoming homeless is a deeply unfortunate drop in one's fortunes, but it is not a sudden or drastic plummet. More often, it is preceded by periods of doubling up with family and gnawing housing insecurity.

Homelessness haunts those who have experienced it and its impact is more than the sum of its awful parts, more than the string of humiliations and traumas (physical, psychological, and sexual) that come with life on the street and in shelters. Once housed, the transience of life and survival, already familiar, may take on greater urgency along with the inescapable fear of suffering it all over again. Add mental illness and addiction to this accumulation of adversity, and it is remarkable that so many find a way to keep going and hope for better times.

Those cumulative adversities continue to exert their influence. This is especially evident when an individual "succeeds" after being housed. We define success as: the mental illness is dormant or under control with medications, addiction is long over (or at least well under control), and the person is ready to return to work, make new friends, and re-establish family relationships.

And yet obstacles still emerge: jobs of all kinds are highly competitive, especially for someone with a high school diploma and a spotty work history. Earning income above a certain level runs the risk of "falling off the cliff," that is, of losing SSI disability income and Medicaid coverage. Making friends is hard when one's primary contacts are case managers, nurses, doctors, and 12-Step sponsors, and when the local neighborhood has more than its share of drugs and illegal activities. Family members have passed away, moved away, or often just stay away.

Repairing relationships with one's children or with surviving relatives takes time and effort.

Exposure to accidents and violence leaves injuries both physical and psychological. Lack of access to medical care—and the side effects of many antipsychotic drugs—predispose one to diabetes, chronic pain, and cardiovascular problems. There are often longstanding unmet needs for specialty treatment from dentists, ophthalmologists, dermatologists, and other health professionals who are difficult to access or afford. Resilience can offset the effects of trauma but the allostatic load of almost-constant stress lasting for decades is difficult to override.

This is not to dismiss the role of individual agency or to promote a naive form of structural determinism. Even with severely limited options, people make bad decisions as well as good ones. But the more popular assumption—that their fates are entirely tied to bad decisions—is more consequential and less grounded in fact.

The Persistence of Structural Barriers

In reviewing the rise of HF and other efforts to end homelessness, three structural barriers stand out as less amenable to a "solution" at the programmatic or individual level. The first and most obvious is the lack of affordable housing. In many U.S. cities, real estate values have skyrocketed along with apartment rents, squeezing out all but the most affluent who can afford to spend several thousand dollars a month to rent (or millions to purchase) their dwelling place. Nationally, the United States continues to lag far behind other Western nations in the provision of housing for low-income families. According to the National Low Income Housing Coalition, for every 100 very low-income households, there are only 30 affordable rental units available and the shortage gets worse with each passing year (http://nlihc.org/unitedforhomes/campaign).

The second structural barrier—availability of living-wage jobs—is on a similar downward trajectory in the United States. The past few decades have witnessed a sharp decline in jobs for those with limited education or experience coinciding with greater concentrations of wealth at the top of the social ladder (Piketty, 2014). Having a job (or multiple low-wage jobs) can still leave one unable to survive financially and with no paths to promotion and higher income (Newman, 2000). A report from the National Alliance on Mental Illness (NAMI) cited a stunning 80% unemployment rate for persons with mental illness compared with 6% in the general U.S. population (Szabo, 2014). Reliance on SSI income—however inadequate—can be a lifeline, but it also creates a situation of labeling and dependency with few exit routes (Hansen et al., 2014).

Mindful of this, homeless and social service organizations link clients to job training, resume-writing, and supported employment programs (Becker, Drake, & Bond, 2011). Some offer "sheltered" employment—clerical, messenger, janitorial services—that is usually part-time minimum-wage work. However, such institutional solutions increasingly are being rejected as inconsistent with constitutional rights of the disabled. "Place then train" approaches to supported employment offer opportunities but are not yet widely used (Drake, Bond, & Becker, 2013; Szabo, 2014).

The third structural barrier—social or community exclusion—is of particular concern to individuals diagnosed with a serious mental illness, but it also affects those living in institutional forms of supportive housing. The latter have faced NIMBY-type responses from neighborhood residents protesting the possibility of institutional forms of supportive housing in their midst. Such overt rejection is, however, less common than the subtle but no less injurious effects of exclusion and stigma acted out in everyday life (Link & Phelan, 2014).

Despite legal and other means of addressing centuries of exclusion and institutionalization, outdated ideas persist that mentally ill persons are dangerous and unable to live and behave "normally." The notion of recovery in and from mental illness is not yet commonplace, and stereotypical portrayals in movies and media do little to promote a recovery orientation.

There is a growing body of research in this area, however, especially on the deleterious effects of stigma (Link & Phelan, 2001; Link & Phelan, 2014; Whitley & Campbell, 2014). Obstacles to community integration of persons with serious mental illness have been the subject of a number of studies (Baumgardner & Herman, 2012; Townley & Kloos, 2011; Wong & Solomon, 2002; Yanos, Barrow, & Tsemberis, 2004; Yanos, 2007). And, although HF provides a built-in advantage when using scatter-site apartments in the community, there is no compelling evidence that community integration is greater for HF clients compared with non-HF clients. Nor is there evidence that living in congregate (vs. scatter-site) living brings more social integration, although Townley and Kloos have reported a greater sense of community felt by residents in a congregate setting (2011). There *is* ample documentation that clients do not prefer living in shared accommodations if given an individual living option (Padgett, Henwood, Abrams, & Drake, 2008; Busch-Geertsema, 2013).

If mental illness brings stigma, so do poverty and homelessness (Hansen et al., 2014; Whitley & Henwood, 2014). Social inclusion is front and center in the European Union's "Europe 2020 Strategy," where poverty reduction is seen as vital (www.feantsa.org), a contrast to the absence of such awareness and political will in the United States. Centuries of scorn and blame directed at the poor are unlikely to melt away, especially given the rising numbers living in poverty in the United States and other nations (Piketty, 2014).

The Olmstead Decision: A Rare Structural Mandate

The right to housing has been asserted in international law for decades, yet the reality of adequate housing remains elusive for much of the world's population (Thiele, 2002). Notwithstanding doubts about the United States as a moral exemplar expressed by its own citizens and others living abroad, the country has pioneered through legislation and litigation some of the strongest civil rights protections for persons with disabilities in the world. Beginning with the Americans with Disabilities Act (ADA) of 1990, persons with disabilities have the right to reasonable accommodations in education, employment, public facilities, and transport. The sweeping impact of the ADA can be seen in public access improvements, but it has also ensured that employers cannot discriminate in job applications nor can educational institutions discriminate in admissions or access.

The ADA enabled persons with psychiatric disabilities to file a lawsuit charging segregation and institutionalization as violations of the Act. On June 22, 1999 the U.S. Supreme Court upheld the ADA (*Olmstead v. L.C.*) and further mandated that such persons must have the opportunity to live in the least restrictive housing arrangements in the community. The impact of the Olmstead decision in the United States was and is profound. With its protections, state and local mental health authorities are mandated to dismantle large facilities such as "adult homes" and "group homes" as violations of Olmstead's provisions.

Further putting teeth into the ruling, the Olmstead decision stated that "intention to discriminate" did not have to be proven, only the existence of unwanted segregation. Further, while states were enjoined to enforce the ruling, not just state-run facilities were affected. Almost any program with any amount of state funding is covered by Olmstead's provision, including private contractors and subcontractors. Many of these facilities correspond directly to the housing options of the staircase model. Not only housing but sheltered workshops and segregated day-treatment programs are potential violations (http://www.ada. gov/olmstead/). By any measure, this was a sweeping ruling. It also lent a huge boost to the HF scatter-site approach.

A leading advocate for the rights of persons with psychiatric disabilities, the Bazelon Center for Mental Health Law, has relied on the success of HF to support its advocacy, stating, "Virtually all individuals with disabilities can live in their own home with supports. Like people without disabilities, they should get to decide where they live, with whom they live, when and what they eat, who visits and when, etc." (Bazelon Center, 2014). Successful legal action against a growing number of states is changing the provision of housing and services. These efforts require a coordinated approach among the Federal government's Department of Justice, local disability advocates, the Bazelon Center, and private law firms (*pro bono* counsel). Of course, Olmstead is only as good as its enforcement.

The Olmstead decision and its consequences can be seen in recent debates on single-site facilities including HF projects.[4] These programs place individuals with disabilities into shared accommodations, a form of institutional living that, under Olmstead, enables residents to seek legal action.[5] However, legal redress is not easy in these situations, a primary reason for the relatively slow rollout of Olmstead mandates in many states. And, to be fair, many single-site facilities are run well and humanely.

Such was not (and is not) the case with adult homes in New York. The adult home controversy in New York State is a rather egregious example of the abuse of disabled men and women and the difficulties of ADA enforcement when there is an organized industry fighting back and state or judicial authorities are slow to act. The controversy began with a searing expose by *New York Times* journalist Clifford Levy in 2002, which led to a lawsuit filed against the state on June 30, 2003 (*Disability Advocates v. Pataki*). As noted by Levy, the industry reaps enormous profits from billing Medicaid to run facilities where adults with developmental and psychiatric disabilities are warehoused in crowded, stultifying conditions with few if any services. Unscrupulous doctors associated with the facilities were increasing profits by billing Medicaid for unnecessary or unperformed procedures and surgeries.[6] Reports confirmed that the bodies of some residents who had died were not found for days due to neglect by staff. Levy's portrayal was an indictment not only of the profiteers but of the State for neglecting to protect the residents in these homes. The defendants in the lawsuit included New York State's Department of Health and Office of Mental Health.

The "homes," mostly institutional-style buildings located in the far reaches of Brooklyn near the waterfront, had alluring names like Surf Manor and Ocean House, but their ambience was more punitive than therapeutic. Residents' SSI checks were cashed by facility owners and small personal allowances doled out weekly. Days were spent standing in line (four times daily for medications and three times daily for meals) and permission had to be sought to leave the premises. Roommates were not chosen but assigned; there were few activities and residents were discouraged from seeking employment or other self-improvement. After all, staff told them, their needs were being taken care of—why leave? Referrals to the homes were typically made upon discharge from a psychiatric hospital, the patient given the choice of a shelter or adult home.

The wheels of justice were slow and at this writing the case awaits a satisfying conclusion. In June 2009, the Eastern District Court of New York found in favor of the plaintiffs, a ruling that pointed to a virtual shutdown of the adult home industry in the state. Some 4,000 residents of 23 homes were affected. A home resident and plaintiff, Ilona Spiegel, responded, "I'm thrilled about this settlement. At my adult home, they don't do anything to inspire you or encourage you to move forward. I know how to take care of myself. I want to work my way back to independence." (Bazelon Center, 2014). The court ruling reads like an extended argument for the benefits of HF, mandating that residents have a right to live in their own homes with supportive services.

This left New York State and the industry's operators responsible for ensuring that residents were transferred to apartments with necessary support services. Jeffrey Edelman, president of New York Coalition for Quality Assisted Living and operator of three such homes, protested the ruling, asserting "... the rights of these adults to live in the homes of their choice, rather than becoming the targets of others' dangerous social experiments." (Secret, 2012, p. A13). To add insult to injury, Edelman charges, the court order requires home operators to develop transition plans for each resident to move into independent supported housing. Quoted in a report from Columbia University School of Journalism's *New York World*, Edelman said of such plans, "They're basically asking you to write your own obituary" (*New York World*, January 28, 2013, http://www.thenewyorkworld.com/2013/01/28/adult-home-exodus/).

Twelve years after Levy's story first appeared in print, only modest progress has been made in carrying out these "dangerous social experiments." New York State filed an appeal and the residents' transfers have been slow despite the State's new operating standards and subsequent offering of contracts to service providers to resettle and house them. Both the Bazelon Center and the U.S. Justice Department under President Obama have been watching the case closely to ensure ADA compliance. The adult home industry, operating in plain sight for decades, will likely be transformed, but not without a fight.

Systems Change Within Homeless Services Revisited: Families and Youth

FAMILY HOMELESSNESS. Efforts to alleviate family homelessness have moved to the forefront in recent years. When the federal Interagency Council on Homelessness (USICH) released "Opening Doors: Federal Strategic Plan to Prevent and End Homelessness" in 2010, a key recommendation was to end family homelessness in 10 years. The National Alliance to End Homelessness (NAEH) convenes an annual conference on family and youth homelessness that draws providers, advocates, and researchers from around the country. Recent concerns about the national priority of assisting the "chronic homeless" and the de facto neglect of families have prompted a re-examination of homeless families and their needs.

Traditional approaches have had limited effectiveness with their practice of rewarding "better behaving" families with earlier access to housing, thus leaving more troubled families in the emergency shelter system. Housing for homeless families also requires support services to help them stay engaged and housed (NAEH, 2004). In a systematic review of the research literature on housing and supports for homeless families, Bassuk and colleagues summarized the findings of six studies and concluded: Postintervention improvements in housing and employment did not result in lasting housing stability or in employment at a living wage (Bassuk, DeCandla, Tsertsvadze, & Richard, 2014). Noting that evidence-based interventions for homeless families are "long overdue" (p 475), Bassuk et al. point to a lack of affordable housing as an obstacle to HF approaches for families. Relatedly, family-size apartments are scarcer and more expensive than one-bedroom and studio apartments.

Not surprisingly, the complications associated with assisting homeless families with young children are of a different order than complications associated with assisting single adults. School authorities and the child welfare system often are involved because children may have to move between school districts, and the status of being homeless is itself cause for concern in child welfare. Rent and support services cannot draw on the inadequate (but regular) monthly disability check—public assistance payments are far less and come with a work requirement.

Child welfare authorities have different goals and priorities, which can stand in the way of a HF approach for families. Their overriding interest in child well-being often puts them in an adversarial position with parents and is typically incident-based, (e.g., a "closed case" is the marker of success). Attitudes toward drug or alcohol use are more zero tolerance than harm reduction; family choice is accorded low if any priority; and the prohibition on a "man in the house" creates obvious dilemmas for single mothers. And yet, as described in an award-winning *New York Times* series about an 11-year-old homeless girl named Dasani (Elliott, 2013), even the presence of a father and mother cannot forestall the cascade of events that results in homelessness, a maelstrom with many causes and too few solutions.

Although families' needs are different, structural constraints are similar to those affecting single homeless adults: Jobs are in short supply and do not pay enough to cover rent and other living expenses. Housing vouchers and public housing units are increasingly scarce and much harder to obtain while homeless. Stigma and victim blaming tend to take precedence over client choice and empowerment.

In the following sections, we offer two examples of research on homeless families, one a "real world" partnership implementing HF and the other a large-scale national randomized trial intended to test various models of housing and services.

HENNEPIN COUNTY, MINNESOTA. With its county seat of Minneapolis, Hennepin County has 1.2 million residents of whom an estimated 4,000 are homeless. Adopting a "high fidelity" version of HF (PHF), the County has forged close working relationships with the state authorities as well as local providers, the faith and business communities, and landlords (a key activity being the annual "landlord appreciation" event). Families targeted for HF assistance by Heading Home Hennepin (the umbrella organization) must have a disabled member who cannot work and be long-term homeless. (On average, families in HF were homeless for six years.)

The opposite of a "hands-off" approach, Heading Home Hennepin has 10 partner agencies to ensure that families get not only a place to live but also receive other assistance needed, including application fees, security deposits, utility services, and household supplies. Over 1,000 families have been placed in apartments with support services. Evaluation of the project has yielded a 91% retention rate after one year (http://www.hennepin.us/~/media/hennepinus/your-government/projects-initiatives/documents/housing-first-partnership-fs-2012.pdf).

THE FAMILY OPTIONS STUDY (FOS). The FOS, funded by the U. S. Department of Housing and Urban Development (HUD), represents one of the most comprehensive evaluations to date of various housing and service configurations for homeless families. Begun in 2008, the FOS enrolled over 2,000 families in 12 communities across the United States, all recruited from emergency shelters where they had spent a minimum of seven days. The study compared (1) community-based rapid re-housing (CBRR), (2) project-based transitional housing (PBTH), (3) permanent housing subsidies (SUB), and (4) usual care (UC) emergency shelter placement.

CBRR provides temporary rental assistance for two to six months (renewable up to 18 months) along with limited housing-focused services to help families secure private-market rental housing. PBTH is temporary housing (up to 24 months, with average expected stays of 6–12 months) in agency-controlled buildings or apartment units with intensive supportive services. SUB is a permanent housing subsidy (usually a Housing Choice voucher), with housing placement assistance but no other targeted services after placement. Finally, UC is the emergency shelter from which families were recruited, along with any housing or services that people would normally access from a shelter in the absence of the first three FOS interventions. Stays of 30 to 90 days are typical.

Recalling the continuum or staircase analogy, UC is the bottom step and PBTH is further up the staircase with institutional housing (clusters of apartments in the same building) where families may share a kitchen and bathroom. The two remaining options, both involving community-based scatter-site housing, offer few services beyond housing placement assistance. CBRR is probably best suited for low-need families in a temporary bind and SUB for families needing long-term rental subsidies but little else in the way of support.

Carried out by Abt Associates and led by Abt's Steven Bell and Professor Mary Beth Shinn of Vanderbilt University, the FOS is a randomized trial examining which of these alternatives works best to promote housing stability, family preservation, self-sufficiency, and adult and child well-being. This is a tall order. Enrollment of 2,282 families—typically mothers in their twenties having one or two children—took over a year and the 18-month follow-up period of observation concluded in September 2013 (U.S. Department of Housing and Urban Development, 2013).

Perhaps not surprisingly, some families in the study had additional problems besides homelessness. Baseline measures showed histories of drug use within the past year by 14% of the adult respondents, 11% reported alcohol abuse within the past year, 22% had symptoms of posttraumatic stress disorder, 22% reported symptoms of serious psychological distress, and 30% reported evidence of one or the other of these psychological problems. The baseline survey explicitly asked families about factors that would affect their ability to find a place to live. Many reported that they either had a poor rental history (26% had been evicted) or that they had never been a leaseholder (35%). Some (14%) reported that at least one adult in the family had been convicted of a felony for drugs or other offenses. In 11% of families, the adult respondent had a felony conviction.

As in all research, study participants in the FOS had the right to refuse participation at any time—and quite a few family heads exercised that right upon being given their random assignment: rejection rates were 71% for PBTH, 51% for CBRR, and 36% for the SUB option. UC was the only assignment that was not an option, given that families were already in that condition. This level of refusal after consenting to be in a randomized trial is unusually high and obviously consequential. The 18-month report released in July, 2015 showed that rapid re-housing was cost-effective but housing subsidies (the SUB option) produced the most positive outcomes.

HOMELESS YOUTHS. Young people in their teens and early twenties face some of the same issues as their older homeless counterparts but with specific problems related to younger age and the systemic options (or lack thereof) available to them. Often runaways (or "throw-aways") from abusive families, homeless youths are more likely to be members of a sexual minority and to come from middle-class backgrounds than are their adult counterparts. At the same time, a significant proportion has aged out of foster care and is not ready or able to assume adult responsibilities (Thompson, 2013).

The perquisites of youth—good health, sexual awakening, and adventure-seeking—can make being homeless a minefield of risk factors for sexually transmitted diseases and other problems (e.g., substance abuse, "survival sex" to make money, and sex trafficking by predatory adults (Milburn et al., 2009). Suspicious of adults (often with good reason), many homeless youth avoid formal services and get caught up in a "street youth lifestyle" (Gaetz, 2014a). Commonly seen in milder climates and tolerant cities such as Portland, Oregon or Austin, Texas, their encampments are an alternative to couch surfing with friends. Less likely to be on the "institutional circuit" experienced by chronically homeless adults (Hopper et al., 1997), homeless youths still have to contend with crowded youth shelters and juvenile detention centers.

Emergency shelter beds for youths are far outpaced by demand. The typical threshold for chronicity—usually set at six months—is telling for this group. The National Alliance to End Homelessness estimates that 550,000 young people in the United States are homeless each year for a week or longer, with 50,000 homeless longer than six months (NAEH, 2014). HUD's single-night count of unaccompanied youths up to age 24 was 194,302 in 2014 (HUD, 2014).

The tenets of HF can be applied to young people if tailored to their needs and capabilities. Living on one's own in independent scatter-site housing is not the norm for this age group (nor could a landlord legally accept such a tenancy without an adult on the lease). In addition, the principle of consumer choice must accommodate legal prohibitions for underage minors as well as their degree of maturity in making consequential decisions. There is a substantial capability gap between a 16-year-old and a 24-year-old, and these developmental variations make any one-size-fits-all approach a poor fit for youths (Gaetz, 2014a).

Research on homeless youths has primarily focused on strategies for engaging this elusive group (Thompson, 2013). To this end, young people are more prone to use social media; Internet access through public libraries, cafes, and youth centers, therefore, provides a ready-made venue for outreach and engagement (Pollio, Batey, Bender, Ferguson, & Thompson, 2013; Rice & Barman-Adhikari, 2014). Residential care—if available at all—has traditionally consisted of dormitory-style quarters with on-site security and varying amounts of support services—not always attractive to young people uncomfortable with rules. Both the scarcity and transitory nature of this type of service delivery has contributed to a scant record of research on housing options for homeless youths.

Steven Gaetz, a professor and leading homeless advocate, has noted that the widespread embrace of HF has yet to be extended to young adults (Gaetz, 2014a). A founder of the Canadian Observatory on Homelessness and The Homeless Hub website (http://www.homelesshub.ca/), Gaetz cites the success of Calgary's Infinity Project operated by the Boys and Girls Clubs. Serving young people 16–24 years old, the project assists homeless youth in attaining permanent housing and self-sufficiency (Gaetz, 2014b). In addition to housing and rent supplements, social services and life skills training are offered. An evaluation of the Infinity Project showed success in housing retention—95% after the first year (Scott & Harrison, 2013).

The expansion of HF to populations not included in the original model—families and youths in particular—is still in its infancy. Similar to the implementation hurdles encountered in new settings, this challenge does not negate the utility of HF but most assuredly requires that specific needs are addressed without sacrificing the basic tenets of choice, self-determination, and access to housing without weighty preconditions. The crux of the matter is this: How compromising are the alterations? Applications of HF with homeless youth are likely to include congregate living and supervision of some kind (at least at the outset). And a "pure" application of HF for homeless families is not to be found in the Family Options Study, where the least restrictive community-based housing options come with the fewest support services and only the most restrictive housing option comes with intensive support services.

Systems Change: Extending Beyond Homeless Services

The reach of HF has begun to affect other systems of care. First and foremost among these is mental health care within homeless services. The transformative message of the mental health recovery movement, a central feature of HF, combines person-centered care with attention to fundamental needs. It is difficult to reconcile mental health recovery with a shelter bed or living in congregate care with other psychiatrically disabled persons. These are persons who, not very long ago, had access to the community only if someone else turned the ward key to open the hospital door. Who, when brought into HF, are given a set of keys to open the door to their own apartment. They are also allowed to come and go as they please, to refuse or accept psychiatric treatment, and to work on their substance abuse without having to sacrifice their housing. This level of decision-making authority and self-determination had not been an option before. In looking back on the history of how mental illness is treated (Whitaker, 2010), this is a quantum leap forward.

In this book, we have seen how the walls separating mental health (and physical health) from housing have started to crumble under HF. Thus, housing authorities became attuned to the needs and life possibilities of HF tenants (with the active assistance of HF staff) and mental health providers came to appreciate the fundamental role of housing in a client's life. Systems change in Europe entailed ending the longstanding separation of social housing from health and mental health provision. In the United States, the joining of housing and support services involved the private housing market, where home visits might be part of the tenant's responsibilities but were not subject to landlord approval (as would be the case with any tenant).

Regardless of venue, the changes introduced by HF were substantial. Housing authorities and landlords had to be convinced to accept clients with no credit worthiness, no letters of recommendation from previous landlords, and limited-to-no income. They learned through experience that the program's support services helped offset the risk, even benefiting them with regular rent payments and someone to call if the tenant was causing problems. For their part, mental health and healthcare providers had to change customary exertions of power over their patients, instead learning to honor consumer choice, cede authority, and work with housing and other providers to get the best results. Changes in practice required moving from the office to the community, in effect, making "house calls." The home visit is an artful combination of engagement, support, and monitoring. As such, it has little in common with the brisk neutrality of an office visit.

Even one of the most resistant-to-change systems of care—substance abuse treatment and its providers—has been gradually adapting to changing times and the growing body of evidence supporting harm reduction (Glaser, 2014). Although the influence of HF on systems change in addictions is still in its early stages, some well-known addiction researchers have tested its impact with this population and found it beneficial (Davidson et al., 2014).

The Dignity of Failure

A sea change in attitudes is the optimal outcome given these cross-system transformations. This refers to a responsible but determined willingness to take the risks needed to be socially inclusive of people with complex needs. It means being tolerant of failure—not every client given the opportunity gets it right the first time (the same can be said for anyone). Such an attitudinal change extends beyond HF and homeless services.

The challenge for extant programs and systems is to expand options and opportunities. As consumer advocate Patricia Deegan cautions, without providing the dignity of failure, a society eliminates the possibility of success (www. patdeegan.com). Openness to risk and change starts at the top—policymakers and governments willing to innovate—but it also reaches down to the organizational, programmatic, and individual level.

The gravitational force of risk aversion is powerful in clinical practice as well as in program development. Leaving the controlled confines of the office, working with clients who are active substance users and unwilling to accept a psychiatric diagnosis (or the prescribed medications), providing injections and blood-draws in less than ideal settings, talking about the effects of the psychiatric medications on weight gain and diabetes risk—all are part of this new way of doing things. Landlords can learn to be more flexible when someone has to move before the lease is up. Employers, friends, and neighbors can be more accepting if someone does not say the conventional thing or does not manage to navigate social cues as expected. Social inclusion is risk and work shared by all.

Housing as Health: The Affordable Care Act

The Affordable Care Act (ACA) passed under President Obama's leadership in 2010 gives states the option to expand Medicaid and Medicare coverage to include "housing as health." By providing financial incentives for health and behavioral health programs to work closely with supportive housing programs, public dollars are directed to housing through Accountable Care Organizations and other health-related venues. Along with other states, New York applied for a waiver under the ACA to use Medicaid dollars to fund capital investment in housing. The rationale is simple yet without precedent at the Federal level: supportive housing significantly brings down healthcare costs, especially of high utilizers (Doran, Misa, & Shah, 2013).

Although still in the early stages, the "housing as health" movement has caught fire in many parts of the country where policymakers desperately have sought to contain skyrocketing healthcare costs. The calculus is rather simple: The costs of stays in hospitals, nursing homes, jails, shelters, and detox centers—not to mention ambulance rides and emergency room visits—are consuming large chunks of state budgets.

The benefits of housing include much more than cost savings (although for some this is sufficient in itself). If one considers the hazards of street life—exposure to hypothermia, infectious diseases, untreated dental problems, disabling injuries—trips to the emergency room are frequently the only (and most expensive) option. Not only does having a home offer shelter from such exposures, it also offers a stable platform for seeking and receiving medical care. Self-care—taking medications, making appointments, maintaining hygiene and nutritional needs—is made infinitely easier in one's home.

The longstanding tradition of biomedicine and health care in the United States—one of cure rather than prevention and of narrowing the window for action to the patient's self-presentation of symptoms—fatefully downplays the influence of the social and physical environment. Yet the "housing as health" movement is not without its downside. Tying eligibility for housing to poor health implies that recovery and better health could bring an end to the housing. The prospect of having to prove ill health to avert homelessness is a form of pathologizing poverty (Hansen et al., 2014), giving the medical establishment the gatekeeping role for what is in most Western nations a social entitlement. In addition, by drawing on Federal funds designated for health care, the movement further relieves the government from responsibility for building and subsidizing affordable housing. As a stopgap measure, "housing as health" is a step forward, but it serves as a Band-Aid solution to a far larger social problem.

Conclusion: Housing First and Systems Change

We end this chapter and this book by noting that the impact of HF on homeless services has been deep and wide. Moreover, its influence in social and behavior health sectors is part of a much-needed movement toward recognizing the salubrious effects of housing. Given that we now know "housing readiness" is unnecessary, and that supported housing, with the right level of support, works for the overwhelming majority, the obvious next step from a policy and funding angle is to focus resources on what ends homelessness rather than on what prepares people to be housed. We also return to an earlier acknowledgement that the staircase—part of the massive homeless services industry—is not yet demolished even as the profound influence of HF chips away at it.

Pivoting from "what has happened" to "what could or should happen" in the wake of HF blends evidence and values—central to what HF stands for. Robust empirical evidence with a strong dose of humanism has changed the conversation about mental illness, homelessness, and even substance abuse. And yet, the homeless services industry remains a lumbering giant, even as HF has prodded it to move away from its expensive and ineffective continuum habits.

Yet, systems change, no matter how impressive, is not the same as structural change. We conclude with an acknowledgment that all that has been wrought by HF has not (yet) changed the world as we know it. Then again, one must start somewhere.

Notes

1. There is a rapidly growing number of successful HF programs for families. The most up-to-date information can be found at www.naeh.org.

2. NAEH Director Nan Roman has worked with the William T. Gates Foundation on applying Housing First to survivors of domestic violence in Washington State (Roman, 2011).

3. According to research by Dennis Culhane, nearly all of the chronic homeless have a disability—mental, physical, and/or substance abuse—and most homeless persons with a disability are not chronically homeless (2014).

4. The second Housing First Partners Conference (HFPC) in March 2014 in Chicago featured keynote talks and public forums for discussing the impact of Olmstead provisions. The third HFPC is planned for 2016 in Los Angeles.

5. Interestingly, single-site housing for individuals with a substance abuse diagnosis (such as Seattle's DESC) is exempt from Olmstead's mandate, because substance abuse is not considered a "disability" under the ADA.

6. Our use of past tense throughout the description of the adult home industry should be observed with caution, because many of the practices described are still happening at this writing.

CODA: The Changing Landscape: A Few Updates

The landscape of homeless services is, to say the least, in flux. In this Coda, we feature a few updates—no doubt many others have been omitted (and for this we apologize in advance). The following appeared the most noteworthy.

PATHWAYS TO HOUSING IN NEW YORK. A regrettable transition occurred on December 31, 2014, when the Pathways Board of Directors decided to close the New York program after 22 years in existence. Its operations and clientele were transferred to a consumer-friendly agency brokered by New York State's Office of Mental Health. Pathways in New York had been struggling financially in recent years, beset by a combination of inconsistent management decisions, lack of support from key government funding agencies, and accumulation of debt. Pathways's closing did not lead to a loss of services or housing for tenants, and its staff were smoothly transitioned to work in the new setting.

This turn of events is not uncommon in the highly competitive and pressured service environment of New York City. Pathways grew to serve over 700 tenants, but by local standards remained a small player—economies of scale favored larger agencies that could sustain temporary losses without sacrificing credit ratings or credibility with funders and state authorities. Meanwhile, the other Pathways agencies in Washington DC, Philadelphia, and Vermont continue to be successful and to grow, with strong local support and funding. Pathways National continues to provide consultation and training to disseminate the Housing First (HF) model.

Nevertheless, the steady stream of national and international visitors who had arrived on New York Pathways's doorstep since 1992—many of whom came in disbelief to see for themselves—will now have to be diverted elsewhere. This phenomenon—"seeing is believing"—has been repeated in a number of places in the United States and abroad.

NEW YORK CITY'S DEPARTMENT OF HOMELESS SERVICES (DHS). If there was ever any doubt about the immensity of the homeless services industry, one need only look to New York City's DHS budget of $1 billion in 2015. One-half of this amount goes to family shelter operations, which frequently benefit private landlords and land owners willing to rent sometimes decrepit motel rooms and apartments at high rates. The second largest budget item is the adult shelter system ($330 million). Some homeless advocates point to the city's right-to-shelter legal obligation as diverting public dollars from more permanent housing solutions. Meanwhile, the city of New York in 2015 had a record-high number of 60,000 homeless persons.

These record levels of spending and homelessness reflect how heavily invested the city's DHS is in the provision of emergency and transitional housing. From the early 1990s to the present, providers of services to the city's homeless have been dominated by nonprofits that dwarf Pathways to Housing (PTH) in size and scope. This did not change despite the growing popularity of HF elsewhere. What did change was the growing influence of HF emanating from this national and international recognition—influence such that the staircase or continuum approach has begun to erode in New York. Yet systems change in the city has been slow, more often consisting of a program adding a top step to the staircase than reversing the order of the steps (or eliminating the stairs altogether).

ENDING SHELTERS: THE PINE STREET INN. Boston's Pine Street Inn is a prime example of how a large service provider can successfully start the transition from shelters to permanent housing and HF. In December 2014, Pine Street announced this major shift after taking a hard inward look at their operations and an outward look at what policy researchers like Dennis Culhane were saying about the 5% or so of chronically homeless individuals who were using the most shelter bed nights. Collecting their own data, Pine Street staff found the same phenomenon as Culhane had found. In 2007, Pine Street initiated a HF pilot project for shelter residents who had lived there for 10 years or more (such long-term habitation a jarring testimony to the service system's overall failings). A year later,

86% remained stably housed—and Pine Street's "rescue mission" focus dating back to 1969 was called into question. Local foundations took notice and offered funds for permanent housing, one foundation executive remarking, "my dream is that Pine Street will be the Museum of Homelessness in Boston" in the future (Haywoode, 2014).

Several cities have announced policy shifts away from shelters to HF, including Phoenix, Arizona, whose mayor Greg Stanton explained the rationale for closing an unsafe shelter and diverting funding to permanent housing: "Real apartments. Real places for people to stay so that they can build some housing stability in their lives. It's the right thing to do" (McClay, 2015). In Salt Lake City, a leading shelter (The Road Home) was facing local opposition when city officials decided to invoke their success with HF as a reason to rethink the need for such shelters (McDonald & Gallivan, 2015). And in Anchorage, Alaska, city and state officials "recognize the effectiveness of the housing first model" (O'Malley, 2015) and in early 2015 began funding two HF programs in the city. This list of cities grows by the day.

ENDING VETERAN HOMELESSNESS. This HUD-VASH initiative has continued to receive national attention for its successes since adopting HF in 2010. In California, 25 cities pledged to end veteran homelessness in 2015, an ambitious goal but one with considerable resources and political will to back it up. Working with the 100K Homes Campaign, HUD-VASH has been extended to homeless vets nationwide, depending on local communities (and VA facilities) for outreach and engagement.

In addition to following HF faithfully and matching support services to veterans' needs, HUD-VASH expanded its assistance through the Supportive Services for Veteran Families (SSVF) program. Focused on prevention, the SSVF has helped veterans and their families at risk of becoming homeless through cash outlays to pay a utility or medical bill, cover the cost of car repairs, or pay for a month's rent. According to Vincent Kane, former Director of the National Center on Homelessness Among Veterans, "Housing First works, because veterans are more likely to achieve stability and improved quality of life when the risks, uncertainty and trauma associated with homelessness are removed."

CANADA'S HOMELESSNESS PARTNERING STRATEGY AND THE AT HOME/CHEZ SOI PROJECT. Have garnered international attention and the Homelessness Partnering Strategy (HPS) has expanded its mandate to implement HF programs to include cities and towns throughout the country. Its positioning of HF as the first priority has met with some opposition (mainly from providers for homeless families and youth because these populations are not included among the chronically homeless) but there has been no retreat from the policy. Since the launch of the HPS in April 2007, the national government has approved over $750 million for projects to prevent and reduce homelessness across Canada. In 2013, it proposed to renew the HPS until March 2019 using a "Housing First" approach. (http://action-plan.gc.ca/en/initiative/homelessness-partnering-strategy). The formation of the Canadian Alliance to End Homelessness (CAEH), a counterpart to the NAEH, began with an annual conference in 2013, its primary goal fostering 10-Year Plans to End Homelessness and a 20K Homes campaign launched in 2015 (www.caeh.ca).

Investigators with the At Home/Chez Soi project have been successful in publishing their findings in a number of journals including a report on the health benefits of HF (Hwang & Burns, 2014). The most comprehensive and widely cited report to date was published in the *Journal of the American Medical Association* (Stergiopoulos et al., 2015). Results from the At Home/Chez Soi randomized trial showed significant improvements in housing stability and cost savings for the HF group, although no group differences in a measure of quality of life. Given the rare recognition of an approving editorial accompanying the article (Katz, 2015), the Stergiopoulos et al. findings were cited as part of the growing evidence base favoring HF and scatter-site living.

NATIONAL ALLIANCE TO END HOMELESSNESS. Led by its indefatigable executive director Nan Roman, NAEH sponsors two annual conferences (one devoted to families and youth) and maintains its national role as a policy-focused champion of ending homelessness. A combination of information clearinghouse and skilled Washington insider, NAEH provides webinars on topics ranging from the annual point-in-time count of homelessness to the latest in rapid rehousing programs for families. NAEH conferences draw an extraordinarily eclectic group of attendees, ranging from faith-based organizations to social enterprises to academic researchers.

In its 2015 annual report, NAEH announced the January 2014 point-in-time count was 578,424 homeless persons, a decrease of 2.3% from the year before. http://endhomelessness.org/library/entry/the-state-of-homelessness-in-america-2015 Although encouraging in its downward trajectory, this trend is taking place in the midst of strong indicators of economic recovery from the 2008 recession, a recovery that has increased wealth for those in higher income brackets and produced widening income disparities affecting everyone else.

BUILDINGS WITH LARGE CAPITAL INVESTMENTS: THE SUGAR HILL RESIDENCE. The business model continues to foster new building projects targeted to reducing homelessness. One formula for this is complicated but not uncommon: Large financial corporations are given tax breaks (under the Federal Low Income Housing Tax Credit Program) in exchange for financing new housing loans for nonprofit organizations and housing authorities. For their investment, these corporations earn a 6% profit (Carrier, 2015). For political and community leaders, the ribbon-cutting ceremony generates good public relations and good will.

Manhattan's Sugar Hill Residence, completed in late 2014, is a shining architectural example of capital investment used for public good. Located on Harlem's Coogan's Bluff, Sugar Hill is the seventh integrated housing residence established by Ellen Baxter's organization, Broadway Housing Communities. The building was financed by the New York City Department of Housing Preservation and Development, which dedicated $10 million in federal funds and $3 million in tax credits, in addition to $3 million in capital funding from the City Council. It has 13 stories and 124 units, 25 of which are reserved for families coming from the shelter system.

Sugar Hill will house support services as well as community amenities, including a children's art program and museum, a preschool, and a daycare facility. The operating premise of Sugar Hill is similar to earlier approaches pioneered by Baxter, namely, mixed or integrated housing, including persons with disabilities and low-income tenants, and affordable, income-calibrated rents.

In October 2014, *New York Times* architecture critic Michael Kimmelman reviewed the Sugar Hill project and stated, "designed by a marquee architect [David Adjaye from Britain], with no concessions to timid taste, the project aspires to must-see status." Kimmelman mixes praise with caution, "Sugar Hill is something of an extravagance and not easily replicable. But it posits a goal for what subsidized housing might look like, how it could lift a neighborhood and mold a generation." The project—with rent-subsidized apartments—will pay one fourth of tenants to watch the front reception area 24/7 and be the "eyes on the neighborhood."

The building has an exterior of dark gray precast concrete with abruptly cantilevered floors, textured surfaces, and idiosyncratic small windows. To accommodate the design, apartments have angled walls, deep-set windows, and uneven layouts. Kimmelman concludes, "Providing poor families with small, distinctive but difficult living spaces to accommodate a striking facade throws the whole design into question, betraying the project's basic mission." (Kimmelman, 2014). Nevertheless, Sugar Hill's success in attracting tenants, given the amenities and affordability, is assured.

SKID ROW IN LOS ANGELES. A latecomer to HF, Los Angeles County in 2014 initiated change with new partners such as the County's Department of Health, which has committed to develop 10,000 units of supportive housing—a decision based in large part on the cost-savings found in research elsewhere. Meanwhile, Skid Row has become a picture of striking contrasts as expensive condominiums encroach upon its borders putting more pressure on supportive housing projects, such as the architecturally modern Starr Apartments.

As of the end of 2014, the United Way of Los Angeles through its Home for Good Initiative was convening monthly strategy meetings aimed at ending chronic and veteran homelessness through a HF approach. At the table are a Who's Who of local homeless services: Los Angeles County's Departments of Health and Mental Health, the Housing Authority of the City of Los Angeles, Los Angeles Homeless Services Authority, the VA Greater Los Angeles Health Systems, the Corporation for Supportive Housing, and the Conrad Hilton Foundation. Using a data-driven approach, the meetings have set a goal of ending veterans' homelessness by the close of 2015 and chronic homelessness by 2016. Although off to a good start, these heroic efforts will be needed to distance Los Angeles and Skid Row from its media notoriety.

With regard to HF in particular, scatter-site living and dispersal from the downtown area have been difficult given the enormous expanses involved in Los Angeles County, namely, nearly 10 million residents living across 4,000 square miles. The combination of geography, lack of public transportation, and scarcity of affordable housing constitute some of the highest hurdles imaginable for HF (although its implementation is in the offing). As the downtown area gentrifies (and complaints from nearby condo owners increase), the pressure to act will intensify. At this writing, Skid Row continues to be a vast open-air encampment with a strong police presence, its rundown buildings housing rescue missions, clinics, and social service programs.

FEANTSA AND THE EUROPEAN MOVE TOWARD HOUSING FIRST. Continues apace with all of the complications inherent to cross-national differences. With funding from the Stavros Niarchos Foundation, an online interactive web guide to implementing HF is being developed. About one half of the 28 EU-member nations are in the process of adopting HF in selected localities, and several are carrying out research on the model's effectiveness. Cities further along in this process include Copenhagen and Odense in Denmark; Stockholm, Gothenburg, and Helsingborg in Sweden; Amsterdam in The Netherlands; and Helsinki in Finland. In January 2015, an Irish charity known as Midlands Simon signed an agreement with Pathways National to implement a high-fidelity HF program in the Midlands region of Ireland. Such formal ties to Pathways are unusual in the

European experience of HF, which is more often informally influenced by in-person visits from Sam Tsemberis.

Although still early on, ripple effects of HF are being noted, including an emphasis on more humane treatment and inclusion of homeless persons' preferences (Liz Gosme, personal communication). At a March 2015 conference in Milan, Italy held for HF providers and foundation representatives, a representative from Bologna noted that their success with HF, albeit on a small scale, had influenced the city's shelter system to eliminate the heavy security guard presence at the shelters. Also featured at the conference was moving testimony from a client in Milan's HF program who spoke of his new home and pursuit of sobriety after years of drinking and sleeping on the street (Alice Stefanizzi, personal communication). Whether needing to see it firsthand or trusting the accumulating evidence, skeptics in Western Europe—like their counterparts in the United States, Australia, and Canada—find it difficult to ignore the transformations in lives and systems wrought by HF.

These updates represent a small portion of the many changes afoot in homeless services in Western nations. Despite significant declines attributable to HF in many localities, the seeming intransigence of homelessness is testimony to the enduring (and expanding) inequalities afflicting these nations. We hope that systems changes gain momentum such that homelessness becomes a thing of the past.

Acknowledgments

This book was made possible by the efforts of many people whose lives inspired us. First and foremost, we are grateful to the (formerly) homeless men and women featured in this book. Their struggles and successes constitute a fundamental reason for telling the story of Housing First. We also salute the providers and front-line staff in homeless services whose involvement in Housing First—whether in support or opposition—is an integral part of the story. We owe gratitude to those who championed Housing First in their respective bailiwicks—and we have sought to showcase their efforts herein.

Key studies whose findings are featured in Chapters 4, 5, and 6 were directed by this book's coauthors and owe their funding to U.S. government sources: The New York Housing Study was supported by the Substance Abuse and Mental Health Services Administration (SAMHSA); both the New York Services Study and the New York Recovery Study were funded by the National Institute of Mental Health (NIMH).

We extend appreciation to the reviewers of the manuscript who gave helpful and supportive comments. We thank Sarah Bones for the photographs featured in Chapter 7. Last but not least, we thank our OUP Editor Dana Bliss for shepherding us through the process with good advice at every turn.

References

Allen, M. (2003). Waking Rip Van Winkle: Why developments in the last 20 years should teach the mental health system not to use housing as a tool of coercion. *Behavioral Sciences and the Law, 21*, 503–521.

Anderson, E. (2000). *Code of the street: Decency, violence, and the moral life of the inner city.* WW Norton & Company.

Ansari, S. M., Fiss, P. C., & Zajac, E. J. (2010). Made to fit: How practices vary as they diffuse. *Academy of Management Review, 35*(1), 67–92.

Anthony, W. (1993). Recovery from mental illness: The guiding vision of the mental health system in the 1990s. *Psychosocial Rehabilitation Journal, 16*, 11.

Anthony, W. A., Cohen, M., & Farkas, M. (1982). A psychiatric rehabilitation treatment program: Can I recognize one if I see one? *Community Mental Health Journal, 18*(2), 83–96.

Anthony, W. A., Cohen, M. R., & Farkas M. (2002). *Psychiatric rehabilitation* (2nd ed.). Boston, MA: Center for Psychiatric Rehabilitation.

Atherton, I., & McNaughton-Nicholls, C. (2008). Housing first as a means of addressing multiple needs and homelessness. *European Journal of Homelessness, 2*, 289–303.

Barrow, S., McMullin, J., Tripp, J., & Tsemberis, S. (2007). Consumer integration and self-determination in homelessness research, policy, planning, and services. National Symposium on Homelessness Research. Retrieved from: http://aspe.hhs.gov/hsp/homelessness/symposium07/

Barry, S. (2014, December 30). Most homeless fight way back to security, says shelter chief. Retrieved from http://www.masslive.com/news/index.ssf/2014/12/as_more_public_funds_are_relea.html

Bassuk, E., DeCandla, C. J., Tsertsvadze, A., & Richard, M. K. (2014). The effect of housing interventions and housing and service interventions on ending family homelessness: A systematic review. *American Journal of Orthopsychiatry, 84*, 457–474.

Battams, S., & Baum, F. (2010). What policies and policy processes are needed to ensure that people with psychiatric disabilities have access to appropriate housing? *Social Science & Medicine*, 70, 1026–1034.

Battilana, J., Leca, B., & Boxenbaum, E. (2009). How actors change institutions: Towards a theory of institutional entrepreneurship. *The Academy of Management Annals*, 3(1), 65–107.

Baumgardner, J., & Herman, D. (2012). Community integration of formerly homeless men and women with severe mental illness after hospital discharge. *Psychiatric Services*, 63, 435–437.

Bazelon Center. (March, 2014). A place of my own: How the ADA is creating integrated housing opportunities for people with mental illnesses. Retrieved from www.bazelon. org/portals/0/Where We Stand/Community Integration/Olmstead/A Place of My Own. Bazelon Center for Mental Health Law.pdf.

Becker, D. R., Drake, R. E., & Bond, G. R. (2011). Benchmark outcomes in supported employment. *American Journal of Psychiatric Rehabilitation*, 14, 230–236.

Benjaminsen, L., Dyb, E., & O'Sullivan, E. (2009). The governance of homelessness in liberal and social democratic welfare regimes: National strategies and models of intervention. *European Journal of Homelessness*, 3, 23–49.

Binder, A. (2007). For love and money: Organizations' creative responses to multiple environmental logics. *Theory and Society*, 36, 547–571.

Bourgois, P. (2009). *Righteous dope fiend*. Berkeley: University of California Press.

Brenner, J. (1987). Feminist political discourses: Radical versus liberal approaches to the feminization of poverty and comparable worth. *Gender & Society*, 1, 447–465.

Brooks, C. (2015, January 2). ARCH working to end homelessness. Retrieved from http:// www.timesnews.net/article/9083800/arch-working-to-end-homelessness

Burt, M. R., & Aron, L. Y. (2000). *America's homeless II: Populations and services*. Washington, DC: Urban Institute.

Busch-Geertsema, V. (November, 2013). Housing First Europe: Results of a social experimentation project. Paper presented at the 3rd Annual Convention of the European Platform. Brussels, Belgium.

Byrne, T., & Culhane, D. P. (2011). The right to housing: An effective means for addressing homelessness? *University of Pennsylvania Journal of Law and Social Change*, 14(3), 379–390.

Byrne, T., Roberts, C. B., Culhane, D. P., & Kane, V. (2014). *Estimating cost savings associated with HUD-VASH placement*. Washington DC: U. S. Department of Veterans Affairs.

Cameron, S., & Makhoul, A. (2009). *Community stories: Alberta's seven cities partnership*. Ottawa, Canada: Caledon Institute of Social Policy.

Carling, P. (1993). Housing and supports for persons with mental illness: Emerging approaches to research and practice. *Hospital and Community Psychiatry*, 44(5), 439–449.

Carrier, S. (2015, March/April). Room for improvement. *Mother Jones*. Retrieved from http://www.motherjones.com/politics/2015/02/housing-first-solution-t o-homelessness-utah

Charmaz, K. (2006). *Constructing grounded theory*. Thousand Oaks, CA: Sage.

Cho, R. S. (2014, June 18). Four clarifications about Housing First. Retrieved from http:// usich.gov/blog/four-clarifications-about-housing-first?utm_source=Housing+First+Gai ns+Momentum&utm_campaign=Housing+First+Newsletter&utm_medium=email

City of Toronto. (2007). *What Housing First means for people: Results of Streets to Homes 2007 post-occupancy research*. Toronto, Canada: City of Toronto, Shelter and Housing Administration.

Clemens, E. S., & Cook, J. M. (1999). Politics and institutionalism: Explaining durability and change. *Annual Review of Sociology, 441–466*.

Cloke, P., Milbourne, P., & Widdowfield, R. (2002). Rural homelessness: Issues, experiences, and policy responses. *Housing Studies, 17*(6), 919–927.

Cohen, M. D., & Somers, S. A. (1990). Supported housing: Insights from the RWJ Program on Chronic Mental Illness. *Psychosocial Rehabilitation Journal, 13*, 43–50.

Collins, S. E., Malone, D. K., & Clifasefi, S. L. (2013). Housing retention in single-site Housing First for chronically homeless individuals with severe alcohol problems. *American Journal of Public Health, 103*(S2), S269–S274.

Corrigan, P. W., & Boyle, M. G. (2003). What works for mental health system change: Evolution or revolution. *Administration and Policy in Mental Health, 30*, 379–395.

Cornelius, N., Todres, M., Janjuha-Jivraj, S., Woods, A., & Wallace, J. (2008). Corporate social responsibility and the social enterprise. *Journal of Business Ethics, 81*(2), 355–370.

Corporation for Supportive Housing. (2014, July). Housing is the best medicine: Supportive housing and the social determinants of health. Retrieved from https://www.health. ny.gov/health_care/medicaid/program/medicaid_health_homes/docs/social_ determinants_of_health_final.pdf

Corrigan, P. W., Salzer, M., Ralph, R. O., Sangster, Y., & Keck, L. (2004). Examining the factor structure of the Recovery Assessment Scale. *Schizophrenia Bulletin, 30*, 11–19.

Cress, D. M., & Snow, D. A. (2000). The outcomes of homeless mobilization: The influence of organization, disruption, political mediation, and framing. *American Journal of Sociology, 105*, 1063–1104.

Culbert, L. (2104, June 27). Participants with mental illness, addictions thrive after being given apartments: Five-year national study. *Vancouver Sun*. Retrieved from http://www. vancouversun.com/news/Participants+with+mental+illness+addictions+thrive+after+b eing+given+apartments+five+year/9979290/story.html#ixzz3955bMXBo

Culhane, D., Metraux, S., & Hadley, T. (2002). Public service reductions associated with placement of homeless persons with severe mental illness in supportive housing. *Housing Policy Debate, 13*, 107–163.

Culhane, D., Metraux, S., Byrne, T., Stino, M., & Bainbridge, J. (2013). The age structure of contemporary homelessness: Evidence and implications for public policy. Retrieved from http://works.bepress.com/dennis_culhane/124

Culhane, D. P. (2014). Non-chronic adult homelessness: Background and opportunities. Presented at the National Alliance to End Homelessness Annual Conference, July 29, 2014, Washington DC.

Damschroder, L. J., Aron, D. C., Keith, R. E., Kirsh, S. R., Alexander, J. A., & Lowery, J. C. (2009). Fostering implementation of health services research findings into practice: A consolidated framework for advancing implementation science. *Implementation Science, 4*(1), 50–59.

Davidson, C., Neighbors, C., Hall, G., Hogue, A., Cho, R., Kutner, B, & Morgenstern, J. (2014, July 15). Association of Housing First implementation and key outcomes among homeless persons with problematic substance use. *Psychiatric Services, 65*, 1318–1324.

Davidson, L., & Roe D. (2007). Recovery from versus recovery in mental illness: One strategy for lessening confusion plaguing recovery. *Journal of Mental Health, 16*, 459–470.

Davidson, C., Neighbors, C., Hall, G., Hogue, A., Cho, R., Kutner, B, & Morgenstern, J. (2014, July 15). Association of Housing First implementation and key outcomes among homeless persons with problematic substance use. *Psychiatric Services in Advance*.

DiMaggio, P. J., & Powell, W. W. (1983). The iron cage revisited: Institutional isomorphism and collective rationality in organizational fields. *American Sociological Review*, 147–160.

Dolbeare, C. N., & Crowley, S. (2007). *Changing priorities: The Federal budget and housing assistance 1976–2007*. Washington DC: National Low Income Housing Coalition.

Doran, K. M., Misa, E. J., & Shah, N. A. (2013). Housing as health care: New York's boundary crossing experiment. *New England Journal of Medicine, 369*, 2374–2377.

Dordick, G. A. (2002). Recovering from homelessness: Determining the "quality of sobriety" in a transitional housing program. *Qualitative Sociology, 25*(1), 7–32.

Drake, R., Bond, G., & Becker, D. (2013). *IPS supported employment: An evidence-based approach*. New York: Oxford Press.

Duneier, M. (1999). *Sidewalk*. New York: MacMillan.

Dupuis, A., & Thorns, D. C. (1998). Home, home ownership, and the search for ontological security. *The Sociological Review, 46*(1), 24–47.

Ellen, I. G., & O'Flaherty, B. (Eds.). (2010). *How to house the homeless*. New York: Russell Sage.

Elliott, A. (2013, December 9). Invisible child: Dasani's homeless life. *New York Times*. Retrieved from http://www.nytimes.com/projects/2013/invisible-child/

Fairmount Ventures, Inc. (2011, January). *Evaluation of Pathways to Housing PA*. Philadelphia, PA.

Falvo, N. (2009). *Homelessness, program responses and an assessment of Toronto's Streets to Homes Program*. Ottawa: Canadian Policy Research Networks, Inc.

Fitzpatrick, S., Quilgars, D., & Pleace, N. (Eds.). (2009) *Homelessness in the UK: Problems and solutions*. Coventry, UK: Chartered Institute for Housing.

Felton, B. J. (2003). Innovation and implementation in mental health services for homeless adults: A case study. *Community Mental Health Journal, 39*(4), 309–322.

Fondeville, N., & Ward, T. (2011, November). *Social situation observatory: Income distribution and living*. Brussels, Belgium: European Commission.

Frazier, I. (2013, October 28). Hidden city. *The New Yorker*, 39–49.

Gaetz, S. (2014a). *Coming of age: Reimagining the response to youth homelessness in Canada*. Toronto: The Canadian Homelessness Research Network Press.

Gaetz, S. (2014b). *A safe and decent place to live: Towards a Housing First framework for youth*. Toronto, Canada: The Homeless Hub Press.

Giddens, A. (1990). *Consequences of modernity*. Oxford, UK: Polity Press.

Gilmer, T., Stefancic, A., Ettner, S. L., Manning, W. G., & Tsemberis, S. (2010). Effects of full service partnerships on homelessness, use and cost of mental health services and quality of life among adults with serious mental illness. *Archives of General Psychiatry, 67*, 645–652.

Gilmer, T., Stefancic, A., Katz, M., Sklar, M., Tsemberis, S., & Palinkas, L. (2014, July 15). Fidelity of the Housing First model and effectiveness of permanent supported housing programs in California. *Psychiatric Services, 65*, 1120–1125.

Gladwell, M. (2006). Million dollar Murray. *The New Yorker*. Retrieved from http://www.gladwell.com/2006/2006_02_13_a_murray.html

Glaser, G. (2014, July 3). A different path to fighting addiction. *New York Times*. Retrieved from http://www.nytimes.com/2014/07/06/nyregion/a-different-path-to-fighting-addiction.html?_r=0

Goering, P. N., Streiner, D. L., Adair, C., Aubry, T., Barker, J., Distasio, J., . . . & Zabkiewicz, D. M. (2011). The At Home/Chez Soi trial protocol: A pragmatic, multi-site, randomized controlled trial of a Housing First intervention for homeless individuals with mental illness in five Canadian cities. *BMJ Open*, 1(2).

Goering, P., Veldhuizen, S., Watson, A., Adair, C., Kopp, B., Latimer, E., Nelson, G., MacNaughton, E., Streiner, D., & Aubry, T. (2014). *National At Home/Chez Soi Final Report*. Calgary: Mental Health Commission of Canada. Retrieved from http://www.mentalhealthcommission.ca

Goffman, E. (1963). *Stigma: Notes on the management of spoiled identity*. New York: Simon & Schuster.

Granovetter, M. (1973). The strength of weak ties. *American Journal of Sociology*, 78, 1360–1380.

Grant, R., Gracy, D., Goldsmith, G., Shapiro, A., & Redlener, I. E. (2013). Twenty-five years of child and family homelessness: Where are we now? *American Journal of Public Health*, 103(S2), e1–e10.

Greenwood, R. G., Stefancic, A., & Tsemberis, S. (2013). Pathways Housing First for persons with psychiatric disabilities: Program innovation, research and advocacy. *Journal of Social Issues*, 69, 645–663.

Greenhalgh, T., Robert, G., Bate, P. Macfarlane, F., & Kyriakidou, O. (2004). Diffusion of innovation in service organizations: Systematic review and recommendations. *Milbank Quarterly*, 82, 581–629.

Greenwood, R. M., Stefancic, A., & Tsemberis, S. (2013). Pathways Housing First for homeless persons with psychiatric disabilities: Program innovation, research, and advocacy. *Journal of Social Issues*, 69(4), 645–663.

Greenwood, R., Díaz, A. M., Li, S. X., & Lorente, J. C. (2010). The multiplicity of institutional logics and the heterogeneity of organizational responses. *Organization Science*, 21(2), 521–539.

Greenwood, R. M., Stefancic, A., Tsemberis, S., & Busch-Geertsema, V. (2013). Implementations of Housing First in Europe: Successes and challenges in maintaining model fidelity. *American Journal of Psychiatric Rehabilitation*, 16(4), 290–312.

Gulcur, L., Stefancic, A., Shinn, M.,Tsemberis, S, & Fischer, S. (2003). Housing, hospitalization, and cost outcomes for homeless individuals with psychiatric disabilities participating in continuum of care and Housing First programs. *Journal of Community and Applied Psychology*, 13, 171–186.

Haggerty, R. (2006). *Smart moves: Spending to save, Streets to Home, Adelaide's thinkers in residence*. Adelaide: Government of South Australia.

Hansen, H., Bourgois, P., & Drucker, E. (2014). Pathologizing poverty: New forms of structural stigma under welfare reform. *Social Science and Medicine*, 103, 76–83.

Harcourt, B. E., & Ludwig, J. (2006). Broken windows: New evidence from New York City and a five-city experiment. *University of Chicago Law Review*, 73, 21–37.

Harding, C. M., Zubin, J., & Strauss, J. S. (1987). Chronicity in schizophrenia: Fact, partial fact, or artifact? *Hospital and Community Psychiatry*, 38, 477–482.

Harding, C. M., Brooks, G. W., Ashikaga, T., Strauss, J. S., & Breier, A. (1987). The Vermont longitudinal study of persons with severe mental illness, II: Long-term outcome of subjects who retrospectively met DSM-III criteria for schizophrenia. *American Journal of Psychiatry*, 144, 727–735.

Harper, D. (2002). Talking about pictures: A case for photo elicitation. *Visual Studies*, 17, 13–26.

Hawkins, R. L., & Abrams, C. (2007). Disappearing acts: The social networks of formerly homeless individuals with co-occurring disorders. *Social Science & Medicine*, 65(10), 2031–2042.

Haywoode, A. (2014, December 3). Pine Street Inn shifts from beds to housing. *Commonwealth Magazine*. Retrieved from http://www.commonwealthmagazine.org/Voices/Perspective/Online-Perspectives-2014/Fall/025-Pine-Street-Inn-shifts-from-beds-to-housing.aspx#.VKdIf2TF9fy

Henwood, B. F., Cabassa, L., Craig, C., & Padgett, D. K. (2013). Permanent supportive housing: Addressing homelessness and health disparities? *American Journal of Public Health*, 103, s188–s192.

Henwood, B. F., Melekis, K., Stefancic, A., & York, N. Y. (2014). Introducing Housing First in a rural service system: A multi-stakeholder perspective. *Global Journal of Community Psychology Practice*, 5(1), 20–25.

Henwood, B. F., Shinn, M., Tsemberis, S., & Padgett, D. K. (2013). Examining provider perspectives within Housing First and traditional programs. *American Journal of Psychiatric Rehabilitation*, 16(4), 262–274.

Henwood, B. F., Stanhope, V., & Padgett, D. K. (2011). The role of housing: A comparison of front-line provider views in Housing First and traditional programs. *Administration and Policy in Mental Health and Mental Health Services Research*, 38, 77–85.

Henwood, B. F., Derejko, K., Couture, J., & Padgett, D. K. (2014). Maslow and mental health recovery: A comparative study of homeless programs for adults with serious mental illness. *Administration and Policy in Mental Health and Mental Health Services Research*, 42, 222–228.

Henwood, B., & Padgett, D. K. (2007). The self-medication hypothesis revisited. *American Journal on Addictions*, 16(3), 160–165.

Henwood, B. F., Padgett, D. K., Smith, B. T., & Tideringon, E. (2012). Substance abuse recovery after experiencing homelessness and mental illness: Case studies of change over time. *Journal of Dual Diagnosis*, 8, 238–246.

Henwood, B. F., Stanhope, V., Brawer, R., Weinstein, L. C., Lawson, J., Stwords, E., & Crossan, C. (2013). Addressing chronic disease within supportive housing programs. *Progress in community health partnerships: Research, education, and action*, 7(1), 67–75.

Herman, D., Conover, S., Gorroochurn, P., Hinterland, K., Hoepner, L., & Susser, E. (2011). A randomized trial of critical time intervention in persons with severe mental illness following institutional discharge. *Psychiatric Services*, 62, 713–719.

Hohmann, A., & Shear, K. (2002). Community-based intervention research: Coping with the "noise" of real life in study design. *American Journal of Psychiatry*, 159, 201–207.

Hombs, M. E. (2011). *Modern homelessness*. Santa Barbara, CA: ABC-CLIO.

Hopper, K. (2003). *Reckoning with homelessness*. New York: Cornell University Press.

Hopper, K. (2007). Rethinking social recovery in schizophrenia: What a capabilities approach might offer. *Social Science & Medicine*, 65, 868–879.

Hopper, K. (2012). The counter-reformation that failed? A commentary on the mixed legacy of supported housing. *Psychiatric Services*, 63, 461–463.

Hopper, K., Jost, J., Hay. T., Welber, S., & Haugland, G. (1997). Homelessness, severe mental illness, and the institutional circuit. *Psychiatric Services*, 48, 659–665.

Hopper, K., Shinn, M., Laska, E., Meisner, M., & Wanderling, J. (2008). Estimating numbers of unsheltered homeless people through plant-capture and post-count survey methods. *American Journal of Public Health*, 98(8), 1438.

Houard, N. (2011). The French homelessness strategy: Reforming temporary accommodation and access to housing to deliver "Housing First": Continuum or clean break? *European Journal of Homelessness, 5*, 83–98.

Houghton, T. (2001). *New York/New York Agreement cost study: The impact of supportive housing on services use for homeless mentally ill individuals.* New York: Corporation for Supportive Housing.

Howie the Harp. (1993). Taking a new approach to independent living. *Hospital and Community Psychiatry, 44*, 413.

Hwang, S. W., & Burns, T. (2014). Health interventions for people who are homeless. *The Lancet, 384*, 1541–1547.

Inciardi, J. A., & Harrison, L. D. (Eds.). (1999). *Harm reduction: National and international perspectives.* Thousand Oaks, CA: Sage.

Jans, L., Stoddard, S., & Kraus, L. (2004). *Chartbook on mental health and disability in the U.S.* InfoUse.

Johnson, G., Gronda, H., & Coutts, S. (2008). *On the outside: Pathways in and out of homelessness.* Melbourne: Australian Scholarly Press.

Johnson, G. R., Parkinson, S. R., & Parsell, C. (2012). Policy shift or program drift? Implementing Housing First in Australia. *American Journal of Psychiatry, 149*(6), 816–823.

Johnsen, S., & Teixeira, L. (2010). Staircases, elevators and cycles of change: "Housing First" and other housing models for homeless people with complex support needs. Retrieved from www crisis.org.uk

Jost, J. J., Levitt, A. J., & Porcu, L. (2011). Street to home: The experiences of long-term unsheltered homeless individuals in an outreach and housing placement program. *Qualitative Social Work, 10*, 244–263.

Kane, V. (2014, December 29). Housing first: Veteran-centered care helping to end homelessness. National Veterans Outreach. Retrieved from http://www.agif-nvop.org/News/tabid/86/EntryId/51/Housing-First-Veteran-centered-care-helping-to-end-Veteran-homelessness.aspx

Katz, M. H. (2015). Housing as a remedy for chronic homelessness. *JAMA, 313*, 901–902.

Keller, C., Goering, P., Hume, C., Macnaughton, E., O'Campo, P., Sarang, A., . . . & Tsemberis, S. (2013). Initial implementation of Housing First in five Canadian cities: How do you make the shoe fit, when one size does not fit all? *American Journal of Psychiatric Rehabilitation, 16*(4), 275–289.

Kelling & Wilson (1982, March 1). Broken windows: The police and neighborhood safety. *Atlantic Monthly.* Retrieved from http://www.theatlantic.com/magazine/archive/1982/03/broken-windows/304465/

Kertesz, S. G., Crouch, K., Milby, J. B., Cusimano, R. E., & Schumacher, J. E. (2009). Housing First for homeless persons with active addiction: Are we overreaching? *Milbank Quarterly, 87*(2), 495–534.

Kertesz, S. G., Mullins, A. N., Schumacher, J. E, Wallace, D., Kirk, K., & Milby, J. B. (2007). Long-term housing and work outcomes among treated cocaine-dependent homeless persons. *Journal of Behavioral Health Services Research, 34,*17–33.

Kimmelman, M. (2014, October 6). Building hope and nurturing into housing. *New York Times.* Retrieved from http://www.nytimes.com/2014/10/07/arts/sugar-hill-housing-w ill-have-a-school-and-a-museum.html?_r=0

Klodawski, F. (2009). Home spaces and rights to the city. *Urban Geography, 30*, 591–610.

Kuhn, T. S. (1962). *The structure of scientific revolutions* (1st ed.). Chicago, IL: University of Chicago Press.

Kusmer, K. L. (2003). *Down and out, on the road: The homeless in American history.* New York: Oxford University Press.

Laing, R. D. (1965). *The divided self: An existential study in sanity and madness.* London: Pelican Press.

Larimer, M., Malone, D. K., Garner, M., Atkins, D. C., Burlingham, B., Lonczak, H. S., ... & Marlett, G. A. (2009). Health care and public service use and costs before and after provision of housing for chronically homeless persons with severe alcohol problems. *JAMA, 301,* 1349–1357.

Link, B. G., & Phelan, J. C. (1995). Social conditions as fundamental causes of disease. *Journal of Health and Social Behavior, 25,* 80–94.

Link, B. G., & Phelan, J. C. (2001). Conceptualizing stigma. *Annual Review of Sociology, 99,* 363–385.

Link, B. G., & Phelan, J. C. (2014). Stigma power. *Social Science & Medicine, 103,* 24–32.

Locke, G., Khadduri, J., & O'Hara, A. (2007). *Housing models.* Cambridge, MA: Abt Associates Inc.

Lockett, A., Currie, G., Waring, J., Finn, R., & Martin, G. (2012). The role of institutional entrepreneurs in reforming healthcare. *Social Science & Medicine, 74*(3), 356–363.

Lofstrand, C. H., & Juhila, K. (2012). The discourse of consumer choice in the Pathways Housing First model. *European Journal of Homelessness, 6,* 47–68.

Lovell, A. M., & Cohen, S. (1998). The elaboration of "choice" in a program for homeless persons labeled psychiatrically disabled. *Human Organization, 57,* 8–20.

Macfarlane, F., Barton-Sweeney, C., Woodard, F., & Greenhalgh, T. (2013). Achieving and sustaining profound institutional change in health care: Case study using neo-institutional theory. *Social Science & Medicine, 80,* 10–18.

MacNaughton, E. L., Goering, P. N., & Nelson, G. B. (2012). Exploring the value of mixed methods within the At Home/Chez Soi Housing First project: A strategy to evaluate the implementation of a complex population health intervention for people with mental illness who have been homeless. *Canadian Journal of Public Health, 103*(7), eS57–eS63.

Maguire, S., Hardy, C., & Lawrence, T. B. (2004). Institutional entrepreneurship in emerging fields: HIV/AIDS treatment advocacy in Canada. *Academy of Management Journal, 47*(5), 657–679.

Mares, A., & Rosenheck, R. (2007). *HUD/HHS/VA collaborative initiative to help end chronic homelessness: National performance outcomes assessment preliminary client outcomes report.* Washington, DC: VA Northeast Program Evaluation Center.

Marlatt, G. A. (1996). Harm reduction: Come as you are. *Addictive Behaviors, 21*(6), 779–788.

Marlatt, G. A., Larimer, M. E., & Witkiewitz, K. (Eds.). (2011). *Harm reduction: Pragmatic strategies for managing high-risk behaviors.* New York: Guilford Press.

McClay, R. (2015, March 31). Protestors march through downtown Phoenix, homeless shelter to close. Retrieved from http://ktar.com/22/1821478/Protesters-march-through-downtown-Phoenix-homeless-shelter-to-close

Mental Illness Fellowship (2014, February 5). *Doorway: Formative evaluation report.* Retrieved from www.nousgroup.com.au

Milburn, N. G., Rice, E., Rotheram-Borus, M. . . . & Duan, N. (2009). Adolescents exiting homelessness over two years: The risk amplification and abatement model. *Journal of Research on Adolescence, 19,* 762–785.

Milby, J. B., Schumacher, J. E., Wallace, D., Freedman, M. J., & Vuchinich, R. E. (2005). To house or not to house: The effects of providing housing to homeless substance abusers in treatment. *American Journal of Public Health*, 95(7), 1259–1262.

National Alliance to End Homelessness (2009). *Organizational change: Adopting a Housing First approach*. Washington DC: Author.

National Alliance to End Homelessness. Youth. Retrieved from http://www. endhomelessness.org/pages/youth

National Alliance to End Homelessness. (2004). *Housing First for Families: Research to support the development of a Housing First for Families training curriculum*. San Francisco, CA: La France Associates.

Nelson, G., Clarke, J., Febbraro, A., & Hatzipantelis, M. (2005). A narrative approach to the evaluation of supported housing: Stories of homeless people who have experienced serious mental illness. *Psychiatric Rehabilitation Journal*, 29, 98–103.

Nelson, G., Sylvestre, J., Aubry, T., George, L., & Trainor, J. (2006). Housing choice and control, housing quality, and control over professional support as contributors to the subjective quality of life and community adaptation of people with severe mental illness. *Administration and Policy in Mental Health*, 34, 89–100.

New Freedom Commission on Mental Health. (2003). *Achieving the promise: Transforming mental health care in America. Final Report*. DHHS Pub. No. SMA-03-3832. Rockville, MD: U. S. Department of Health and Human Services.

Newman, K. (2000). *No shame in my game: The working poor in the inner city*. New York: Vintage.

Nussbaum, M., & Sen, A. (Eds.). (1993). *Quality of life*. New York: Oxford Press.

O'Connell, M., Tondora, J., Croog, G., Evans, A., Davidson, L. (2005). From rhetoric to routine: Assessing perceptions of recovery-oriented practices in a state mental health and addiction system. *Psychiatric Rehabilitation Journal*, 28, 378–386.

O'Dwyer, P. J., & Alexander, E. (2014, March 12). Aging gracefully: An anticipated future in Housing First. Paper presented at the Second Housing First Partners Conference. Chicago, IL.

O'Hara, A. (2007). Housing for people with mental illness: Update of a report to the President's New Freedom Commission. *Psychiatric Services*, 58, 907–913.

O'Sullivan, E. (2012). Varieties of punitiveness in Europe: Homelessness and urban marginality. *European Journal of Homelessness*, 6, 69–96.

Ornelas, J. (2013, September 20). *Housing First: An ecological approach to support community integration*. Paper presented at the European Research Conference, Berlin, Germany.

Padgett, D. K. (2007). There's no place like (a) home: Ontological security among persons with serious mental illness in the United States. *Social Science & Medicine*, 64(9), 1925–1936.

Padgett, D. K. (2012). *Qualitative and mixed methods in public health*. Thousand Oaks, CA: Sage.

Padgett, D. K., Struening, E. L., Andrews, H., & Pittman, J. (1995). Predictors of emergency room use by homeless adults in New York City: The influence of predisposing, enabling and need factors. *Social Science & Medicine*, 41(4), 547–556.

Padgett, D. K., Gulcur, L., & Tsemberis, S. (2006). Housing first services for people who are homeless with co-occurring serious mental illness and substance abuse. *Research on Social Work Practice*, 16(1), 74–83.

Padgett, D. K., Hawkins, R. L., Abrams, C., & Davis, A. (2006). In their own words: Trauma and substance abuse in the lives of formerly homeless women with serious mental illness. *American Journal of Orthopsychiatry, 76*(4), 461.

Padgett, D. K., Henwood, B., Abrams, C., & Davis, A. (2008). Engagement and retention in services among formerly homeless adults with co-occurring mental illness and substance abuse: Voices from the margins. *Psychiatric Rehabilitation Journal, 31*(3), 226.

Padgett, D. K., Henwood, B., Abrams, C., & Drake, R. E. (2008). Social relationships among persons who have experienced serious mental illness, substance abuse, and homelessness: Implications for recovery. *American Journal of Orthopsychiatry, 78*(3), 333–339.

Padgett, D. K., Stanhope, V., Henwood, B. F., & Stefancic, A. (2011). Substance use outcomes among homeless clients with serious mental illness: Comparing Housing First with treatment first programs. *Community Mental Health Journal, 47*(2), 227–232.

Padgett, D. K., Smith, B. T., Henwood, B. F., & Tiderington, E. (2012). Life course adversity in the lives of formerly homeless persons with serious mental illness: Context and meaning. *American Journal of Orthopsychiatry, 82*(3), 421–430.

Padgett, D. K., Smith, B. T., Derejko, K., Henwood, B. F., & Tiderington, E. (2013). A picture is worth? Photo-elicitation interviewing with formerly homeless adults. *Qualitative Health Research, 23,* 1435–1444.

Parsell, C., Fitzpatrick, S., & Busch-Geertsema, V. (2014). Common Ground in Australia: An object lesson in evidence hierarchies and policy transfer. *Housing Studies, 29,* 69–87.

Parsell, C., Tomaszewski, W., & Jones, A. (2013). An evaluation of Brisbane Street to Home: Final Report. Brisbane, Australia: Institute for Social Science Research, University of Queensland.

Parvini, S. (2014, May 27). In helping L.A.'s homeless population, advocates must strike a "delicate balance." Retrieved from http://www.kcet.org/news/agenda/homeless/when-it-comes-to-helping-las-homeless-population-advocates-must-strike-a-delicate-balance.html

Patton, M. Q. (2002). *Qualitative research and evaluation methods* (3rd ed.). Thousand Oaks, CA: Sage.

Pearson, C., Montgomery, A. E., & Locke, G. (2009). Housing stability among homeless individuals with serious mental illness participating in Housing First programs. *Journal of Community Psychology, 37*(3), 404–417.

Pearson, H. (2014). Collective impact: Venturing on an unfamiliar road. *The Philanthropist, 26,* 49–53.

Perlman, J., & Parvensky, J. (2006). *Denver Housing First Collaborative: Cost benefit analysis and program outcomes report.* Denver: Colorado Coalition for the Homeless.

Piat, M., Polvere, L., Townley, G., Nelson, G., Macnaughton, E., Egalite, N., & Goering, P. (2012). *Baseline consumer narratives of lived experience of the Mental Health Commission of Canada's At Home/Chez Soi project: Cross-site report.* Toronto: Mental Health Commission of Canada.

Piketty, T. (2014). *Capital in the twenty-first century.* Cambridge, MA: Belknap Press.

Pollio, D. E., Batey, D. S., Bender, K., Ferguson, K., & Thompson, S. J. (2013). Technology use among emerging adult homeless in two U.S. cities. *Social Work, 58*(2), 173–175.

Price, M. (2014, March 23). Charlotte's apartments for homeless save money. Retrieved from http://www.charlotteobserver.com/2014/03/23/4787934/study-concludes-charlotte-homeless.html

Quigley, J. M., & Raphael, S. (2004). Is housing affordable? Why isn't it more affordable? *Journal of Economic Perspectives, 18,* 191–214.

Quinn, B. (2014, June 13). Anti-homeless spikes are part of a wider phenomenon of "hostile architecture." *The Guardian.* Downloaded from http://www.theguardian.com/artanddesign/2014/jun/13/anti-homeless-spikes-hostile-architecture

Rao, H., & Giorgi, S. (2006). Code breaking: How entrepreneurs exploit cultural logics to generate institutional change. *Research in Organizational Behavior, 27,* 269–304.

Rhenter, P., & Girard, V. (2014, March 14). Marx and not Freud: What are the social and political factors that influence the paradigm shift in public policies? Paper presented at the Second Housing First Partners Conference, Chicago, IL.

Rice, E., &Barman-Adhikari, A. (2014), Internet and social media use as a resource among homeless youth. *Journal of Computer-Mediated Communication, 19,* 232–247.

Ridgway, P., & Zipple, A. M. (1990). The paradigm shift in residential services: From the linear continuum to supported housing approaches. *Rehabilitation Journal, 13*(4), 11–31.

Robbins, P. C., Callahan, L., & Monahan, J. (2009). Perceived coercion to treatment and housing satisfaction in Housing First and supportive housing programs. *Psychiatric Services, 60,* 1251–1253.

Rogers, E. M. (1962). *Diffusion of innovations.* New York: Simon and Schuster.

Roman, N. (2011, September). Building on our past, learning as we go. Keynote remarks given at the Domestic Violence Housing First Symposium. Seattle, WA: Bill and Melinda Gates Foundation.

Roos, L. E., Mota, N., Afifi, T., Katz, L. Y., Distasio J., & Sareen, J. (2013). Relationship between adverse childhood experiences and homelessness and the impact of Axis I and II disorders. *American Journal of Public Health, 103,* s275–s281.

Sadowski, L. S., Kee, R. A., VanderWeele, T. J., & Buchanan, D. (2009). Effect of a housing and case management program on emergency department visits and hospitalizations among chronically ill homeless adults: A randomized trial. *JAMA, 30,* 1771–1778.

Sahlin, I. (1998). *The staircase of transition. European Observatory on Homelessness. National Report from Sweden.* Lund, Sweden: Department of Sociology.

Salyers, M., & Tsemberis, S. (2007). ACT and recovery: Integrating evidence-based practice and recovery orientation on ACT teams. *Community Mental Health Journal, 43,* 619–641.

Sampson, R. J., Raudenbush, S. W., & Earls, F. (1997). Neighborhoods and violent crime: A multilevel study of collective efficacy. *Science, 277*(5328), 918–924.

Santos, F. (2014, January 16). Program to end homelessness among veterans reaches a milestone in Arizona. *New York Times,* p. A14.

Scott, W.R. (2001). *Institutions and organizations.* Thousand Oaks, CA: Sage.

Scott, F., & Harrison, S. J. (2013). Calgary, Alberta: The Infinity Project. In S. Gaetz, F. Scott & T. Gulliver (Eds.), *Housing First in Canada: Supporting communities to end homelessness* (pp. 61–75). Toronto: Canadian Homelessness Research Network.

Secret, M. (2012, April 7). Court upends 9-year fight on housing mentally ill. *New York Times,* p. A13.

Shern, D. L., Tsemberis, S., Anthony, W., Lovell, A. M., Richmond, L., Felton, C. J., Winarski, J., & Cohen, M. (2000). Serving street-dwelling individuals with psychiatric disabilities: Outcomes of a psychiatric rehabilitation clinical trial. *American Journal of Public Health, 90,* 1873–1878.

Shibusawa, T., & Padgett, D. (2009). The experiences of "aging" among formerly homeless adults with chronic mental illness: A qualitative study. *Journal of Aging Studies, 23*(3), 188–196.

Shinn M. B., & Baumohl, J. (1999). Re-thinking the prevention of homelessness. Retrieved from http://www.huduser.org/portal/publications/homeless/practical.html

Shinn, M. (2010). Homelessness, poverty and social exclusion in the United States and Europe. *European Journal of Homelessness, 4*, 19–44.

Shinn, M. B., Greer, A., Bainbridge, A., Kwon, J., & Zuiderveen, S. (2013). Efficient targeting of homeless services for families, *American Journal of Public Health, 103*, S324–S330.

Shore, M. F., & Cohen, M. D. (1992). Observations from the program on chronic mental illness. *Health Affairs, 11*, 227–233.

Slade, M., Amering, M., & Oades L. (2008). Recovery: an international perspective. *Epidemiologia e Psichiatria Sociale, 17*, 128–137.

Snow, D. A., & Anderson, L. (1987). Identity work among the homeless: The verbal construction and avowal of personal identities. *American Journal of Sociology, 92*, 1336–1371.

Snow, D. A., Soule, S. A., & Cress, D. M. (2005). Identifying the precipitants of homeless protest across 17 US cities, 1980 to 1990. *Social Forces, 83*, 1183–1210.

Sobell, L. C., Sobell, M. B., Leo, G. L., & Cancella, A. (1988). Reliability of a timeline method: Assessing normal drinkers' reports of recent drinking and a comparative evaluation across several populations. *British Journal of Addiction, 83*, 393–402.

Stanhope, V., & Dunn, K. (2011). The curious case of Housing First: The limits of evidence-based policy. *International Journal of Law and Psychiatry, 34*, 275–282.

Stanhope, V., Henwood, B., & Padgett, D. (2009). Understanding service disengagement from the perspective of case managers. *Psychiatric Services, 60*, 459–464.

Stefancic, A. (2014). *"If I stay by myself, I feel safer": Dilemmas of social connectedness among persons with psychiatric disabilities in Housing First.* (Doctoral dissertation UMI No. 3644245). Retrieved from http://dx.doi.org/10.7916/D83B5XSS

Stefancic, A., Henwood, B. F., Melton, H., Shin, S. M., Lawrence-Gomez, R., & Tsemberis, S. (2013). Implementing Housing First in rural areas: Pathways Vermont. *American Journal of Public Health, 103*, S206–S209.

Stefancic, A., Tsemberis, S., Messeri, P., Drake, R., & Goering, P. (2013). The Pathways Housing First fidelity scale for individuals with psychiatric disabilities. *American Journal of Psychiatric Rehabilitation, 16*(4), 240–261.

Stefancic, A., Schaefer-McDaniel, N. J., Davis, A. C., & Tsemberis, S. (2004). Maximizing follow-up of adults with histories of homelessness and psychiatric disabilities. *Evaluation and Program Planning, 27*(4), 433–442.

Stefancic, A., & Tsemberis, S. (2007). Housing First for long-term shelter dwellers with psychiatric disabilities in a suburban county: A four-year study of housing access and retention. *Journal of Primary Prevention, 28*(3–4), 265–279.

Stein, L. I., & Test, M. A. (1980). Alternatives to mental hospital treatment. *Archives of General Psychiatry, 37*(4), 392–397.

Stergiopoulos, V., Hwang, S.W., Godzik, A., Nisenbaum, R., Latimer, E., Rabouin, D., . . . & Goering, P. N. (2015). Effect of scattered-site housing using rent supplements and intensive case management on housing stability among homeless adults with mental illness: A randomized trial. *JAMA, 313*, 905–915.

Stid, D. (2012, April 25). Dismantling the social services industrial complex. *The Washington Post.* Retrieved from http://www.washingtonpost.com/national/on-innovations/dismantling-the-social-services-industrial-complex/2012/04/25/gIQAuTcMhTstory.html

Substance Abuse and Mental Health Services Administration. (2007). National Registry of Evidence-based Programs and Practices: Pathways' Housing First Program. Retrieved from http://www.nrepp.samhsa.gov/programfulldetails.asp?PROGRAM_ID=195

Suddaby, R. (2010). Challenges for institutional theory. *Journal of Management Inquiry*, 19, 14–20.

Suddaby, R., & Greenwood, R. (2005). Rhetorical strategies of legitimacy. *Administrative Science Quarterly*, 50(1), 35–67.

Surowiecki, J. (2014, September 22). Home free? *The New Yorker*, p. 42.

Szabo, H. (2014, July 10). Bleak picture for the mentally ill: 80 percent are jobless. *USA Today*. Retrieved from http://www.usatoday.com/story/news/nation/2014/07/10/high-unemployment-mentally-ill/12186049/

Thiele, B. (2002). The human right to adequate housing: A tool for promoting and protecting individual and community health. *American Journal of Public Health*, 92, 712–715.

Thomas, L., Shears, J. K., Pate, M. C., & Priester, M. A. (2014, February 14). *Moore Place permanent supportive housing evaluation study*. Charlotte, NC: University of North Carolina–Charlotte, Department of Social Work.

Thompson, S. J. (2013). Homeless and runaway youth. *Encyclopedia of Social Work*. New York: Oxford University Press.

Tinland, A., Fortanier, C., Girard, V., . . . & Auquier, P. (2013). Evaluation of the Housing First program in patients with severe mental disorders in France: Study protocol for a randomized controlled trial. *Trials*, 14, 309–319.

Toro, P., Tompsett, C. Lombardo, S . . . & Harvey, K. (2007). Homelessness in Europe and the United States: A comparison of prevalence and public opinion. *Journal of Social Issues*, 63, 505–524.

Townley, G., & Kloos, B. (2011). Examining the psychological sense of community for individuals with serious mental illness residing in supported housing environments. *Community Mental Health Journal*, 47, 336–346.

Townley, G., Miller, & Kloos, B. (2013). A little goes a long way: The impact of distal social support on community integration and recovery of individuals with psychiatric disabilities. *American Journal of Community Psychology*, 52, 84–96.

Tsemberis, S. (1999). From streets to homes: An innovative approach to supported housing for homeless adults with psychiatric disabilities. *Journal of Community Psychology*, 27, 225–241.

Tsemberis, S. (2010). *Housing First: The pathways model to end homelessness for people with mental illness and addiction*. Minneapolis, MN: Hazelden.

Tsemberis, S., & Asmussen, S. (1999). From streets to homes. *Alcoholism Treatment Quarterly*, 17, 113–131.

Tsemberis, S., & Eisenberg, R. F. (2000). Pathways to housing: Supported housing for street-dwelling homeless individuals with psychiatric disabilities. *Psychiatric Services*, 51(4), 487–493.

Tsemberis, S., Gulcur, L., & Nakae, M. (2004). Housing First, consumer choice, and harm reduction for homeless individuals with a dual diagnosis. *American Journal of Public Health*, 94(4), 651–656.

Tsemberis, S., Kent, D., & Respress, C. (2012). Housing stability and recovery among chronically homeless persons with co-occurring disorders in Washington, DC. *American Journal of Public Health*, 102(1), 13–16.

Tsemberis, S., Moran, L. L., Shinn, M., Asmussen, S. M., & Shern, D. L. (2003). Consumer preference programs for homeless individuals with psychiatric disabilities: A drop-in center and a supported housing program. *American Journal of Community Psychology, 32*, 305–317.

U. S. Department of Housing and Urban Development. (2010). *The 2010 Annual Homeless Assessment: Report to Congress.* Washington, DC. Retrieved from http://www.hudhre. info/documents/2010HomelessAssessmentReport.pdf

U. S. Department of Housing and Urban Development. (2013). Interim report: Family Options Study. Retrieved from http://www.huduser.org/portal/family_options_study. html

U. S. Department of Housing and Urban Development. (2014). FY2013 Annual Performance Report. Retrieved from http://portal.hud.gov/hudportal/documents/huddoc?id=HUD_ FY13APR_FY15APP.PDF

U. S. General Accounting Office. (1994). *McKinney Act programs provide assistance but are not designed to be the solution.* Washington DC: Author.

U. S. Interagency Council on Homelessness. (2010). *Opening doors: Federal strategic plan to prevent and end homelessness.* Washington, DC: Author.

U. S. Interagency Council on Homelessness. (2013). Ending veterans homelessness: HUD-VASH makes housing first a priority. Retrieved from http://usich.gov/population/veterans/veterans_homelessness_in_focus/ ending_veterans_homelessness_hud_vash_makes_housing_first_a_priority/

Vitullo-Martin, J. (2007, January 18). Homeless in America. *Wall Street Journal.* Downloaded from http://www.manhattan-institute.org/html/_ wsj-homeless_in_america.htm

Weber, M. (1952). *The Protestant ethic and the spirit of capitalism.* New York: Scribner.

Wewerinke, D., & Wolf, J. (2014). *Strengthening the social inclusion of Housing First participants.* Nijnegen, Netherlands: Raboud University Medical Centre.

Wewerinke, D., Wolf, J., Maas, M., & Al Shamma, S. (2012) Discus Amsterdam: Housing First. *Housing First: A Key Element of European Homelessness Strategies.* Unpublished conference proceedings. Retrieved from http://feantsa.horus.be/code/EN/ pg.asp?Page=1409

Whitaker, R. (2010). *Mad in America.* New York: Basic Books.

Whitley, R., & Campbell, R. D. (2014). Stigma, agency and recovery amongst people with severe mental illness. *Social Science & Medicine, 107*, 1–8.

Whitley, R., & Henwood, B. F. (2014). Life, liberty and the pursuit of happiness: Reframing inequities experienced by people with severe mental illness. *Psychiatric Rehabilitation Journal, 37*, 68–70.

Wilkerson, I. (2011). *The warmth of other suns: The epic story of America's great migration.* New York: Vintage Books.

Willse, C. (2010). Neo-liberal bio-politics and the invention of chronic homelessness. *Economy and Society, 39*, 155–183.

Wilson, W. J. (1997). *When work disappears: The world of the new urban poor.* New York: Vintage Books.

Wilson, W. J. (2012). *The truly disadvantaged: The inner city, the underclass and public policy* (2nd ed.). Chicago, IL: University of Chicago Press.

Winnicott, D. W. (1964). *The child, the family and the outside world.* London: Pelican Books.

Wong, Y. L. I., & Solomon, P. L. (2002). Community integration of persons with psychiatric disabilities in supportive independent housing: A conceptual model and methodological considerations. *Mental Health Services Research, 4,* 13–28.

Wright, J. D. (1989). *Address unknown: The homeless in America.* New York: Aldine.

Yanos, P. T. (2007). Beyond landscapes of despair: The need for new research on the urban environment, sprawl, and community integration of persons with severe mental illness. *Health & Place, 13,* 672–676.

Yanos, P. T., Barrow, S., & Tsemberis, S. (2004). Community integration in the early phase of housing among homeless persons diagnosed with severe mental illness: Successes and challenges. *Community Mental Health Journal, 40,* 133–150.

Index